Essay Index

THE WORLD'S LEADING POETS

HOMER, VIRGIL, DANTE, SHAKESPEARE, MILTON, GOETHE

HOMER

THE WORLD'S LEADING POETS

HOMER, VIRGIL, DANTE, SHAKESPEARE, MILTON, GOETHE

BY

H. W. BOYNTON

WITH PORTRAITS

Essay Index Reprint Series

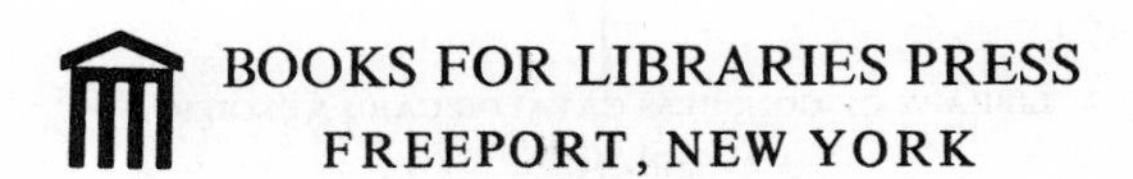

BOOKS FOR LIBRARIES PRESS
FREEPORT, NEW YORK

First Published 1912
Reprinted 1968

Originally published in
THE WORLD'S LEADERS, edited by W. P. Trent

LIBRARY OF CONGRESS CATALOG CARD NUMBER:
68-8439
PRINTED IN THE UNITED STATES OF AMERICA

CONTENTS

PORTRAITS

THE WORLD'S LEADING POETS

HOMER

ANY sort of book about the great poets of the world would naturally begin with Homer. Unfortunately, there is no place for him in a book of biographies, since no material for biography exists. But, that so great a name may not be altogether passed by, we may find space even here for a few words of conjecture as to what human being may have borne that name, and as to where and when he may have been alive.

The difficulty is not that the modern world — the world since the birth of Christ — has been heedless of the poet of the *Iliad* and the *Odyssey*. On the contrary, during all that period, there has been a vast amount of interest in the matter, and great expense of scholarly labor and romantic imagination. Even before the Christian era, various alleged "Lives" of Homer had been contrived. They were chiefly built upon the ingenious plan of attributing to the author of the two great epics, whoever he might be, many other poems of miscellaneous sorts. Hymns, popular songs, riddles, and humorous poems like *The Battle of the Frogs and Mice* were all cheerfully and confidently linked with the name of Homer. From such a mass of poems it was easy to glean and to piece together a fabric of more or less credible allusions to the experience of an actual human being in the flesh.

Later, this pleasing structure was undermined by the application of a little common sense. It came to be acknowledged that very little was known about the man Homer. Later still, the theory was advanced that Homer was not author of the *Iliad* and the *Odyssey* as we have them. It was argued that Homer had merely written, or composed and handed down by word of mouth, a series of detached lays, which were collected and given unity centuries after his time by Pisistratus or some other. Now it is no doubt true that the Homeric epics, like most other long poems, were built of materials which the poet found ready to hand. As we see in studying Shakespeare, for example, mere invention of plot is a matter of little moment to genius of the first order. But it is not clear why Homer may not have assembled and perfected his material at least as well as, say, Pisistratus.

But this was not the last denial of Homer that should be made by admirers and profound students of his work. The final crushing blow to the hero-worshiper was dealt by the skeptical eighteenth century. It was done most effectively in the book of a German scholar named Wolf, the *Prolegomena,* published in 1795. That authority asserted, with Gamp-like directness, that there was no such person as Homer! Thus began a famous controversy which is not yet ended. But the world's second thought has been in the main that of Goethe. He was at first so possessed by Wolf's theory that he toasted him as " the man who has delivered us from the name of Homer "; but three years later we find him writing to Schiller: " I am more than ever convinced of the indivisible unity of the *Iliad;* the man lives not, nor ever shall be born, who shall destroy it." In short, we may, better than not, believe that some ten centuries or more before Christ, there lived in Greece the great poet whom we call Homer: and who so nobly sang his own heart, his own age, as to sing the heart of all mankind in every age.

There is an old couplet to the effect that:

> Seven cities claimed Homer dead,
> Where Homer living begged for bread;

from which it would appear that there are the very oldest precedents for starving genius. But no doubt the comparatively modern person who built that jingle was only fitting a stately name to his own wretched experience. The places which have claimed Homer are not limited to the magical number seven, and there is no evidence that he ever begged in any of them.

Yet although we know so little about the life of the man Homer, the *Iliad* and the *Odyssey* do not leave us in absolute ignorance as to the kind of man he must have been. It may be that he was born in Smyrna, it may be that he died on the island of Ios;

we do not know. But we do know his temper, his heart, his mind, his way of looking at life.

His kind of poetry, whether written or not, was far more distinctly the popular utterance of that primitive age than the novel is of our own. No doubt he found his materials in folk legend and song, but he made them his own as clearly as Shakespeare made Plutarch and Holinshed and the Italian novelists his own. Folk-poetry, the poetry which grows as a people grow, and springs no man knows whence, is often "simple, sensuous, impassioned," as Milton said all poetry should be; but it is only the hand of genius that can give it the supreme quality, the quality of great poetry — nobility. Homer's possession of this quality has given him his power through the centuries. And by nobility I do not mean sublimity,— the lofty imagination and lofty style for which we give honor to Milton. Homer has his passages of unrivaled sublimity, but it is rather his calm and equable temper, his sturdy and even joyful acceptance of all life has to offer, that gives him his perennial hold upon the hearts of men.

Wherever and whenever he lived, Homer must have been an active man, a fighting man. Napoleon declared that when Homer wrote about war he knew what he was talking about. "The journal of Agamemnon," he said, "could not be more exact as to distances and time, and in the lifelike character of the military operations, than is the *Iliad*. Homer describes a fight not like an onlooker, but like a man who has a part in the thick of it. When Homer is busy with a battle, he is absorbed in it; he thinks of it all the time and of nothing else; he feels the exhilaration of it, the earnest satisfaction, the joy of action and achievement, he deals every blow he describes, and exults whenever the blow does its work." All life presents itself to him in terms of war. To live successfully is to fight and to win. This is no doubt a boyish point of view. It was a boyish age, and Homeric warfare is in some ways more like a street fight than a chivalrous contest. This is why all boys like the *Iliad*. Two gangs meet, one called the Greeks, the other the Trojans. There is some cause for "trouble" between them, but half the time they forget what it is. For a while they will have a general scrimmage. Then they will draw apart for breath, and a big boy steps forward from one side and dares any big boy from the other side to come on, picturing in blunt terms what he purposes to do to him if he does come on. The other big boy is forthcoming, has his say, and they are at it. The age of Homer was not the age of chivalry, its notion of military honor was not ours (speaking as adults). But this is a question of manners. What noble use Homer can make of the figure of warfare, you may see in Sarpedon's speech to Glaucus: "Friend of my soul, were it that, if we once escaped from this war, we should live forever without old age or death, I should not fight myself among the foremost, nor would I send thee into the battle that gives men glory; but, for a thousand fates of death stand over us, which mortal man may not flee from nor escape, let us go on, and give glory to another or win it ourselves." To live boldly, generously, for glory — which is to say for a fairly earned happiness — with keen enjoyment of the act of living, without unmanning thought of the end: this is the Homeric way.

For one reason, at least, it is proper, even necessary, to say a few words about Homer in such a book as this. He was the first of the great line of poets not only in time but, as it were, in blood. Without Homer, Virgil could not conceivably have been what he was, as without Virgil, we should have had a different Dante. Before beginning our brief sketch of Virgil's life, we may do well to say what is to be said about his relation to Homer.

The Augustan age differed more radically from the age of Homer than the eighteenth century differed from the tenth. We may take Nettleship's summary of the situation at the time when Virgil began to write: "It was given to the Greeks to attain an independent national development, uninfluenced for the most part by any civilization other than their own. Hand in hand with their national and political growth, their poetry advanced from the simple elements of myth and lay and epic to elaborate forms of lyric and drama, until it expired in the learned labors of the Alexandrian school, and the delicate prettinesses of the *Anthology*. The Italians, on the other hand, never developed a national literature on its own lines. The influence of Greece was too strong for them; as early as the time of Pyrrhus (about 280 B. C.) Greek historians were busy with Rome, and easily overwhelmed the too docile Italians, who had had no time to cultivate a learning of their own, with a deluge of second-hand and second-rate mythology. The last poem of importance composed in the national Italian metre was the *Punic War* of Nævius, written towards the end of the third century before Christ. From this time onwards Greek metres reigned supreme in Italy. Ennius wrote his great epic chronicle of Roman history in hexameters, Plautus and the other dramatists used the Greek iambic and trochaic. Although the Italians had plenty of original power, and must have been conscious of it, the study and imitation of Greek models in regard both to metre and handling of the subject matter, was henceforth regarded by them as their first duty, and on this principle they continued to work without question and with unceasing care till the time of Virgil, Horace, and Ovid, when, indeed, it was not abandoned, but when new models, accepted by subsequent generations as classical, were formed within the domain of Roman literature itself."

The chief interest of Virgil's contemporaries was not in Homer or the great Greek dramatists, but in the Alexandrian school which had intervened. Virgil's own early poems showed his familiarity with this inferior literature, though a sound taste protected him from the worst extravagances of his models. But there is little trace of the Alexandrians in the *Æneid,* and a great deal of Homer. It was a period of imitativeness and dilettantism. Virgil, like his contemporaries, chose his models in Greece, but chose the most robust. Many motives, scenes, phrases even, in the *Æneid* are transferred almost bodily from Homer, and much unnecessary talk has been made about this natural fact from Virgil's time to ours. The world is but now reluctantly beginning to accept the fact that genius cannot plagiarize: the terms are contradictory. If one man's work is so far influenced by another's as to lose its own character, then its character can have been hardly worth saving. Homer's important service to Virgil consisted in his serving, not as a treasury of detail, but as a guide to a larger world than was contained in the traditions and the coteries of Augustan Rome. "He brought him into a world of men, where, like Odysseus, he might see the cities of many and learn their minds. He showed him the energies, the passions, and the infinite life of men and women, in a larger air and on a grander and simpler scale than he could find it elsewhere, in art or in what people call real life. He showed him a broad, wide world, a world of battle and seafaring, of city and forest, where warrior, sailor, counselor, fisherman, shepherd, all pursue their task with that keenness of interest, that calm in the face of danger and obstacle, and that fundamental content, which a great poet can see, where a lesser finds only failure and despair, broken hopes and baffled endeavors. The minor poets,— the people whom Goethe calls 'the lazaretto poets'— are overcome by the sense of man's failure, but Homer's note is different. In him man triumphs over the world because he can and will look it full in the face and find in the human spirit something to overcome the world." This serene and triumphant mood, at least in the process of creation, we shall find to be the common possession of all the great poets whose lives and characters are to be sketched in this book.

VIRGIL

A REALLY great name has a way of losing its personal meaning, and getting to be simply a label for something done. We know that it stands for genius, but we have a feeling that supreme genius is a sort of disembodied quality, so that if a great name usually means something to us, it rarely means somebody. And yet it often might, if we were to stop thinking of it as a thing to be found on the backs of books or the pedestals of statues. There is no reason why we should not have some measure of acquaintance with the man Dante, or Shakespeare, or Milton, or Goethe, — yes, or even Virgil. We have the best of them, no doubt, in their immortal poetry, and it would be an impertinence for us to pry unduly into the conditions and events of their mortal life, yet they did live once, and they must have been worth knowing. Virgil's fame expanded in a way rather monstrous after his death — like the form of the genie after he had escaped from the bottle. Up to the end of the Middle Ages, up to the time of Dante and beyond, he lived in the popular mind not only as the greatest of poets, but as a magician, a bogy-man, a name for mystics to conjure with. Yet the records of his contemporaries show him simply a man like other men, except as he

VIRGIL

was marked by high poetic gifts. There was nothing sensational about his career, nothing exceptional, unless it were for the steady increase of a worldly prosperity which has been the portion of talents of the second order oftener than of the first.

Virgil (Publius Virgilius Maro) was born on October 15 of the year 70 B. C., in the village, or district, of Andes, near Mantua. Andes, Virgilius, and Maro have all been said to be names of Celtic origin; and from this saying has derived a theory of his mixed race. But the theory has not been proved, and leaves us very much where it found us. A passage in the tenth book of the *Æneid* seems to give a hint of its possible truth; that in which Virgil speaks of Mantua as "rich in ancestry, yet not all of one blood, a threefold race, and under each race four cantons; herself, she is the cantons' head, and her strength is of Tuscan blood." Pliny speaks of Mantua as "the last Etruscan relic across the Po." Even in Imperial times the little city remained in literal insulation, untroubled by the affairs of Rome. Virgil was a provincial, therefore, in a sense beyond that in which Horace, Ovid, and other prominent poets of his time were provincials.

Like Horace, he was of humble birth. As a young man his father had lived in Cremona, in the service of a courier (*viator*). Whatever his origin, he was evidently a man of ambition, worked hard and well, and married his master's daughter. There are odd analogies in these matters. Shakespeare's father, Milton's father, Goethe's grandfather, were all men who lifted themselves from a low social plane to a higher by unusual industry and by favorable marriages. Virgil was born in the first consulship of Pompey and Crassus. The republic had virtually received its deathblow, and the years which followed were still years of public disorder. It was at this time, perhaps, that Virgil's father found it possible to buy up certain tracts of woodland. At all events, he seems during the poet's youth to have been farmer, forester, and bee-keeper, and perhaps kept up his trade of courier as well. There are innumerable traces in Virgil's poems of his familiarity with the soil. His first-hand knowledge gives a note of sincerity to his *Eclogues* and *Georgics* which is rare in pastoral verse, and which would have been otherwise unthinkable in so artificial an age as the Augustan. His knowledge of practical forestry has been testified to by experts, and his love of trees must be obvious to any reader of his poems. There is no finer praise of the forest than that of the second *Georgic*. Especially significant of his early experience is the passage which bewails the necessity of turning woodland into arable, destroying not only the trees, but the homes of countless wild creatures. He feels the forest not only as a haunt of beauty but as a commonwealth. It has some such place in his imagination as the sea has in Homer's. Odysseus finds the nether world by the path of the sea; Æneas in the depths of a forest. In the fourth *Georgic* is a pleasant and vivid reminiscence of his father's bee-keeping — an important industry in the days when honey was both honey and sugar. Another relic of his youth was the rustic and slightly awkward manner which he never outgrew, and for which the Roman wits were wont to ridicule him after he had become a famous man.

The courier-father had advanced himself in the world, and was in a position to start his sons toward a yet higher step of the ladder. There were two other sons beside Virgil, and for anything that we know to the contrary, they were all given equal opportunities. But one of them died in boyhood, and the other hardly reached manhood. It may be that Virgil showed special ability which led his father to determine upon educating him thoroughly. Perhaps he was not physically robust enough to promise well for active life. At all events, we know that he received a training far superior to what might have been expected from his father's station and the remoteness of his birthplace. A courier must be, at least, something of a man of the world. Virgil's father of course knew, as the ordinary farmer and woodsman would not know, what the uses of an education were, and where it might be got. The boy studied first at Cremona, then at Milan, and finally at Rome. At fifteen he assumed the *toga virilis,* and so technically became a man.

We have a book of minor poems, called the *Cata-*

lepton, attributed to Virgil. His authorship of some of the poems included has been disputed, and in one or two cases virtually disproved. But most of them we may accept as the *juvenilia* of a great poet. Traces of Catullus are naturally very numerous. He was Virgil's earliest master, and his influence was not a passing one. Both Lucretius and he were at the height of their fame when Virgil reached the most impressionable age. Lucretius died when Virgil was sixteen years old, and Catullus not much later. What Latin poetry had become in their hands is best described by M. Patin: "There is for a literature a moment, slow to come and swift to pass, when the language, polished and made pliant by use, lends itself to the most vivid and most exact expression of conceptions which have themselves been developed by the long labor of genius. It was thus with Latin literature, when from that branch long since severed from the old Homeric trunk, which two centuries of culture had accustomed to the sky and soil of Latium, Virgil and Horace came to gather the fruits of poetry, mature at last. All that the epic poetry of Nævius and Ennius, the tragedy of Pacuvius and Attius, the comedy of Plautus and Terence, the satire of Lucilius, the efforts of poets of every class, had accumulated in the poetic treasury of the Romans — well-defined terms, subtle shades of meaning, natural analogies, graceful turns of expression, happy phrasing, striking images, harmonious combinations of words; that precision of form, that art in composition, upon which the easy inspiration of Lucretius lighted by happy chance, and which the skill and industry of Catullus sought and found — all this, such was the fortune of their birth, fell to Virgil and Horace to inherit, and entered into the formation of their genius, very much as at the same time the various powers of the republican constitution gathered together into one single hand to form the absolute authority of their imperial protector."

Catullus was a master of style, and it was from him rather than from any other that Virgil got his extreme scrupulousness in matters of form, his sedulous pursuit of refinement as well as vigor of expression.

The *Catalepton* not only contains a parody of Catullus and several imitations, but the flavor of the whole collection is his. It must have been shortly after his death that the slim boy Virgil, now at Rome, composed the most spirited and delightful of these pieces. His ambitious father had probably intended him for an advocate, and he had been set to study rhetoric under the best masters, one of them being Epidius, the master of Antony and Octavian. But Virgil had no knack for speaking, and hated the formal exercises of the rhetoricians. He is said to have appeared just once as an advocate, with what mediocre effect may be judged from the marked absence of comment upon his performance. He was finally released from rhetoric and began the study of Philosophy under Siro, a noted philosopher of the Epicurean school.

And the boy Virgil, overjoyed at the exchange, sings his little song of defiance and triumph, and addresses it to the new master: "Away with you, empty color-bottles of the rhetoricians, words swollen with water, but not of the dews of Greece, away with you, Stilo, Tarquitius, and Varro, you nation of pedants soaking with fat, you tinkling cymbals of the class-room. Farewell, too, Sabinus, friend of all my friends; farewell from henceforth, all my beautiful comrades. We are setting our sails for the havens of blessedness, going to hear the learned words of great Siro, and mean to redeem our life from all distraction. Farewell, too, sweet Muses, for to tell the truth I have found how sweet you are; still I pray you sometimes, but with modesty and at rare intervals, to look on my pages again." That is the whole poem, and a little gem it is, worthy to be read by the modern schoolboy who thinks of Virgil as a rather stupid old gentleman, some time dead, who wrote a lot of stuff in hexameters which the school-boy would willingly let die. Here is indeed a note of buoyancy, of boyish ardor and hope, which we do not find in the poet's mature work. No doubt he failed to find all the ills of life cured, all the problems fully solved, by the learned words of great Siro. But it is certain that this teacher meant much to him. During the next ten years, at least, the Epicurean philosophy had strong hold upon him. At about the time when his studies under Siro began, the masterpiece of Lucretius was given circulation. Here was a master in whom, with a beauty of manner equal to Catullus's, there was also a firmness of substance of which Catullus was incapable. And Lucretius was a follower of Epicurus.

The Muses, meantime, had refused to take Virgil's farewell seriously. There is no doubt that by the time he had entered his twenties, he had begun to see that his career was to lie in poetry rather than philosophy. Somewhere about the age of twenty-seven, he apparently returned to Mantua, to his father's house, with no very promising record behind him, it may be, from the paternal point of view. He had made his one unsuccessful attempt at the bar, he had written some poems which in private circulation had won some commendation from good judges. According to Suetonius, he had tried his hand during these years at a poetical history of Rome, but had wisely given up the project. There is a passage in one of the *Eclogues* which probably alludes to this incident: "When I was trying to sing of kings and battles, Apollo touched my ear, and warned me to desist." In short, he realized that he was by nature a poet and not a historian, and had better stick to his last. If his return to Mantua meant in a sense that he was back upon his father's hands, it meant quite as probably that his presence at home was important. There seems to have been some such perfect sympathy between father and son as was to exist between the two John Miltons. And Virgil's father was rapidly growing blind,— an added call upon Virgil's loyalty. A year or two after the return from Rome, events occurred which tested this loyalty, and showed further that, even from a material point of view, his time in Rome had not been wasted.

There was every reason why Virgil, like other Mantuans, should have been a strong Cæsar's man. Julius Cæsar had been patron of Transpadane Gaul, the district in which Mantua lay, almost since Virgil's birth. In the year 49 he crossed the Rubicon, and made the inhabitants of this whole region Roman citizens. Cæsar's assassination in 44 no doubt aroused quite as much grief in Mantuans as in Romans. The years of confusion and prolonged civil bloodshed which followed brought their share of terror to the people across the Po. In 41 much of their territory was confiscated by the victorious triumvirs, Antony, Octavian, and Lepidus, and distributed among their veterans. Among the estates disposed of in this summary way was that of Virgil's father. But Virgil, unlike most of the victims, among them certain brother-poets, was equal to the emergency. When the barbarian, the strange soldier, came to take possession, the young poet was able to find a place of refuge to which he could bear his old and half-blind father, if not literally as Æneas bore Anchises, surely in the same filial spirit. This was the villa of Siro, his old master in philosophy, which is apostrophized in one of the poems of the *Catalepton:* "I commit myself to thee, and with myself those whom I have always loved, if perchance I should hear any gloomy news of my country. Above all shalt thou shelter my father; to him thou shalt be what Mantua and Cremona once were." It is not known where Siro's villa was, but there for a time Virgil remained with his father and mother, and perhaps his brother. For his father he evidently had a special tenderness. It has been suggested that the episode of Iapis in the *Æneid* could have been written only by a devoted son. "To him Apollo himself offered his own arts, his own gifts,—augury and the lyre and archery; but he, to prolong the life of his father who lay dying, chose rather to know the virtues of herbs and the craft of healing, to ply inglorious a silent art." Virgil's resources did not end with the finding of a temporary retreat. He knew Rome, and had made important friends there. Thither he went, and through Varus, governor of Transpadane Gaul, Gallus and Pollio (poets as well as men of affairs) and, it is said, Mæcenas, actually secured a restoration of the Andes estate. It must have been a difficult negotiation, as to prove himself an "Indian-giver" to his veterans must have been the last thing the wily Octavian would have wished to do. Two of the *Eclogues*, the first and the ninth, clearly enough allude to this episode. The *Eclogues* as a whole are dedicated to those who had helped the poet in his time of trouble. The ninth, under the veil of the pastoral figure, describes how he, "Menalcas," was driven by force from his home, in spite of his pleadings and, as it seems, resistance: in spite of his reputation as a poet. Or, we should rather say, his services as a poet. For in the age we call Augustan, which really began a generation before the title of Augustus was given to Octavian, the practice of letters, and especially of poetry, was esteemed a public service, and almost as a requisite for a public career. Imagine a king or a president of our day who should feel it necessary, in order to keep or to extend his prestige, to encourage poets! Augustus did feel that, as the rulers of the rather feeble Augustan age of England felt it,— much to our amusement!

It was in the pastoral form, a form developed in Greek literature which had not yet been conveyed effectively into the Roman,— that Virgil first seriously challenged his world. Conington says that "the history of pastoral poetry shows how easily the most simple form of composition may pass into the most artificial." The idyl of Theocritus represents the original and simple form,— a short poem, often in dialogue, representing some simple scene or episode of country life. The shepherds and milkmaids,— the nymphs and swains,— are real persons though idealized, if we may so put it: at all events they are not mere lay figures to hang poetical conceits upon — as they are, for example, in the pastorals of Ambrose Philips or Pope, which represent the form at its nadir, and whose absurdities are hit off so perfectly in the travesties of the flippant Gay and the bitter Swift.

But there was an intermediate form between these extremes. "The pastoral character of the poem became a mere form or setting, in which the poet suggested, as in a kind of allegory, a reference to events in his own life and times. . . . In Virgil's eclogue the shepherd speaks, not only in his own person, but in that of the poet, and the names of his companions are chosen to denote well-known persons in whom the interest of the poet happens to center." In plan and phrase, Virgil's pastorals closely imitate their Greek original. Even the names and scenes employed are often Greek or Sicilian rather than Italian. Yet the *Eclogues* are not mere exercises: in a large sense, they ring true, and they give a new melody to the Latin tongue, too much hitherto a tongue of and for the market and the forum. As mere exercises they would have been worth while, for, as Mr. Woodberry says of the pastoral in this connection, "its small scale enforces attention to detail and encourages perfection of phrase, line and image in the workmanship, and condensation in the matter, while its variety of description, dialogue, and inserted song and its blend of lyric and dramatic moods give scope to a mind experimenting as it learns. It is for this reason that so many of the world's great poets in their youth have tried their wings in these numbers, brief, composite, academic, so well fitted for the exercise of growing talents, already touched with scholarship, in a world not too real to be lightly held, not so fantastic as to preclude truth of feeling. Virgil derived the proper good from the imitation of a great master by developing through it his native power. Theocritus remained the master-singer of the idyl; but before the different genius of Virgil passed on to its own toils, he had left the sweetness of his youth here in the pastoral like a perfume forever."

Our concern is with the human and personal side of his poetry. It is significant that in the opening eclogue, expressing his gratitude to Augustus for the kindness which has restored to him the home acres, he also expresses sorrow for the fellow-exiles who have not been equally favored. The good fortune which followed him steadily for the rest of his life did not make him careless, though he continued to be grateful for it. Suetonius says that when on one occasion Augustus offered him the estate of an exile, Virgil could not bring himself to accept it.

The *Eclogues* are now arranged in chronological order. The fifth probably dates back to the period of Julius Cæsar's death, or shortly after. It is written in a strain of eulogy whose fulsomeness, if we must call it that, is due rather to the hour than to the poet. "Daphnis," it runs, "is now a god, and in the brightness of his divinity looks for the first time on the threshold of heaven and sees the clouds and the stars beneath his feet." It must be recalled that within a year of his death, Cæsar was formally declared Divus, and a proper object of worship. It was one of the old Greek fashions which Rome had adopted, to confer, as it were, an honorary deity upon the memory of their greatest men. Consequently when Virgil calls Cæsar a god, he is simply using an intelligible term of the day. No especial obsequiousness or extravagance can be charged against him for his use of such phrases. There is no doubt that he had a sincere personal admiration for Cæsar. Certainly he had a real regard for Augustus. Even in his own day he was accused of servility and sycophancy. The favors he received from his great patrons naturally seemed indecent, a proof of shame, to persons who were not treated in the same way. The most that can fairly be alleged against Virgil was that he evidently kept still about matters of which he did not approve. He was not a satirist, not a man of impatient temper.

As early as the year 40, when Octavian was more than nominally sharing the power with Antony and Lepidus, Virgil probably anticipated the passage written many years later in the sixth book of the *Æneid* in which he prophesies that Augustus is to restore the golden age. Octavian had recently been married. The fourth *Eclogue* is an ode to a child presently to be born: " The golden age is to return, and the generations are to begin their course anew. The newborn child is to be initiated into the life of the gods, to walk with demi-gods and heroes, and to rule the world with the manly virtues of his father; he is the offspring of gods, and another Jove is to spring from him. To greet him the earth will blossom with her fairest flowers, the goats will return unbidden to the milk-pails, the lion will lie down with the lamb, there will be no more serpents or poisonous plants, and as he grows up, the fields will be yellow with corn, and the brambles will bear the ruddy grape. When he is come to manhood, all the evil ways of men shall cease; there shall be no more building of ships, no commerce, no tilling of the soil; the earth shall bear all things everywhere, and there shall be no need of harrow or pruning-hook. The glory of the age is born, who shall wipe out all traces of former guilt and govern the world in righteousness." This eclogue was dedicated to Asinius Pollio, trebly distinguished as orator, poet, and statesman; and in the long discussion which arose as to the meaning of the prophecy about the child, it became known as "the Pollio." In the early centuries of the Christian era, it was supposed to refer to the birth of Christ, and had much to do with the growth of a belief in Virgil's supernatural powers. There are of course striking coincidences of thought and phrase between the passage and certain ancient Hebrew prophecies concerning the Messiah. It was long believed that there had been numerous unconscious prophecies of Christ in the "heathen" world, from the utterances of the Cumæan Sybil down.

Those who have taken the poem more literally have

been divided as to whether the child foretold was a child of Pollio, or of Octavian or some other. But Pollio's descent was not especially noteworthy, while Octavian not only was of the race of the deified Julius, but claimed descent from Venus, and consequently from Jupiter. "He is the offspring of gods, and another Jove is to spring from him"; surely it is reasonable to suppose that the prediction connects itself in some way with the Octavian who was soon to be Augustus. Perhaps the most reasonable interpretation of all is that it is a prophecy after the fact — that Virgil means Augustus himself. In this case the composition of the poem may belong to a later date.

Certainly it seemed to Virgil, as to most of his contemporaries, that the rule of Augustus actually brought to pass a condition of things almost ideal. For a century before he gathered the reins of power so gradually and firmly in his hands, Italy had been torn by political dissensions and bloody factional war. The first thing to be desired by most Italians was a stable peace, and this Augustus gave them. With peace came prosperity of various kinds, and a special prosperity for poets. Prose-writers did not fare so well. Livy is the only brilliant name in a generation of poets, and he plainly alludes to the difficulty of writing sincere prose under an absolute monarchy. Poetry, on the other hand, was likely to be encouraged because of its habit of dealing with agreeable abstractions. What Augustus chiefly wanted of his poets was the glorification of things as they were under his rule, in contrast with things as they had been in the immediate past; or, to put it more flatteringly, what he wanted was to hear the Augustan age spoken of as a return to the ancient and legendary glories of Rome — with improvements. There is no denying that Virgil was prepared to give him this satisfaction, and that with perfect sincerity. If his phrases are often extravagant to our ears, we must remember that Augustus was not only his sovereign but his patron. His tone toward Mæcenas is hardly less obsequious. A certain formal adulation was looked for toward the patron from that time to the very threshold of our own. Recall Dante's attitude toward Can Grande, Shakespeare's toward Southampton. A last relic of this convention in our own times is the English laureateship.

There is a legend to the effect that Virgil was driven a second time from his estate by soldiers, that he offered some resistance, was forced to fly, took refuge from his pursuers in the house of a charcoal-burner, from whose back door he again escaped, and swam across the river Mincio to safety. According to this story he again made plea to Rome, and was again restored to his home. Whether he was once or twice evicted, it is certain that it was this business of the estate which first brought him to the notice of Octavian. From this time on the benefactions of his two patrons raised him to a level of worldly prosperity which has hardly been equaled by any poet in the world's history. He had a house in Rome and a villa at Naples: when he died he left the equivalent of something like half a million dollars. These facts may easily be dwelt upon too much. He was not a lover of luxury, and the story of his later life is a story of very serious devotion to his poetic calling.

The *Eclogues* had so vast a success as to make Virgil at once a public figure in Rome. An astonishing indication of the popularity of poetry in that time is the fact that these pastorals were read in the theaters; and Tacitus says that on one occasion a great audience rose on Virgil's entrance, an honor commonly given only to Augustus. For some years after his adoption by Augustus and Mæcenas he probably spent a good deal of time at Rome. There he found himself presently the chief among a group of poets whom the generous Mæcenas had gathered about himself. "Mæcenas, the center of the group, owes his immortality to his poet friends. With their aid and that of other writers, who have preserved memories of him, we can see him still — statesman, fop, husband, and friend, a man of affectations in dress and jewel, and precious beyond intelligibility in language, who quarreled a thousand times with his wife, and had as many reconciliations, though without excessive faithfulness on either side; who flaunted his dislike for the toga so far as to refuse to wear it even when acting as the Emperor's deputy; who tormented his friends with his complaints about health, gave them estates, listened to their poetry, and won their love; and who, finally, was a shrewd and moderate statesman, sparing the sword, never abusing his power, and guilty of no outrage but upon his mother-tongue." Horace and Varius were the two other poets of the group with whom Virgil seems to have been most intimate. Unfortunately most of the poems of Varius have been lost, but he held a high place in his day, and Virgil's regard is shown by the fact that he made him his chief literary executor. Horace had been introduced to Mæcenas by Virgil himself, and the relation between the two poets is one of the most memorable among literary friendships. It is supposed that in the early days of their acquaintance they may have spent some time together at Tarentum. There are allusions in the verses of both poets which seem to bear out the supposition, and the scenery described in several of the *Eclogues* is said to be more appropriate to the neighborhood of Tarentum than to the Mantuan country. "The friendship of the two poets," says Nettleship, "was of great importance for the future of Latin literature. Though they followed different lines, their styles are curiously akin; and elsewhere I have collected passages from their works which seem to show that they must sometimes have worked and almost thought together. It was a fashion of the time for one poet to use, sometimes unaltered, sometimes with slight alterations, the verses of another whom he loved or admired; and there are several instances of this kind which attest, in their way, the intimacy of Virgil with Horace." They were of very different character and tastes. Horace was preëminently the man of the world, the man about town, elegant, urbane, fond of the best society. He perhaps represents the Augustan age as it was, Virgil as it might have been. Hence we have the curious paradox of greater apparent servility on the part of the larger-minded poet. Horace chose to live in the town, and owned to his fondness for the society of the rich and powerful. But he saw through Rome and its Augustus as Virgil did not. He also, when in the mood, celebrated the virtues and the godhead of Augustus in terms which eclipsed Virgil. But there was a vein of sturdiness in him. He refused to be the Emperor's private secretary, or to write an epic for him which he doubtless saw must be but a eulogy on a great scale. He also refused personal favors such as Virgil did not scruple to accept. The Emperor did not like to have his poets get out of hand, and Suetonius gives letters from him, accusing Horace of a contempt for his friendship, and asking him if he feared posterity would judge it a disgrace for him to have been the intimate of Augustus.

With Virgil the facts were precisely reversed. He was, according to a contemporary, of rustic manner, "very slow of speech, and almost like an uneducated person": not at all the kind of man to get on easily in polite circles. He must have been made uncomfortable, too, by the character of many of the people who surrounded Augustus. The court of the new Emperor was not unlike that of Napoleon. Few of the old aristocracy were to be found there, many tools and partizans who had been useful to Octavian before he became Augustus, military adventurers, men who had made their fortunes by blood-money and confiscation. The blessings of the Emperor's rule were genuine, and Virgil's satisfaction in them was sincere. But for that reason he must recoil from reminder of the means by which Augustus had gained his power, and of some of the means by which he kept it secure. At all events, the poet chose to spend most of his later years away from the atmosphere of the court, away from Rome. So he was able to keep his idol unblemished before his imagination, to accept the imperial bounty without question, and to put his whole heart into the task of writing an epic for Augustus, and largely in his honor.

Indeed, it is impossible to separate any of Virgil's work from the thought of Augustus. The *Georgics* were inscribed to Mæcenas, but in substance they are continually recurring to the greatness of Augustus and his cause — the regeneration of Italy. Seven or eight years seem to have been occupied in the writing of these poems, the last of which cannot have been finished before the year 29. They constitute a celebration of husbandry, and it is said that a chief object was to renew the ancient zeal for the art of agriculture with which such havoc had been made during the civil disturbances of the preceding century. The first book deals with the cultivation of the land, the second with forestry, the third with cattle-raising, and the fourth with bee-culture. Here again the Italian finds his models in Greece — Hesiod and others; but he improves upon them as he cannot be said to have improved upon Theocritus in the *Eclogues*. His farm and field lore are often sound: through all one feels his unfeigned love for the soil and the open air. And more: if the poet is now singing in the middle of that golden age which Augustus had brought, it is not the golden age of the early eclogue — when there should be "no tilling of the soil, no need of harrow and pruning-hook." Nor is it the golden age of his piping shepherds, with their pleasant tasks — half play,— and their leisure for Amaryllis and the rest. Here, on the contrary, is a celebration of toil, endless and heart-breaking toil — the lot of the farmer from time immemorial. Over and over again, year by year must be the plowing, the pruning, the "eternal" hoeing,— toil, toil, and exhaustion as the price of sleep. No wonder Burns the plowman, who well knew the racking labor of the fields, thought the *Georgics* "by far the best part of Virgil."

So did Dryden, for that matter, and so have others to whom husbandry was but a name: a sure sign of their vitality as poetry. One of their charms is the vein of gentle humor which plays always about Virgil's description. He, like Burns, has a whimsical tenderness for the "timorous beastie" who must be regarded as a pest in the soil, and who yet has his own home and his own rights in the eye of nature. And there is a strain of deeper philosophy underlying both humor and didacticism. The influence of Lucretius is still strong upon him. "There are passages . . . which seem to show that his greatest ambition would have been to have sung, like Lucretius, of the secrets of nature rather than either of heroic legends or of country life. And here and there, throughout these books of the *Georgics,* wherever he has the opportunity, he forgets the farmer in the natural philosopher, and breaks off in the midst of some practical precepts to indulge in speculations on the hidden causes of nature's operations, which would have sorely puzzled a Roman country gentleman or his bailiff, if we could suppose that the work was really prepared with a view to their practical instruction."

Though Virgil was of halting speech, he was an effective reader. He is said to have read the whole of the *Georgics* to Augustus,— except certain portions which Mæcenas read, to spare the poet's voice. The reading took four days. Suetonius says that Virgil sometimes read his poems to others beside Augustus, "but not often, and generally passages about which he was doubtful, with a view to criticism." A minor poet who had heard him "used to say that he would steal Virgil's voice and pronunciation and delivery, if he could, for verses would sound well when he read them which from any other lips were empty and dumb." We have also the story of his reading passages of the *Æneid* to Augustus and his sister Octavia. Marcellus, Octavia's son, had died not long before, and Virgil's rendering of the passage in the sixth book in praise of Marcellus was so moving that Octavia fainted.

The *Georgics* were finished in 29, the year in which Augustus returned in triumph from the East. The last ten years of Virgil's life were given to the writing of the *Æneid*. Most of his time was spent at Naples. It will be recalled that he had early thought of attempting an epic on the early history of Rome, but had been warned off by Apollo. Before he had finished the *Georgics*, he had pretty well made up his mind to another undertaking. In the prelude to the third *Georgic* he distinctly says that he is going to tell of the battles of Cæsar, by which he means, of course, the story of Augustus's recent successful campaigns in the East. There are certain passages in the *Æneid*, — the description of the battle of Actium, for instance, — which may perhaps be fragments of such a work actually begun. The *Æneid*, in fact, is virtually a combination of the two projects. Instead of dealing with the early kings and wars of Rome,— a theme which had been often handled in prose and verse,— Virgil turned to its legendary history. The subject offered much better and safer material for his idealizing imagination, material for the glorification of Augustus as well as of Rome. It was a fad among the Roman aristocrats to trace a fancied descent from the heroes of the Homeric epics. Julius Cæsar had claimed descent from Iulus, son of Æneas, son of Venus, and Augustus was the nephew of Julius Cæsar. As Æneas was the traditional founder of the Roman empire, Virgil evidently had a pretty complete set of materials for his epic at hand. "The story of the wanderings of Æneas from Ilium to Italy is a chapter in a large body of fables which must have grown up as the foundation of Greek colonies in Sicily and the south of Italy brought Greece and Italy into nearer contact with each other. Two main features distinguish this mythology from that represented by the Homeric poems. First, the heroes of the Trojan war appear as migrating westward to Sicily and Italy; secondly, they are not like Achilles and Ulysses, the destroyers, but like Æneas and Antenor, the founders, of cities. Their glory is as much in peace as in war; in law-giving as in conquest." In this respect again the subject is fit for Virgil's hand. Peace, order, justice, not military conquest, really appeal to him, really move him to admiration and love. He has none of Homer's fighting blood. If Napoleon found the strategy and the tactics in the *Iliad* perfect, he judged Virgil's warcraft very differently. He dismisses it as absurd, declaring that Virgil "was nothing but the regent of a college, who had never gone outside its doors, and that he did not know what an army was." In short,

Virgil's descriptions of battles are a part of his task, and nothing more. No wonder he thought better of the project of making himself official poetical chronicler of Augustus's campaign. He could by no means have done for Achilles what he did for Æneas.

Neither from the Greek point of view nor from the modern is Æneas an heroic figure. He is too helpless a puppet of the gods. He deserts Dido because the gods will it; and it is on this occasion that Mercury utters the famous adage, "Varium et mutabile semper femina," — which seems a good deal like adding insult to injury, as poor Dido is faithful enough in all conscience! He conquers Turnus and becomes master of Italy by trickery, and again by the interference of the gods. In Homer also the gods take an often disconcerting hand in events; but there are elements of sturdiness, of honor, in Achilles, yes, in the crafty Ulysses even, which the pious Æneas totally lacks. Gladstone had a theory that Virgil himself preferred Turnus: "that although he made Æneas victorious, as was required in order to carry out the complimentary reference of the Roman origin to Troy, still the young chief of native Italian blood, maintaining a gallant struggle for his rights against gods and men, and only conquered at the last by supernatural force and fraud, was purposely held out to popular admiration." Virgil may very well have done this unconsciously; for it would be at this point that his two motives — the praise of Italy and the praise of Augustus — would conflict. Whatever of matter and general method the *Æneid* may owe to Greece and her great master of the epic, its feeling is intensely Italian, even Roman. Virgil's gods are Roman. Sainte-Beuve has illustrated the fact by comparing the Æolus of Homer with the Æolus of Virgil. In Homer he is "a good enough fellow, a genuine patriarch among his family, given over on his island to enjoyment, to mirth and good cheer," while in Virgil he is "this subaltern of a god, somber, uninquisitive, a little bored upon his rock. . . . There is something of the centurion about him." So in Homer an assembly of the gods is a pleasant convivial affair; in Virgil it is a session of the Roman senate.

The *Æneid* stood as we have it in the year 19 B. C. But it was not finished, it must always remain a fragment, a rough sketch. Virgil had planned to spend three years more in polishing and refining it, and meant then, when he should have completed his masterpiece, to abandon poetry (as Horace had already done) and give himself to reading and philosophy. Augustus showed a deep interest in the plan and progress of the poem, and Suetonius speaks of letters written from the field during the Spanish campaign "full of playful entreaties and equally playful menaces to wring from him either a first draft of the poem, or at any rate some part of it." A letter from Virgil to Augustus has been preserved, which would seem to have been written at this time, in which he says, "As to my Æneas, if

I really had him in a state worthy of your ears, I would gladly send him; but the subject I have taken in hand is so vast, that I feel it was madness to attack so big a work, particularly when I have, as you know, to devote other and more important study to that work." Surely here was a poet who took his task with almost appalling seriousness. He depended upon no sudden afflatus; his method was most painstaking. He himself said that he had to lick his verses into shape as a bear might her cubs. He would write a few lines, and then spend much time in revising them, adding much less than he threw away.

For ten years he worked upon the *Æneid,* and at last got it into such shape that he felt he could profitably leave it for a time. So he set out on a tour through Greece and Asia Minor. Before leaving Italy he had authorized his friend and fellow-poet Varius to burn the *Æneid* if anything should happen to him upon his journey. Varius had refused to promise anything of the kind, but apparently the manuscript had been left in his hands. Virgil had cause to fear that something might happen to him. He had never been a thoroughly well man, his throat and digestion were both weak, and he was liable to hemorrhages. He had got as far as Athens, when he met Augustus, who was on his way back to Rome from one of his expeditions into the East. Virgil decided to return with the Emperor, instead of going on with his journey. By an irony of chance, this was a fatal decision. The day before they were to start on their return, he went with Augustus to see Megara. It was an extremely hot day, and Virgil was ill when they started on their voyage home. By the time they landed at Brundisium he was much worse. There he died a few days later, on September 21, of the year 19. In his dying hours he kept begging his friends to bring him the manuscript of the *Æneid*, so that he might destroy it. But this they refused to do, and as a last chance of suppressing the unfinished poem, he left all his writings to Varius and another friend, Tucca, with the provision that they were not to publish anything which he had not already put forth himself. However, it was not likely that Augustus would allow any arrangement of this sort to stand. He gave Varius and Tucca authority to edit and publish the *Æneid*. They seem to have used all possible discretion in handling the work, making only a few obvious corrections in a manuscript which was confessedly incomplete.

There is no doubt that Virgil was deeply lamented by his friends. We have not only the testimony of Horace and other contemporaries that he was one of the most lovable of men, but that of the affection in which his memory has always been held. This in spite of the fact that the world has also held him in awe: his power for fifteen centuries was enormous. Mr. Woodberry has written eloquently of it: "Virgil is that poet whose verse has had most power in the world. He was the poet of Rome, and concentrated in his genius its imperial star; so long as that ruled the old Mediterranean world, with the great northwestern and eastern hinterlands, Virgil summed up its glory for the human populations that fleeted away in that vast basin; in a world forever mightily changing, his solitary preëminence was one unchanging thing, dimmed only as the empire itself faded. His memory illumined the Dark Ages. He rose again as the morning star of the Latin races. He penetrated the reborn culture of Europe with the persistency and pervasiveness of Latinity itself; not only was knowledge of his works as widespread as education, but his influence on the artistic temperament of literatures, the style of authors, and even the characters of men in their comprehension of the largeness of life, was subtle and profound, and was more ample in proportion to the nearness of the new nations to the direct descent of civilization."

The new Italy was of course in nearest descent from the old; and it may be worth while to say a word here of Virgil's influence upon the great spokesman of that New Italy, Dante, of whose life we have next to tell. When Virgil was accused of stealing from Homer, he challenged their accusers to try it themselves. Said he, "You will find it easier to rob Hercules of his club than Homer of a single verse." Though he drew a good deal of material from Homer, his chief debt to him, as we have seen, was for an inspiration which he could not have got elsewhere. The same thing may be said of Dante's debt to Virgil. Virgil was his exemplar in elevated feeling and pure and noble expression. Moreover, Virgil represented the culmination of antiquity to him as he himself represents the culmination of medievalism to us. As we shall see, Dante knew Greek literature only as it had come, greatly diluted, through the Roman. Consequently, though Homer is one among the five poets whom Dante meets in Hell, he seems almost to be included out of compliment to Virgil. Virgil speaks of Homer as "the sovereign poet," but is himself hailed by them all as the "loftiest poet." Dante is given the sixth place. The other three are Ovid, Horace, and Lucian.

"Master Virgil" held a remarkable place in the medieval mind. He was not only the greatest of poets, but the greatest of magicians. All sorts of magical powers were attributed to him. Strange and elaborate legends came into being, relating to the feats of magic he had performed. The Sortes Virgilianae were used from the time of the Roman emperors to our own day. Before Dante was born, his name had become connected in the popular mind even with diabolism and the black art. All this was an outgrowth of the respect at first accorded to him as a poet. In no long time after his death it had begun to seem that if Cæsar was a god, his favored friend could not have been much lower. Silius Italicus started the fashion of celebrating Virgil's birthday, of making pilgrimages to his tomb, and offering sacrifices there, as to a god. " Statius alluded to Virgil's tomb as to a temple. Martial declared that, as Diana had rendered sacred the Ides of May, and Mercury those of August, so Maro consecrated the Ides of October. . . . . In thus offering divine honors to the memory of Virgil, these poets opened the way for those miraculous stories that began soon to be related." Dante of course did not hold with the grosser superstitions which had gathered about Virgil's name in his time, but it is clear that he did add to his admiration of him as a poet, a reverence for him as one of powers which at least approached the supernatural. When Beatrice, at the instance of the Virgin and St. Lucia, determines to attempt the salvation of Dante, it is naturally Virgil who is chosen to act as his guide through Hell and Purgatory. Being a Pagan, he can go no farther, but whatever human intellect, and such experience as intellect can have in both worlds, are able to offer, is at his command. The Hell of Dante, in nature and topography, is that of Virgil, and there are many details of the great poem in which the influence of Virgil upon either thought or diction can be easily traced. For the rest, there was a special bond of race between them; they were both not only of Italy but of Tuscany, and the tongue of Virgil was not yet a dead tongue to Dante, though he himself chose to use the vernacular for the most part.

In one respect, one would think, Dante must have

found himself far apart from Virgil: in his attitude toward woman and the love of women. Romantic love between the sexes was as unknown in Virgil's age as in Homer's. Domestic affection was of course understood, though not greatly valued in Augustan Rome. Now and then we find a poet groping toward the idea of a feeling between man and woman which should be independent of either affection or passion. But there was no vocabulary to express such a feeling. Consequently we find Horace telling Lesbia that he wishes to love her not as one loves his mistress, but as a father loves his sons and sons-in-law! There is a touch of whimsical incongruity, from this point of view, in Virgil's being despatched by Beatrice to save Dante. How amazed the real Virgil would have been at the thought of such a relation between human beings! And yet how much, in purity of purpose, in steadfast effort, in beauty of style, these two great poets had in common!

DANTE ALIGHIERI
From Giotto's fresco in the Bargello, Florence

DANTE

DANTE was born "in the sign of the Twins," that is to say somewhere between the middle of May and the middle of June, 1265. It has been supposed, from his numerous allusions to St. Lucia and her influence upon his life, that he may have been born on her saint-day, May 30. It is St. Lucia who with the Virgin suggests to Beatrice that she come to the aid of Dante at the time when he finds himself in greatest danger from worldly sins.

Dante is a contracted form of Durante, a not uncommon name in Florence. Family names were just beginning to be used, chiefly by the higher nobility, among whom they were derived from estates or castles. Contemporary lists of the Florentine nobility do not contain the name Alighieri. Alighiero was the Christian name of Dante's father and great-grandfather. His grandfather was known as Bellincione. Yet Dante undoubtedly laid claim to noble blood, and there is no good reason to doubt the claim, though he cannot have been of the "Grandi," or greater nobles. In the fifteenth canto of the *Paradiso* he meets the first of his noble ancestors, his great-great-grandfather, Cacciaguida, who, after descanting upon the simple virtues of the Florence of his day, says: "To such a tranquil, to such a beautiful life of citizens, to such a trusty citizenship, to such a sweet inn, Mary, called on with loud cries, gave me, and in your ancient baptistery I became at once a Christian and Cacciaguida. Moronto was my brother, and Eliseo; my dame came to me from the valley of the Po, and thence was thy surname. Afterward I followed the Emperor Conrad, and he belted me of his soldiery, so much by good deeds did I come into his favor. Following him, I went against the iniquity of that law whose people usurp your rights, through fault of the shepherd. There by that base folk was I released from the deceitful world, the love of which pollutes many souls, and I came from martyrdom to this peace." That is, he went with Conrad III. of Suabia upon the second crusade, was knighted by him, and died in the Holy Land. His wife was of German birth, hence the name Alighiero, or Aldighiero as its older form appears to have been. In short, Dante was called Dante Alighieri precisely as he might have been called James Johnson in England. "He himself, if we may trust the evidence of letters ascribed to him, seems to have written 'Dantes Aligherius,' while his son calls him 'Dantes Aligherii,' and himself 'Petrus Dantis Aligherii,' Peter, son of Dante, son of Alighiero. In the official Florentine documents, where his name occurs, it is 'Dantes Allegherii' or 'Dante d'Alighiero,' and no more. The form 'degli Alighieri,' which would indicate a true family name, we find in no undoubtedly contemporary document." If Dante's origin had not been in some degree noble, he would hardly have been admitted to marriage with a daughter of the Donati, one of the proudest of Florentine families. Many of these families, as we shall see, bore surnames of German derivation. The name "Aldighiero" is said, curiously enough, to come from "Aldiger," which means much the same thing as "Shakespeare." The arms of the family were, with almost fantastic appropriateness to the career of its great son, a golden wing in an azure field.

Whatever may have been the rank of his distant forbears, Dante's father seems to have been of very little consequence personally. When the Guelf nobles were banished from Florence, some five years before the poet's birth, Alighiero was apparently allowed to stay in the city — by no means a tribute to his importance. It is strange that with all his fondness for biographical details, his full mention of his friends and acquaintances, and even of his wife's relations, Dante nowhere makes mention of any member of his immediate family. His mother died when he was very young — perhaps at his birth. His father married again, a woman of a lower class, who brought him a son and a daughter; and himself died while Dante was still a boy. His half-brother helped him more than once in money matters: and this is all we know of Dante's family.

The Florence of Dante's day had already achieved

great things, in spite of the state of political and social turmoil in which it had been born and, as it were, brought up. Originally an offshoot of the neighboring city of Fiesole, it had long overtowered the parent stock. In due time Charlemagne found it a point of vantage, deposed the Longobards, and instituted a line of German margraves as rulers, about whom gathered a German aristocracy. Hence the predominance of German names among the leading families of Tuscany thereafter. But the vitality of the native race was not destroyed; and long before Dante was born the people had begun to assert themselves against the nobility. "The names of 205 castles which existed in the county about the year 1200 have been preserved, but there undoubtedly were many more of them. One after the other fell in those endless little wars, being either razed, occupied, or subjected. . . . One lordly race after the other — the Aldobrandeschi, the Buondelmonti — were constrained to pass a part of the year in the town, and so become members of the commune. In the year 1108 the Alberti, descended from the blood of Frankish Dukes, were made to swear 'in a doleful voice' to renounce all taxes which until now they had levied from the citizens passing through their territory. Such was also the fate of the Adimari. The wars against the Guidi were never ended."

At the beginning of the thirteenth century the struggle was still between the *Grandi,* or old nobility, and the people. But matters were presently to become far more complicated with the rise of the lesser nobility and the growth of other distinctions of class, as between the *popolo grasso* or class of wealthy merchants, the lesser guilds, and the *plebe minuta,* or working class. The institution of the *podestà,* during the early part of the century, shows how impossible the different elements found it to unite in a stable government, for the common welfare. The *podestà* was a nobleman of foreign birth, elected to the chief judicial office in the state. "His courts and his chancery, his notaries, judges, armed men afoot and on horseback, his marshals and knights, were all foreigners, whom he brought with him. . . . During his term of office he was neither allowed to leave the town, nor to dine out with any of the citizens, nor even to have social intercourse with them, so deep was the mistrust of the parties." The city was already active and successful in commerce and the arts; but the Florentine was no fonder of a bargain than of a pageant or a fight. Fifty-six holidays were kept in the course of the year. The dwellings of the nobility were strongly fortified, and the town was dotted with the towers of the independent corporations. Every man's hand was against his neighbor, in business, war, and love: yet, somehow, the little city throve.

And there arose a great feud among the nobility which gradually absorbed to itself, on one side or other, citizens of all other classes and factions, and finally spread far beyond the borders of triple-walled Florence. The origin of the strife between the Guelfs and the Ghibellines is in doubt, but we have at all events no more authentic explanation of it than that given by old Villani; it seems to have been believed in by Dante. Villani's story, at all events, breathes the very air of the Florence into which Dante was born.

"In the year of Christ 1215, one Messer Bondelmonte, of the Bondelmonti, a noble citizen of Florence, having promised to take to wife a damsel of the house of the Amidei, honorable and noble citizens; as this Messer Bondelmonte, who was a gay and handsome cavalier, was riding through the city, a lady of the Donati family called to him, speaking evil of the lady who had been promised to him, how that she was not fair or fitting for him, and saying: 'I have kept my daughter here for you,' showed him the maiden; and she was very fair. And straightway falling enamored of her, he gave her his troth, and espoused her to wife; for which cause the kinsfolk of the first promised lady gathered together, and being grieved for the shame that Messer Bondelmonte had wrought them, they took on them the accursed quarrel whereby the city of Florence was laid waste and broken up." The offense was the worse because Bondelmonte (or Buondelmonte) was not of the older Florentine nobility. Villani goes on to describe his assassination by a band of the older nobles: "For the which thing's sake, the city flew to arms and uproar, and the death of Messer Bondelmonte was the cause and the beginning of the accursed Guelf and Ghibelline parties in Florence, albeit that before this the factions among the nobles of the city had been plenty, and there had been the parties I have said, by reason of the conflicts and questions between the Church and the Empire." Bondelmonte was a Guelf (as were most of the newer nobility) and the Guelfs favored the rights of the Church, while the Ghibellines were for the Empire; but each party was for itself rather than for any cause, as is the way of parties. The truth of the matter has been excellently put by Karl Federn: "All the countless causes of dissension which can and will arise in a country so torn in itself, all the many conflicting interests, the differences of races, classes and rival cities, the combat of great ideas as well as the smallest local enmities and family feuds, were covered, and in each town differently, by the names of the two great parties. The only thing common to all was strife." Dante's family was of the Guelf faction, and as we shall see, he took the matter seriously enough. The Alighieri owned houses and land, but apparently lacked money. Dante was born in one of their houses in St. Peter's Gate, near the Piazza San Martino. Not far off were the greater families of the Donati and the Portinari, one of which was to give him his wife, the other his Beatrice.

Few facts about Dante's childhood can be absolutely verified, and many of the details furnished by Boccaccio and Villani and long in general acceptance have come to be discredited by our skeptical generation. He was probably a lonely and sensitive child, eager to learn, wistful in all senses. His mother he never knew; his father died, according to one Leonardo Aretino, while he was yet a child. Good teachers he must have had, but who they were, with one possible exception, we do not know. In the fifteenth canto of the *Inferno,* Dante is accosted by the spirit of Brunetto Latini, with whom he talks at some length, and of whom he speaks as "my master." The shade foretells his fate at the hands of the Florentines: "If thou follow thy star, thou canst not miss the glorious port, if in the beautiful life I discerned aright. And if I had not so untimely died, seeing Heaven so benignant unto thee I would have given cheer unto thy work. But that ungrateful populace malign which descended from Fiesole of old, and smacks yet of the mountain and the rock, will hate thee because of thy good deeds; and this is right, for among the bitter sorb-trees it is not fitting the sweet fig should bear fruit. Old report in the world calls them blind; it is a people avaricious, envious, and proud; from their customs take heed that thou keep thyself clean. Thy fortune deserves such honor for thee that one party and the other shall hunger for thee; but far from the goat shall be the grass. Let the Fiesolan beasts make litter of themselves, and touch not the plant, if any spring still upon their dungheap, in which may live again the holy seed of those Romans who remained there when it became the nest of so much malice." To the substance of this prophecy we shall have cause to recur. For the moment, the interesting thing is Dante's reply: "If all my entreaty were fulfilled," replied I to him, "you would not yet be placed in banishment from human nature; for in my mind is fixed, and now fills my heart, the dear, good, paternal image of you, when in the world hour by hour you taught me how man makes himself eternal: and in what gratitude I hold it, so long as I live, it behoves that on my tongue should be discerned." In parting, the master commends to Dante his *Treasure,* in which, he says, he still lives.

Brunetto Latini was one of the most learned and accomplished of thirteenth century Florentines. Villani said that he did much to refine the Tuscan idiom; but Latin and French were the literary tongues to him as to other Italians before Dante — as they were to Englishmen before Chaucer. The *Treasure* to which he alludes was a work published in French under the title *Li Trésors,*— a summary of medieval learning which had many forerunners and successors. The writer was a Guelf, and went into exile with his party five years before Dante's birth. He wrote and published *Li Trésors* in France, and it may be that there was a touch of policy in his prefatory praise of French as "more delightful and more common than all other tongues." The old notion that he was literally Dante's tutor seems improbable. After the return of the Guelfs he held high office in the state, and was a person of commanding influence in many ways. But it is equally unnecessary to hold, as certain cautious biographers have held, that Dante knew him only through his books. "When in the world hour by hour you taught me how man makes himself eternal" more naturally suggests some sort of actual intimacy than not. Dante was a man before Brunetto's death. He had friends among the younger nobles; and had made himself known among the learned men of Florence. There is no reason why he may not have known Brunetto.

In that age a man might "take all knowledge to be his province," and really compass the *omne scibile.* What was this precious learning? Let us glance at the *Treasure* of the man Dante was proud to call master. Its ancient history is a jumble of Hebrew scripture and classical Greek myth. Its modern history — the story of the Roman Empire — is extremely incorrect. Its science is childlike: "The circumference of the earth measures exactly 20,427 Lombard leagues in length, the size of the sun is just 166 3-10 times as great, while the distance of the firmament, that is of the heaven of fixed stars, from the earth, is 10,066 times as long as the earth's diameter." Under the name of geography we are told of strange races, men born old, men who have no heads, but eyes in their shoulders; and so on. Its natural history is that of Pliny — with variations. The crocodile, the hippopotamus, and the siren, are fishes; the ant and the chameleon are mammals. Under the heading of snakes (which hide their poison under a stone while they drink) we find the basilisk, the dragon, and the salamander.

This is the science of the Middle Ages, which is to say of antiquity, for there was little progress made during medieval times. There is no doubt that Dante accepted it as a whole, and was content with it. The cosmography of the *Divine Comedy* is that of Brunetto — is that of the day. But he learned what could be learned, and made the most of it. "As to the nature of his studies," says Lowell, "there can be no doubt that he went through the trivium (grammar, dialectic, rhetoric) and the quadrivium (arithmetic, music, geometry and astronomy) of the then ordinary university course. To these he afterward added painting . . . theology and medicine. He is said to have been the pupil of Cimabue, and was certainly the friend of Giotto, the designs for some of whose frescoes at Assisi and elsewhere have been wrongly attributed to him, though we may safely believe in his helpful comment and suggestion." He is credited by his early biographers with having studied at Bologna, Padua, Naples, Paris and Oxford. There is no evidence that he was ever in England, but he may easily enough have visited Paris either before or after his exile; perhaps both. Much of his wide reading was no doubt done in later years, but wherever or whenever he may have studied, he certainly became master of the learning and literature known to his time. His reading included much Latin, some Hebrew and Arabic, and a little Greek. Aristotle he knew chiefly through the version of Albertus Magnus. He calls him, with the schoolmen, "the philosopher," and cites him oftener than any other writer. However limited and unreliable this maximum of Dante's learning may appear, it was a maximum. Its mastery meant that he had done the utmost that was possible for him, and his use of it presently showed that it had given him sufficient training for the development of his genius. To the modern reader who tries to approach Dante from the modern point of view he must often seem pedantic. In reality, to him as to all the greatest minds, learning was of importance only as a means toward wisdom. So we find him saying in the *Convito:* "He is not a true lover of wisdom who loves it for the sake of gain, as do lawyers, physicians, and almost all churchmen, who study, not in order to know, but to acquire riches or advancement, and who would not persevere in study should you give them what they desire to gain by it."

Dante speaks here of the wisdom which is the fruit of study — of philosophy in something approaching the scholastic sense. But he had other sources of wisdom. Dreamer that he was, there was nothing of the recluse about him. He had much of Shakespeare's active step and inquiring eye as well as much of Milton's inward absorption. His mysticism often obscures the extreme directness of his thought. He followed the fashion of the time in expressing everything by allegory and symbol. He said that all worthy and noble poetry was allegorical, and that only dunces wrote otherwise. "He himself seems to have been versed in every form of symbolism from the Kabbala down, and the mystic relation of numbers, the significance of colors, the secret properties of gems, the influences of the stars, the hidden meanings of the poets and the Scriptures, and even the mysteries concealed in their use of certain letters and words, were equally intelligible to him." All this lore was a natural accumulation not only from books but from the talk of his associates from early childhood.

Who his childish friends were we do not know. They were probably of his own class, and would not necessarily include the children of the important nobility, such as the Donati and the Portinari. And this brings us to Beatrice.

Boccaccio is responsible for the statement that the Beatrice of Dante's lifelong dream was none other than Beatrice Portinari, who was a year younger than Dante, married Simone de' Bardi, of a great banking family, and died about the year 1390. This theory has been unnecessarily discredited in modern times. Boccaccio was born eight years before Dante's death, and was nothing if not a Florentine. He had every reason to know whatever could be known about Dante by tradition and hearsay. No reason appears why he should have invented so specific a statement, and it was apparently not denied by any of the numerous survivors of Dante's time. On the other hand, it would not be sensible to identify this flesh-and-blood Beatrice literally and wholly with the lady of the poet's soul, or to take with perfect literalness his account of their relation in life.

To understand this we must try to forget the centuries that have intervened, and take ourselves back to the medieval attitude toward women, which was Dante's attitude. In the Dark Ages woman had been debased to the lowest position, moral and social. In the tenth and eleventh centuries, chiefly in southern France and Moorish Spain, developed what we call "chivalry." This was not an institution but a tone of life; as it matured it came to involve not only adventurous valor but refinement of manners and feeling. And so the cult of woman arose, and with it what is most distinctive in modern civilization. All modern life and modern poetry are tinged with the sentiment of the troubadours.

It was in Provence that this new religion took rise, — Provence with its individual tongue, its fiery and poetic heart, its mind alert before all others to the abuses of monkery. "The Provençal tongue was the earliest of all Romance tongues, and its poetry was the oldest romantic poetry. It was the first poetry of a civilized European nation since the fall of the antique, and it developed unbiased by any antique influence; the themes which the poets liked to treat, their forms, and the way in which they looked on life, were quite different and new." And the newest thing of all, and the most enduring, was the worship of women which is reflected in all their poetry. The dominance of the monks had been largely responsible for the degradation of woman, and Provence was first to cast off the monkish rule. "Viler than a priest" became a proverbial phrase, and the troubadour's mockery of the clergy was the obverse and complement of his praise of women. Provençal was the admitted tongue of chivalry; even the troubadours of Italian birth who were presently to be heard in the courts of Northern Italy used that tongue as a matter of course. There is little doubt that Dante himself wrote songs in Provençal; in the last circle of Purgatory the shade of a troubadour answers him in that romantic speech. It was a gracious and sensuous life of which the troubadours were the ornament. "In your courts," writes one of them to his patron, "everything graceful is to be found: liberality and courtesy to women, beautiful dresses and fine armor, trumpets, games, violins and songs:" a quaint and suggestive inventory. When Provence was crushed by papal decree, Italy became the shrine of woman-worship. The rites became more and more refined. Whatever of sensuality and mere gallantry had lurked in the amorous devotions of the troubadours gave place to a spiritual conception of woman as identified with all that is highest in human nature. More, the love of man for woman came to seem a symbol of divine love: "It became spiritualized and platonic in that high sense in which Plato really meant it. This poetry is soft, sweet, and mystical, full of enthusiasm and secrecy, as remote from the sensual love-poetry of Ariosto and Swinburne as from the sentimental lays of the Provençal."

The creator of this "sweet new style" in Italian poetry, as Dante calls it, was one Guido Guinicelli of Bologna. He died when Dante was eleven years old, but Dante may already have come under his influence. At all events, he calls Guinicelli "my sweet master." As Dante grew toward manhood, he found himself one of a group of young Florentine singers in this style. There were six or eight of them, all acquaintances, and given to exchanging sonnets in friendly rivalry. The most important of them in every way was Guido Cavalcanti, of whose friendship with Dante something is to be said. He was ten years older than Dante, who calls him "the first of his friends." He belonged to one of the greatest families among the Guelf nobles. Boccaccio has an anecdote about him in the *Decameron*. "Messer Guido di' Cavalcante de' Cavalcanti not only was one of the best logicians that the world held, and a surpassing natural philosopher, but he also excelled in beauty and courtesy, and was of great gifts as a speaker, and everything it pleased him to do, and what best became a gentleman he did better than any other." He was brave, proud, and generous, and had much influence on Dante at an important moment. By all accounts it was he who persuaded Dante to write the *Vita Nuova* in the vernacular rather than in the Latin which would have been more naturally used for a work of such dignity. One of Dante's early sonnets throws light upon the pleasant relations of these two, as well as upon their romantic pursuits:

> Guido, I wish that Lapo, thou, and I,
> Could be by spells conveyed, as it were now,
> Upon a barque, with all the winds that blow
> Along all seas at our good will to hie.
> So no mischance or temper of the sky
> Should mar our course with spite or cruel slip;
> But we, observing old companionship,
> To be companions still should long thereby.
> And Lady Joan and Lady Beatrice,
> And her the thirtieth on my roll, with us
> Should our good wizard set, o'er seas to move:
> And they three ever to be well at ease,
> As we should be, I think, if this were thus.

Lapo Gianni was another of the group of sonneteers. It seems that the friends had made a list of the sixty fairest ladies in Florence, and Lapo's maiden is mentioned quaintly by number, like a convict.

Beatrice, we must note, is here spoken of as a human maiden among others. Two years after the death of Beatrice Portinari, Dante wrote the *Vita Nuova,* a book of mystical confidences, in which are gathered together the poems of the preceding decade, linked by a liberal commentary in prose. In this record are joined, and indeed identified, the story of his love for a real Beatrice, whether Beatrice Portinari or not, a maiden of flesh and blood; and the story of his passion for the ideal of spiritual purity and beauty of which he makes her name, her idea, the symbol.

The plain facts would seem to be that as a child on the verge of boyhood he saw and loved a little girl in a red dress. He sees her after that many times, but he is a boy on the verge of manhood when the first salutation passes between them. They meet after that as acquaintances till she dies. After her death he is tempted to be unfaithful by responding to the pitying love of another woman. But he is successful in resisting the temptation, or yields to it only for the moment, and dedicates his life anew to her service.

The *Vita Nuova* was probably written when Dante was in his twenty-eighth year. His conception of Beatrice did not yet approach the grandeur of his later conception. But it had by that time come far on its road from a human passion towards a spiritual ideal. The devices of symbolism are deliberately made use of in the narrative: all the dates, for example, are multiples of nine. He first sees Beatrice in his ninth year; their first greeting takes place in his eighteenth — and so on. The fact that it is nowhere suggested by Dante that his Beatrice is married has been taken to indicate that she is not to be identified with Beatrice Portinari. But for that matter he evidently does not regard his own later marriage as having any bearing whatever on his love for Beatrice. This is altogether natural according to the code of the day. The romantic love of chivalry was, at its highest, a disembodied love, altogether independent of crude physical or legal relation. The smile and speech of his lady are the end of Dante's desires,— or seem to have been as he looks back upon the great experience. The supreme experience, the virtual deification of Beatrice, was yet to come.

But if Beatrice, or what she stood for, early occupied his imagination in its nobler moods, it must not be supposed that his youth was given up to mooning. It is matter for rejoicing that he could, as a very young man, write such poems as this sonnet, which loses marvelously little in Rossetti's translation:

Last All Saints' holy-day, even now gone by,
I met a gathering of damosels;
She that came first, as one doth who excels,
Had Love with her, bearing her company;
A flame burned forward through her steadfast eye,
As when in living fire a spirit dwells;
So, gazing with the boldness that prevails
O'er doubt, I knew an angel visibly.
As she passed on, she bowed her mild approof
And salutation to all men of worth,
Lifting the soul to solemn thoughts aloof.
In heaven itself that lady had her birth,
I think, and is with us for our behoof:
Blessed are they who meet her on the earth.

But, as Giotto's charming early portrait suggests, the young Dante was a very different person from the stern abstracted poet of later years. He has his eager hours of study, his friendships; above all, his share in the brilliant life of the liveliest of Italian cities. "We must imagine him in the gay feasts of Florence, of which the chroniclers tell, with their baldachins and tribunes hung with wreaths of flowers, the great festival on St. John's Day, when the young men, clad in white, led by Signor d'Amore, went singing and dancing up the street of Santa Felicita, and women and girls, also in wreaths of flowers, partook of the festivities, and music and songs and ringing bells filled the air with joyful sounds."

And he had no sooner reached manhood than he began to take a part in the sterner activities, the wars and hatching of wars, in which the city was perennially engaged. Those were stirring times in Florence, and one could never tell what ingredient would rise to the top of the pot. Within two years of Dante's birth, the Ghibellines had been driven from the city, and never after regained their foothold as a party. It presently appeared how little the Guelf allegiance to the Church amounted to when their own interests were threatened. Pope Gregory X. visited Florence, and did his best to bring about a reconciliation between the parties. He had little success, and promptly placed the city under interdict. Gregory died a year and a half later, and "by his death," says

Villani, "the Guelfs of Florence were greatly cheered, by reason of the ill-will which he had towards them."

If a house divided against itself were always doomed, Florence would have had short shrift with fate; for the expulsion of the Ghibellines by no means gave the city peace. Here again we may best quote Villani:

"In those times, the Guelf nobles of Florence, reposing from their foreign wars with victory and honor, and fattened upon the goods of the exiled Ghibellines, and by reason of their other gains, began, through pride and envy, to quarrel among themselves, whence came to pass in Florence more feuds and enmities between the citizens, with slayings and woundings. Among them all the greatest was the quarrel between the house of Adimari of the one part, who were very great and powerful, and on the other side were the house of the Donati; in such wise that nearly the whole of the city took sides, and some held with one party and some with the other, whereby the city and the Guelf party were in great danger."

Once again a Pope intervened, and this time to such good effect that the factions were nominally reconciled, and a government by fourteen "good men" was instituted under which for several years the Florentines succeeded in living without serious feuds among the nobles. But the fourteen "good men" were disposed to oppress the people, and a bitter contest of classes began, which resulted, in 1282, in an entirely new form of government. This was a government of the people, or rather of the guilds. There were seven greater guilds and five lesser, and from these guilds six "Priors" were chosen by ballot of a limited number of electors. The Prior's term of service was only two months; and his administrative powers were held in check by a complex system of councils. Every possible precaution was taken to prevent any party or faction from getting a lasting majority. Nobles could become eligible to office only by becoming members of some one of the guilds. It was in this way that Dante later became Prior; at the time this government was established he was only seventeen. From that time on Florence prospered greatly in commerce and the arts. The exiled Ghibelline leaders were continually plotting to recover their lost position in Florence. Arezzo became for a time their chief headquarters, and in 1289 the battle of Campaldino was fought. The Ghibellines were defeated and Arezzo punished; and among victorious Florentines was Dante. It was not his first battle, for of Campaldino he says: "I was present, not a boy in arms, and I felt much fear, but in the end the greatest pleasure, from the various changes of the fight." He was among the Florentine troops at the siege of Caprona in the following year, as a passage in the *Inferno* proves: "And all the devils pressed forward, so that I feared they would not keep their compact. And thus I once saw the foot-soldiers afraid, who came out under pledge from Caprona, seeing themselves among so many enemies." Yes, those were stirring days, and it is clear that Dante had his full part in them. The surrender of Caprona took place in August, 1290. Beatrice Portinari had died a few months earlier, and it may be that he was glad to incur the risks and the excitement of the campaign.

There is no doubt that the death of Beatrice affected him deeply. She was the human being who, in whatever sense, meant most to him. When she vanished from the earth, his youth was over. The next ten years mark a second distinct period in his life. There is a tradition that the death of Beatrice so overwhelmed him that for a time his friends despaired of his life. But this is probably a romantic exaggeration. There are indications that he tried the familiar consolations of dissipation, study, and religion. The restraining presence of Beatrice had kept him from the sowing of wild oats till this time. But now there probably came a natural relaxation, and a freedom of life which he afterward regretted. To this time apparently belongs the beginning of his intimacy with Forese Donati, who later was to become his brother-in-law, and who belonged to what we should now call a "fast set." Dante meets him in Purgatory, and says that the memory of the life they once led together can hardly lessen his suffering. And certain sonnets have been preserved, written by Dante and Forese in the coarse vein of the "man-about-town." We have also a sonnet of a different sort and addressed to Dante by his older and worthier friend, Guido Cavalcanti, which is worth quoting for its testimony to Dante's mood at this time:

> I come to thee by daytime constantly,
> But in thy thoughts too much of baseness find;
> Greatly it grieves me for thy gentle mind,
> And for thy many virtues gone from thee.
> It was thy wont to shun such company,
> Unto all sorry concourse ill-inclined:
> And still thy speech to me, heartfelt and kind,
> Had made me treasure up thy poetry.
> But now I dare not, for thine abject life,
> Make manifest that I approve thy rhymes;
> Nor come I in such sort that thou mayst know.
> Ah! prythee read this sonnet many times:
> So shall that evil one who bred this strife
> Be thrust from thy dishonored soul and go.

Whether this alludes to Forese or to some other seducing companion we cannot know. It is pretty clear that within a year or two of Beatrice's death Dante became infatuated with another woman. To her he wrote various sonnets which are preserved in the *Convito;* her he eventually identifies with Philosophy, insisting that it is always the spirit of philosophy which he invokes in her name. So in the *Convito* he says: "When I had lost the first delight of my soul, I remained so absorbed in sorrow that no comfort availed me. . . . And just as if a man should go about looking for silver, and apart from his purpose should find gold; so I, who sought to console myself, found not only a remedy for my tears, but knowledge of authors and of sciences and of books; considering which, I soon decided that Philosophy, who was the sovereign lady of these authors, these sciences, and these books, was the supreme thing. And I imagined her as a noble lady; and I could not imagine her as other than merciful; therefore so willingly did my thought dwell upon her that it could hardly be diverted from her. And on account of this imagination I began to go where she in truth showed herself, that is, in the schools of the religious and the disputations of the philosophers; so that in a little while, perhaps thirty months, I began to be so deeply aware of her sweetness, that the love of her banished and destroyed every other thought." So "the spirits of his eyes became her most devoted friends:" in other words, he gave himself absolutely to study for some time. Dante evidently meant to have it thought that the noble lady whom he mentioned at the end of the *Vita Nuova,* and who is the theme of his canzones in the *Convito* was merely an allegorical figure. He had then become ashamed of his love-songs, and declared that they should be read only figuratively: a statement which encouraged disbelievers in a flesh and blood Beatrice. But it is safe to say that these different ideals had their living prototypes. Who this second "noble lady" was, and how long her physical sway lasted, is a matter of pure guesswork.

Some commentators have held it to be his wife, but this seems unlikely, as his avoidance of mentioning her elsewhere is marked. His marriage must have taken place at some time before 1295. It was in about his thirtieth year that he took to wife Gemna Donati, a kinswoman of Corso Donati, head of the most powerful of Florentine families. Boccaccio hints that it was an unhappy marriage. We simply do not know. It probably was an ordinary marriage by arrangement — a "good match" for Dante, surely, in the social sense. They lived together till his exile, and several children were born. But his family did not share his exile, and it is not absence from them, but absence from the city of his birth, that he laments in later years.

The tyranny of the Guelfs after the expulsion of the Ghibellines finally resulted in a popular uprising. Under a noble, Giano della Bella, they succeeded (1293) in seizing the reins of government. Certain "ordinances of justice" were passed, which vested all powers in the Priors of the trades, nobles being debarred from all part in the government of the city. It was at this time, a year or two after his marriage, that Dante entered political life. To do this to any purpose he had to put himself on the citizen level by joining one of the guilds. His name is to be found upon the books of one of the greater guilds, that of the physicians and apothecaries, where he is characterized simply as "poet." Dante very soon proved his capability. He served several times as member of the

Council of the Hundred. He acted as ambassador, probably more than once. At San Gemignano, one year, he is recorded to have moved the annual renewal of the Guelf League. In 1300 he became one of the six Priors. "This unhappy Priorate," he had too good cause to declare later, "was the cause of all my misfortune."

Before this time new factional troubles had arisen which threatened to become as serious as the Guelf-Ghibelline feud. A family quarrel in Pistoia had resulted in the growth of two factions known as the Black and the White; and the Florentines, always ready for a quarrel, took the matter up among themselves. Corso Donati, Dante's connection by marriage, was at the head of the Blacks. Dante, though nominally a White, in practice remained neutral, and as soon as he was in office did his best to make peace. Guido Cavalcanti was on the White side. In the year 1300 the trouble reached its height. "Wherever members of both parties met, insults and quarrels were the consequence. At the burial of a lady of the Frescobaldi family, a man's movement, that had been misunderstood, had caused bloodshed. The Donati had been the aggressors. A few days later Guido Cavalcanti, riding the streets with a small party of other young men, chanced to meet Corso on the way with his son Simone and others, and in sudden anger spurred his horse directly against him, and the people asserted that in riding up to him he threw his lance or dagger at Donati. Corso, Simone and Cecchino de Bardi instantly pursued him with drawn swords and threw stones at him."

At this unlucky moment Dante became Prior. Almost at once the Priors, it is said by his advice, took radical means to restore civil peace in Florence by banishing the leaders of both factions. Among them were not only Corso Donati, but Dante's friend Guido, who as an unforeseen result of his banishment, died a few months later. But Dante's own time in Florence grew short. It appears that this plan of getting rid of the leaders might have resulted in peace for Florence if a Pope had not interfered.

This was Pope Boniface VIII., an unusual man, whose career was most extraordinary. On the death of Nicolas IV. in 1292, the electoral conclave could not agree upon his successor. Finally chance suggestion "stampeded" them toward a Franciscan hermit known as Peter, who lived in solitude and self-discipline on a mountain in the Campagna. He was said to be a worker of miracles. When they told him that he was elected Pope, he ran away, thinking they were mocking him. But his fellow-Franciscans pursuaded him to take the office. Of course, he was unfit for it, and fell at once into the hands of the Cardinal Cajetano, who in due time caused him to resign and had himself elected as Pope under the name Boniface VIII. In his reign the Church reached the height of its power. He refused to confirm Albert of Hapsburg as Emperor, with the plain remark: "Ego sum Imperator." He made his cardinals princes, and dressed them in purple. He confiscated property, burned cities, sent his personal enemies to the galleys, declared that every human creature was his subject. He was about to excommunicate and depose Philip the Fair of France, when he himself was seized and imprisoned by a band of French sympathizers, and died shortly after, mad from the shock of that act of sacrilege.

Now there were reasons for his regarding Tuscany as the property of the Holy See, and he showed a disposition from the beginning of his reign to interfere in the affairs of Florence. When the trouble arose between the Blacks and the Whites, therefore, he saw a chance to assert his authority under the guise of making peace. The Cardinal whom he sent as legate was a tactless and overbearing man, and gave great offense. His only proposal toward the improvement of affairs at Florence was that the Priors be chosen by lot instead of by vote. When he asked for a Florentine troop of a hundred men to help the Pope in his campaign against the Colonna, Dante, who was then in the Council of the Hundred, is reported to have proposed the pithy motion: "Nihil fiat."

The Whites were in control of affairs in Florence, and consequently we find the Blacks in secret league with the Pope, doubtless with the understanding that Florence and Tuscany were to be turned over to his sovereignty when the Blacks were put in their rightful place at the top of the heap. It is supposed that the Blacks even suggested the intervention of the French. At all events, it was brought about that Prince Charles of Valois should be the next "pacificator" despatched to Florence by the Pope. In the autumn of 1291 he actually entered the city with an unarmed train, but, as Dante says, bringing with him "the lance of Judas." Before his entry the Priors had sent ambassadors to him, and he had pledged his word in writing not to assume control of Florence or to make any change in her laws. There is a tradition that at about this time Dante was sent on an embassy to Rome; and it is in this connection that the famous speech is attributed to him: "If I stay, who goes? and if I go, who stays?"— a speech which, according to Villani, gave some offense among his colleagues. Dante was quite capable of this kind of Napoleonic utterance, but there can hardly have been occasion for it at that time. If indeed he was of such prominence as some of the biographers would have us think, he would have been all the less likely to be sent on such a mission. For he had consistently opposed all encroachment upon the affairs of Florence by the Church, as well as by the French.

Charles of Valois had not been long in Florence before active trouble began to brew,— especially for the Whites, who had been thus far in control in spite of the fact that the Guelf "captains" were Blacks.

Armed men in ever greater numbers gathered about the French prince, there was increasing unrest among the populace, and the Priors did not know what to do. "Their hearts failed," says one of them: "Never would I have believed that so great a lord, and one of the royal house of France, ever could break his word and oath." Charles began to exact tribute, and, finding himself still practically unopposed, finally allowed Corso Donati and a large band of his Black followers to enter the gates. The great bell was rung to call the people to the defense of the city, but there was no response. Indeed, it is probable that the mass of the people did not greatly care whether Black or White were in control. The French Prince was already virtual master of the city; Corso Donati was a picturesque swaggerer; and the short of the matter was that the populace welcomed the excuse for pillage with cries of "Long live Lord Charles and the Baron (Corso)!" "Many shameful crimes were perpetrated," says Dino, the Prior just quoted, "on women and maids, houses were pillaged, the weak were bereft of their goods, or they hunted them out of the town. Many did whatever they pleased, the accused were forced to confess, and there was no succor." And now one Messer Cante de' Gabriele d'Agubbio was made *podestà,* and began to administer justice according to the desires of Charles and the Blacks. Hundreds of the White party were proscribed and banished. And presently he issued a decree which will keep him from being forgotten more surely than if he had been the most upright judge of his century. This decree is still to be found in the archives of Florence. It is dated January 27, 1301. In very bad Latin it accuses Dante and four others of "peculation, fraud, extortion, bribery, rebellion against the Pope and Charles, breach of the peace, and the like." More specifically, it charged them with "the use of public money to resist the entrance of Charles of Valois, and the interference in the affairs of Pistoia with the view of securing the expulsion from that city "of those who are called the Blacks, faithful men devoted to the Holy Roman Catholic Church," which had taken place in May, 1301. It is stated that, having been duly summoned, "they had contumaciously absented themselves, which seems to show that they were not in Florence; and they are sentenced to pay five thousand florins apiece within ten days, or, in default, to be banished and have their houses destroyed and their goods confiscated, and in any case they were banished for two years." In March the sentence was confirmed and made to include ten others, and all of them were pronounced exiles and outlaws forever, and condemned to be burnt alive if they should ever be taken on Florentine soil.

From all this it would appear that Dante and some others among the leading Whites had fled from Florence some time before the passage of the first decree: perhaps at the time when Donati entered the city and the supremacy of the Whites was without doubt at an end. The charges against him and his companions were clearly trumped up, so far as they implied dishonesty or treachery of any sort. It is true that Dante had been in debt for a year or two before his exile, but that is not exactly a proof of peculation. There is a good deal of space given in the *Inferno* to this particular crime,—an indication perhaps that Dante was anxious to put on record his abhorrence of it. Villani, who sided with the Black party, and was a Prior of Florence not many years after Dante's exile began, virtually controverts these charges by ignoring them: "His exile from Florence was for the reason that when Lord Charles of Valois, of the house of France, came to Florence in 1301 and drove out the White party, as is mentioned under the date, the said Dante was one of the chief governors of our city, and belonged to that party, Guelf though he was; and therefore, for no other fault, he was driven forth and banished with the said White party from Florence."

So, at all events, Dante's lifelong exile began. It is necessary to understand something of what that exile meant to him in order to make anything of his subsequent life and work. In the first place, he had a burning sense of the injustice of the thing. He had been the faithful servant of his country (and it must be kept in mind that Florence, rather than Italy, was his country), and he had been cast forth. Then there was the injury to his pride; for he was above all a proud man, with a raw sensitiveness to anything approaching indignity to his person or his name. These two feelings find expression again and again in the *Divine Comedy.* Very plainly they appear in this passage from the *Convito,* which was written within a decade of his banishment: "Since it pleased the citizens of the fairest and most famous daughter of Rome, Florence, to cast me forth from her most sweet bosom (wherein I was born, and nourished up to the climax of my life, and wherein, by their good leave, I long with all my heart to rest my weary soul, and to end the days allotted to me)—since then I have wandered a pilgrim, wellnigh a beggar, through almost every region where her language is spoken, displaying against my will the wounds of fortune, which are often wont to be imputed unjustly to the wounded one himself. Truly have I been a vessel without sail and without rudder, borne to divers ports and shores and havens by the dry wind that blows from dolorous poverty; and have appeared vile in the eyes of many who, perhaps, through some fame of me had imagined me in other guise; in whose consideration, not only did I in person suffer abasement, but all my work became of less account, that already done as well as that yet to do." Evidently the pride of the poet (though never the self-respect), has suffered bitterly during these years.

But above all we must feel the sheer grief of the

banished man. In the Middle Ages, as in antiquity, exile was looked upon as a penalty almost more bitter than death. His heart must continue to beat, he must eat and drink and move about among men. But he was bereft, accursed, he could not take root in alien soil. He must move always upon the outskirts of life, cherishing the forlorn hope of return to Florence, his land, his home. One may think that Dante, with his great mind and strong heart, should have been superior to this feeling. Why was it not simple for him to leave one Italian city for another: to find a new object for his devotion, to carve out a new career? He was but thirty-seven years old when Florence cast him forth, and had not yet reached his full power. But Florence was more than a city: it was a state, a fatherland; for Dante the rest of Italy, the rest of the world, was but a limbo in which his restless, homeless spirit was doomed to wander,— always with the desperate hope of return. Through all those years of wandering he signed himself "Dantes Aligherii Florentinus exul immeritus." Bitterly he speaks of the ingratitude of Florence, but thither his thoughts turn to the last. Even toward the end of the *Divine Comedy* we find him preöccupied with the thought that his great poem may at last prove a mediator between himself and the beloved city: so that he may at last return, "with other voice, in other garb, a Poet, and at the font of his baptism take the laurel."

During the early years of his exile he no doubt had

lively hope, and even expectation, of return. But the downfall of the Whites proved final, like that of the Ghibellines. The two defeated factions became practically one: but Dante was not long among them. At first, apparently, he was active in the councils of the exiles, but it is evident that he quickly grew impatient of their spirit and methods. In truth, the rank and file of the Whites were no better than the Blacks, of the Ghibellines than the Guelfs. He probably found more self-love than love of Florence among his companions. He himself was stern, uncompromising, and probably haughty and domineering in manner. Before long he left them to their own resources, and he probably had no part in the several futile attempts which were made in the following years to force a way back to Florence. In the testimony of his ancestor, Cacciaguida, which takes the form of prophecy (*Paradiso,* XVII.) Dante has left his own clear commentary on this experience:

> Each thing beloved most dearly thou wilt leave,
> And this is but the earliest dart which fares
> From the bow of exiles, when it shoots to grieve,
> Thyself wilt prove what bitter taste there bears
> The alien's bread, and what a weary road
> Is climbing and descending alien stairs.
> And that which most of all thy back will load,
> Will be the evil troop with whom thou'lt fall
> Into this valley, scattered all abroad.
> For all ungrateful, mad, and impious all,
> Against thee will they act, but very soon,
> Their brows, not thine, will bear shame's reddened pall.

Of their bestiality their progress on
 Will be the proof, to thee it will be fair
 To have made thy party by thyself alone.

So Dante became undisguisedly what in some sense he must always have been, his own party. He might be doomed to eat other men's bread and mount other men's stairs, but always as his own man. It is impossible to imagine him a suppliant — unless to his Florence to take him back — or a parasite to any great man. He seems to have been well treated wherever he went. Only a year or so after his banishment we hear of him as in Verona, the guest of two princely houses in succession. On an old palace in that city is still to be found a tablet commemorating the fact that the great poet was once a guest within those walls. Another year or two, and he is heard of as under the roof of a certain Marquis in Lunigiana. It was probably during these years that he studied at Padua, Bologna, even Paris. "During the nineteen years of Dante's exile," says Lowell, "it would be hard to say where he was not. In certain districts of Northern Italy there is scarce a village that has not its tradition of him, its *sedia, rocca, spelonca,* or *torre di Dante;* and what between the patriotic complaisance of some biographers overwilling to gratify as many provincial vanities as possible and the pettishness of others anxious only to snub them, the confusion becomes hopeless."

It appears from the words he puts into the mouth of

Cacciaguida, that either in fact or in fancy he found himself everywhere met, if with consideration, with the reservation due to the man who has been denounced and outlawed. Even the poetry for which he had been commended before his exile was now held in less regard. There was no doubt some basis in fact for the feeling. This continual brooding upon a real wrong, this unflagging consciousness of a real if unmerited humiliation, would have unstrung and demoralized a lesser poet, a lesser man. It merely served to bring out all that was finest and noblest in Dante's genius: "We will not complain of Dante's miseries," says Carlyle in his Hero-Worship lecture; "had all gone right with him as he wished it, he might have been Prior, Podestà, or whatever they call it, of Florence, well-accepted among neighbors,— and the world had wanted one of the most notable words ever said or sung. Florence would have had another prosperous Lord Mayor, and the ten dumb centuries continued voiceless, and the ten other listening centuries (for there will be ten of them and more), had no *Divina Commedia* to hear! We will complain of nothing. A nobler destiny was appointed to this Dante; and he, struggling like a man led toward death and crucifixion, could not help fulfilling it. Give *him* the choice of his happiness! He knew not, more than we do, what was really happy, what was really miserable."

Boccaccio asserted that Dante had various love-affairs during these years of exile, and several instances not mentioned by him were later alleged by other ingenious gossips. Some of these stories were no doubt pure fiction. But indeed we can hardly wish to think of Dante as going through those years without warm human attachments. Tenderness and passion are as clearly elements in his nature as lofty imagination. As his feeling for Beatrice became more and more spiritualized, it became more and more disembodied. He was a prophet, but not an ascetic. Though with the passing of youth he ceased to be a troubadour, he remained a lover of whatever was fairest and noblest in his kind. That a woman had become the symbol of all his highest aspirations attracted him to all womanhood. It is clear that in exile he not only continued to make friendships among men, but was led by his love of beauty and need of feminine sympathy into certain romantic relations for which, in the *Divine Comedy,* he unsparingly censures himself. But in the mere sensuality which was meat and drink to Boccaccio, he can have had no part.

After some five or six years of exile, we find him at work upon the *Convito,* and *De Vulgari Eloquentia* (Of Eloquence in the Vernacular). The latter was a treatise, the first of its kind, upholding the merits of the common Italian (or rather Tuscan) speech as a literary vehicle. In the *Convito,* the general proposition has already been laid down in the vernacular. It was a novel and heretical opinion to be advanced by a man with pretensions to learning: but Dante was presently to enforce it, to impose it, in a way utterly without parallel in the history of literature. He gave permanent life to the living but naturally ephemeral speech of his time and day. Half a century later, Chaucer was to do something of the same kind for the English vernacular. But modern English is in many ways unlike Chaucer's — in many ways radically unlike it, while modern Italian is essentially the Italian of Dante. It was four centuries before the common speech of Germany successfully asserted itself; and Milton was by no means the last Englishman to hesitate between Latin and the common speech, great as were the achievements of which it already could boast. In the *De Vulgari Eloquentia* (written in the polite speech that it might appeal to scholars), Dante advanced certain linguistic theories which have been verified by philologists of much later date.

The *Convito* (Banquet) is a work of more importance. In certain early editions it is styled the *Convivio Amoroso;* but no English reader need take it up in the expectation of finding anything either convivial or (if he follows the author's instructions) amorous. At twenty-five Dante had written the *Vita Nuova,* a mystical interpretation of the Beatrice experience. Now, at forty-three or thereabouts, he gives an account, equally mystical though more severe in manner, of his relation with the other "noble lady," whom he identifies with learning or philosophy.

The *canzones,* or love-poems which serve as texts, had probably been composed many years before the commentary: into their lines he reads, with all possible elaboration, the record of a pursuit of divine philosophy. It is to the modern mind an extraordinary figure, this identifying of an intense human passion with the love of learning. Listen, for example, to the opening sentences of the Second Book:

"As we have said in the last book, my second love had its beginning in the compassionate looks of a lady; which love then, finding my life responsive to its ardor, like a fire, from a small, kindled into a great flame; so that not only waking, but sleeping, its light shone in on my brain. And how great was the desire to behold her, with which love inspired me, can be neither told nor understood. And this desire was not for her alone, but for all persons having any relation with her, either by acquaintance or kindred. Oh! how many were the nights when the eyes of others were closed in sleep, that mine were gazing eagerly on the habitation of my love! And as such a rapidly growing fire must needs burst out (for it was impossible that it should remain concealed), I was seized with a desire to speak of love, which I could no longer restrain."

If this be not the voice of human love, what is? And yet we must regard it at the time when the *Convito* was written, at least, as expressing to his mind the love of abstract knowledge. What Dante was proposing to himself (and only partially succeeded in doing, for only four of the fourteen chapters he had planned were actually written) was certainly to present in this figurative form, and in the vernacular, some such compendium of the learning of the day as his confessed master Brunetto Latini had achieved in *Li Trésors*. The first book is chiefly given up to a defense of his use of the "vulgar tongue." At the beginning of the second book he lays down the theory (many centuries old in his time) "that books can be understood, and ought to be explained, in four principal senses: namely, the literal, the allegorical, the moral, and the anagogical (or mystical)." As we shall see, he later conceived and interpreted his masterpiece in each of these four ways.

The banquet he offers, accordingly, is a feast of philosophy, of learning, the best that he is able to command. And he offers it not with the arrogance which he sometimes shows, but with excuses of himself as a scholar who has but picked up what he might, and speaks by the authority of his superiors: yet, "though he had not himself been sitting at the blessed table, he yet had sat at the feet of those who are gathered round it, and had collected the crumbs that had fallen from their feast."

That the full number of courses were not served was due perhaps to the fact that in 1310 an event occurred which for the moment gave Dante the liveliest hopes of a return to his beloved Florence. He had been a Guelf, a member of the party which, for reasons however selfish, had stood in the main on the side of the Church as against the Empire. After his exile he had joined the Ghibellines, or at least his sympathies became theirs rather than those of the party which had disgraced him. But he was always a devout Catholic. He indignantly protests against the outrage visited upon Christ through his Vicar in the rough usage suffered by Boniface VIII., though he detested that enemy of Florence as a man, and repeatedly scores him for his faults in the *Divine Comedy*. But in the *Convito* we find him arguing at length that the head of the Roman Empire has a majesty and authority the highest in human society. And in the treatise *De Monarchia,* which probably belongs to the same period, he defends at length the same idea. In the hands of Albert of Hapsburg, the power of the Empire had greatly waned. The succession of Henry of Luxemburg, in 1308, promised better things. The Ghibellines took heart, and with them the exiled Dante. "In the year 1310 Henry of Luxemburg came to Italy. By no one was he saluted with such exultation as by Dante. He wrote letters full of wild and triumphant joy to Rome and Florence and to all the princes of Italy. He had an audience with the Emperor; in his letters he called him the 'New Moses,' and 'The Lamb of God'; he was full of the most ardent hopes." But the Italian states had been for a long time in possession of virtual independence. They did not wish to be united, even by the historic bond of the Empire. Whatever chance of success there may have been, Henry squandered in delays and unnecessary pomps — being confirmed as Emperor at Rome, and receiving the iron crown of Lombardy. Pope Clement was really intriguing in the interests of the French King. The people rallied to the support of the Guelf leaders. An attempt on the part of the Emperor's forces failed, and shortly after, worn out, it is said, by the cares of his office, he died.

So vanished Dante's only real chance of return to Florence. It must not be supposed that his adherence to the Emperor showed a disposition to ruin Florence for the sake of vindicating himself. However mistakenly, he imagined that the Guelfs were now the enemies of Florence, and that their defeat and the return of the Ghibellines under the control of the Emperor would restore her fortunes. It is clear, moreover, that some vision of the unification of Italy was in his mind — a dream that was not to be realized for many centuries. A good many of the exiles had been recalled to Florence at the moment when she seemed most in danger from Henry. If Dante had not declared himself so strongly on the Imperial side he might have been included among the number. As it was, in that same year the sentence against him was repeated. And this was to happen yet again, with an addition which might lead us to suspect that the lion had cubs. The death of Henry was not the end of the Ghibelline attempts against Florence. New leaders arose, among them a Pisan, who took the field with energy, and under whom some advantage was gained in Tuscany. In 1315 he defeated the Florentines on their frontier, but the city itself stood firm. Then followed a decree against Dante in which his sons are named with him: "as Ghibellines and rebels against the Commonwealth and the people of Florence and the statutes of the Guelf party, to be beheaded wherever taken." It may be that Dante was known to have had a hand in these latest demonstrations of the exiled Florentines.

Still later, to be sure (December, 1316) a general amnesty was offered, permission being given to all exiles to return on conditions of fine and penance. An eloquent letter has been preserved, which is said to have been written by Dante, indignantly rejecting this offer. Its authenticity has been denied, and there is no way of absolutely proving it Dante's. If it is an invention, it is written in the very spirit of the man: "Is this then the glorious return of Dante Alighieri to his country after nearly three lustres of suffering and exile? Did an innocence patent to all suffer this? — this, the perpetual sweat and toil of study? Far from a man, the housemate of philosophy, be so rash and earthen-hearted a humility as to allow himself to be offered up bound like a school-boy or a criminal! Far from a man, the preacher of justice, to pay those who have done him wrong as for a favor! This is not the way of returning to my country; but if another can be found that shall not derogate from the fame and honor of Dante, that I will enter in with no lagging steps. For if by none such Florence may be entered, by me then never! Can I not everywhere behold the mirrors of the sun and stars? speculate on sweetest truths under any sky, without first giving myself up inglorious, nay, ignominious, to the populace of Florence? Nor shall I want for bread."

Bread at least he did not want. During the next, and last, five years of his life he was the guest of various noble and princely houses at Verona, Ravenna, and elsewhere. His most powerful host and patron was Can Grande della Scala, a prince who held court at Verona, one of the greatest of his day. To him the poet inscribed his masterpiece. At Ravenna Dante seems to have had some diplomatic post, if we are to believe the tradition that it was while on a mission to Venice that he contracted his fatal illness. He died September 13th or 14th, 1321. He was buried at Ravenna, where a monument was raised to him by Guido Novello. On this monument were inscribed certain lines said to have been dictated by Dante on his deathbed, and which, as doggerel, vie with the epitaph on Shakespeare's grave. Lowell notes this analogy and says, "In both cases the rudeness of the verses seems to us a proof of authenticity" ; why, he does not make clear. But whatever may be said of the form, the substance is "Dantesque" enough. Here it is, with Lowell's translation:

"Jura monarchiæ, Superos, Phlegethonta, lacusque
Lustrando cecini volverunt Fata quousque;
Sed quia pars cessit melioribus hospita castris,
Auctoremque suum petiit felicior astris,
Hic claudor Dantes patriis extorris ab oris,
Quem gentit parvi Florentia mater amoris."

"The rights of Monarchy, the Heavens, the Stream of Fire, the Pit,
In vision seen, I sang as far as to the Fates seemed fit;
But since my soul, an alien here, hath flown to nobler wars,
And, happier now, hath gone to seek its Maker 'mid the stars,
Here am I Dante shut, exiled from the ancestral shore,
Whom Florence, the of all least-loving mother, bore."

So passed Dante out of life, to experience in reality that other world which his imagination had painted with such vividness. Did he find Beatrice there? and did he cease to long for Florence as he took his place beside her?

We have many portraits of Dante, several of them nearly or quite contemporary. One of the most appealing is the fresco by Giotto, discovered fairly in our own time. The hawk nose and slightly protruding jaw of the later portraits are here, but the face is full of sensibility as well as strength: this is the Dante of youth, of the *Vita Nuova*. Boccaccio, who was born early enough to have seen him, paints the older Dante in these words: "Our poet was of middle height, his face was long, his nose aquiline, his jaw large, and the lower lip protruding somewhat beyond the upper; a little stooping in the shoulders; his eyes rather large than small; dark of complexion; his hair and beard thick, crisp, and black; and his countenance always sad and thoughtful. His garments were always dignified; the style such as suited ripeness of years; his gait was grave and gentlemanlike; and his bearing, whether public or private, wonderfully composed and polished. In meat and drink he was most temperate, nor was ever any more zealous in study or whatever other pursuit. Seldom spake he save when spoken to, though a most eloquent person. In his youth he delighted especially in music and singing, and was intimate with almost all the singers and musicians of his day. He was much inclined to solitude, and familiar with few, and assiduous in study as far as he could find time for it. Dante was also of marvelous capacity and the most tenacious memory." Villani, who also knew Dante in the flesh, makes one significant remark: "This Dante, on account of his learning, was a little haughty, and shy; and disdainful; and like a philosopher almost ungracious; knew not well how to deal with unlettered folks."

Dante was an aristocrat as well as a philosopher, and although he held office under a republican government, he had no respect for the rule of the majority. His manner may have had something of the arrogance of birth as well as of wisdom. It must be remembered that the medieval republics were not democracies of either the ancient or the modern type. There was no general suffrage in Dante's Florence. He became a member of a guild so that he might bear a hand in the government of the city, but he did not regard the prior system as an ideal form of government. He makes clear his contempt for the nobleman, Gian della Bella, who had deliberately fouled his own nest by bringing about the law which forbade nobles a share in the government of Florence. And, as in Paradise he listens to the voice of his knightly ancestor, he glories in his noble blood. While the *Divine Comedy* was being written, a great Swiss struggle for independence was going on, but there is no echo of it in Dante's verse. There is an eloquent passage in the *Convito* which shows that this pride of the noble was a matter of instinct rather than opinion: for here he not only upholds rigorously the principle of *noblesse oblige,* but asserts that a true nobility is independent of birth. "Let not the Uberti of Florence, or the Visconti of Milan, say: 'Because I am of such a family I am noble,' for the divine seed does not fall upon a family, that is, a race, but upon individuals, and the race does not ennoble the individuals, but the individuals ennoble the race." He gives blunt judgment upon the excesses of the medieval noble: "Ah, miscreants, born under an evil star! ye who plunder widows and orphans; and with it furnish forth banquets, give away horses and arms, robes and money; wear superb clothing, build magnificent edifices, and believe this to be liberal!" There are, he says, many "who, being of famous and ancient lineage, or descended from excellent fathers, believe themselves to be noble, although there is no nobility in them." He believed in the rule of the best, not of the many. He believed, further, that the temporal authority of the Roman Emperor was as directly God-given as the spiritual authority of the Pope. Consequently his chief hope for Florence, as for all Italy, lay in the restoration of the Imperial power in secular affairs. But this was not destined to come about, and Dante closed his career as the faithful champion of a lost cause.

The title of the *Divine Comedy* was bestowed upon Dante's masterpiece in a casual way. The title he gives it in his letter to Can Grande is simply "the Comedy." The "Divine" was added long after Dante's death by enthusiastic Italian admirers, and applies rather to the sublime quality of the poem than to the sacred nature of its theme. Various early editions have *The Vision,* and it is a pity that the title was not adopted. In the letter, Dante says that he calls it comedy because of its happy ending: "Comedy begins with a certain asperity, but its matter ends prosperously. . . . Likewise in their manner of speech do tragedy and comedy differ from each other; for one speaks in an elevated and sublime, the other in a weak and humble style. . . . By this it is made evident why the present work is called a comedy, because, if we consider the matter thereof, in the beginning it is horrible and fetid, being Hell, in the end prosperous, desirable, and pleasant, being Paradise. If we consider its language, it is humble and weak, because it is the vulgar tongue, which women ever use." So, with the quaint ingenuousness which marked the most learned discourses of that age, he goes on to analyze the poem.

When the different cantos of the poem were written we do not know, all, probably, within the last quarter-century of his life. Boccaccio says that the first seven cantos were written before his exile, that Dante left them behind in Florence, that they were discovered by accident and sent to the Marchese Malespina, with whom he was staying four or five years after his banishment: that Dante acknowledged the verses as his, and went on with them at the urgent request of the Marchese. It seems very doubtful that Dante could have left any part of the work to such a chance, for he knew perfectly well what its importance was. He may of course have left a draft in Florence which might have been called to the attention of his host. Boccaccio has a similar legend to record about another part of the poem. The last thirteen cantos, he says, were missing at Dante's death, and in spite of much searching could not be found. At last, after some months, Dante appeared to his son Jacopo in a dream, and told him where he could find them. There is nothing to be verified in either of these traditions, but they are interesting as examples of the legends which, almost immediately after his death, began to spring up about his memory. Indeed, it is certain (as is indicated by the nature of the second of the traditions just mentioned), that during his last years Dante was already famous. It is very probable that parts of the *Comedy,* at least, had been in circulation for some time before his death. Hence the legend of his being pointed out with awe by the women of Ravenna, as he walked the streets in stern abstraction, as the man who had been in Hell. The experience of his imagination as well as of the events of his life in the flesh no doubt were terribly real to him, and had left their mark upon his features. The face of this man who had been in Hell, the face of all the later portraits, is the subject of one of Carlyle's most striking bursts of imaginative description:

"To me it is a most touching face; perhaps of all faces that I know, the most so. Lonely there, painted as on vacancy, with the simple laurel wound round it; the deathless sorrow and pain, the known victory which is also deathless; significant of the whole history of Dante! I think it is the mournfulest face that ever was painted from reality; an altogether tragic, heart-affecting face. There is in it, as foundation of it, the softness, tenderness, gentle affection as of a child; but all this as if congealed into sharp contradiction, into abnegation, isolation, proud hopeless pain.

A soft ethereal soul looking out so stern, implacable, grim-trenchant, as from imprisonment of thick-ribbed ice! Withal it is a silent pain, too, a silent scornful one; the lip is curled in a kind of godlike disdain of the thing that is eating out its heart,— as if it were withal a mean insignificant thing, as if he whom it had power to torture and strangle were greater than it. The face of one wholly in protest, and lifelong unsurrendering battle, against the world. Affection all converted into indignation: an implacable indignation; slow, equable, silent, like that of a god! The eye, too: it looks out as in a kind of *surprise,* a kind of inquiry, Why the world was of such a sort? This is Dante: so he looks, this 'voice of ten silent centuries,' and sings us 'his mystic unfathomable song.' "

A mystic unfathomable song it is by all accounts — by Dante's own account. In the letter to Can Grande, he says, " There are six things that must be sought out in beginning any instructive work, that is to say, the subject, the agent, the form, the end, the title of the book, and the nature of its philosophy." . . . " The meaning of this work is not simple, but rather may be called complex, that is to say, it has many meanings; because the meaning of the letter is quite different from that of the things signified by the letter. The first is called *literal,* the second *allegorical* or *mystical.*" This is by no means all, however. " The form is duplex, that is, the form of the work and the form of its treatment. The form of the work is triplex, according to its triple division. The first division is this: the whole work is divided into three canticles; the second, each canticle is divided into cantos, the third, each canto is divided into rhythms. The form, or rather the mode, of treatment is *poetic, figurative, descriptive, digressive, abbreviative;* and besides, *definitive, divisive, probative, improbative,* and *positive in examples.*" Modern readers may be moved by all this to breathe a sigh of relief that other poets have not thought it necessary to exhibit the bare bones of their discourse in this fashion. But Dante's pedantry, his store of medieval learning, were matters which he took with perfect seriousness. In his mind this song, in order to prove its right to exist, must prove itself unfathomable. The feeling which underlies Dante's apparent scholasticism has been beautifully defined by Lowell: "Where, as in Dante, the religious sentiment and the imagination are both organic, something interfused with the whole being of the man, so that they work in kindly sympathy, the moral will insensibly diffuse itself with beauty as a cloud with light. Then that fine sense of remote analogies, awake to the assonance between facts seemingly remote and unrelated, between the outward and inward worlds, though convinced that the things of this life are shadows, will be persuaded also that they are not fantastic merely, but imply a substance somewhere, and will love to set forth the beauty of the visible image because it suggests the ineffably higher charm of the unseen original."

The literal meaning of Dante's Comedy, or Vision, is this: On Maundy Thursday of the year 1300 Dante finds himself lost and mazed in a dark wood, at the bottom of a gloomy valley. How he had come there he hardly knew. Fear took hold upon him, but as he looked upward, he saw the sun shining over the top of a mountain which enclosed one side of the valley. He began to climb toward it, but his path was crossed by three terrible beasts, and he was about to retreat when a figure appeared before him. This turned out to be the shade of Virgil, who assured him that there was no sure escape from those beasts in this world, but offered to lead him through Hell and Purgatory, and to provide him with another guide to Paradise. Dante with trembling consented, visited Hell and Purgatory with Virgil as Guide, and Heaven under the convoy of Beatrice herself. The whole journey took up eight days; when Dante returned to the world, now in less peril of the three menacing beasts, and free to take up human life again with the advantage of his supernatural knowledge. The most obvious secondary sense of the poem is that Dante found himself in middle life threatened by the vices of luxury, pride, and greed, and was saved by a supernal vision especially vouchsafed to him — on condition, the implication is, that he shall give the benefit of it to mankind. A third meaning would relate to the journey of mankind from sin toward salvation. Beyond this I need not here go: the libraries are full of books interpreting the great poem. What we are concerned with is the light it throws on the life and character of the poet.

From the opening verse of the poem, "midway upon the journey of life," it is generally thought that Dante meant to refer the experience it records to the year 1300, when he was thirty-five years of age. It is his habit to speak precisely on all such matters. It must have been about then, for events which happened before that date are spoken of as past, while later events are given as prophecy. One of its prophecies, to be sure, that of Virgil about a certain "hound" which was to deliver Italy from her misrule, has never found any accepted interpretation, though it may allude to Can Grande in the way of pure prophecy. But for the rest, we find the prophetic form used to record events in the life of Italy between the beginning of the fourteenth century and Dante's death. Here is a commentary in imaginative form upon the chief happenings in Dante's life, and in that life of Florence and Italy which he personally knew. Here are an infinite number of allusions, direct and indirect, to the factional strife of the Guelfs and the Ghibellines, the Blacks and the Whites; to the struggle between Church and Empire. Here, most interesting of all to the biographer, is a mass of personal allusions, or rather judgments, which give us the best possible light upon the heart and mind of the poet. You may judge pretty well what a man is from the way he speaks of his friends and his enemies,— always supposing you understand the language in which he speaks. Dante speaks in terms of his own day. The dreadful scenes he describes in *Hell* and *Purgatory* must be misunderstood by a modern reader who reads them as he would modern poetry. The fact that so many of the victims are specified by name has led to charges of harshness toward his friends and gloating cruelty toward his enemies on the part of Dante. Lowell has said all that need be said in connection with this theory of Dante's personal vindictiveness: — "We are not greatly concerned to defend him on that score, for he believed in the righteous use of anger, and that baseness was its legitimate quarry. He did not think the Tweeds and Fisks, the political wire-pullers and convention-packers, of his day merely amusing, and he certainly did think it the duty of an upright and thoroughly trained citizen to speak out severely and unmistakably. He believed firmly, almost fiercely, in a divine order of the universe, a conception whereof had been vouchsafed him, and that whatever and whoever hindered or jostled it, whether wilfully or blindly it mattered not, was to be got out of the way at all hazards; because obedience to God's law, and not making things generally comfortable, was the highest duty of man, as it was also his only way to true felicity. It has been commonly assumed that Dante was a man soured by undeserved misfortune, that he took up a wholly new outfit of political opinions with his fallen fortunes, and that his theory of life and of man's relations with it was altogether reshaped for him by the bitter musings of his exile. This would be singular, to say the least, in a man who tells us that he 'felt himself four-square against the strokes of chance,' and whose convictions were so intimate that they were not merely intellectual conclusions, but parts of his moral being. Fortunately we are called on to believe nothing of the kind."

It cannot be denied that there was a deep tinge of personal bitterness in Dante's later attitude toward the city which had cast him out; and he is too ready, perhaps, to identify Florence with the small faction which ruled her at the time of his misfortune. He urged Henry of Luxemburg to crush first Florence, as the "Hydra and Myrrha," the root of all Italy's ills. The full title of his great work, as given in the letter to Can Grande, reads, "Here begins the Comedy of Dante Alighieri, Florentine by birth, not by customs:" a final shaking of the dust more uncompromising than in such a place was clearly called for. But if there is something implacable in his attitude of injured pride toward the city of his birth, it is because she seems to him to stand for all human injustice and dishonor. And so it is in his attitude toward the individual culprits whom he has known personally, as they lived. One may hold that there is a sort of blasphemy in his readiness to assume divine powers of judgment, and yet may be unable to deny the majesty with which he plays the part. There is nowhere in his prose or verse a touch of that scurrility of which even Milton, in moods of partizan heat, is guilty. Horrible his pictures often are, and all the more so for his minute realism of method. This was the method by which he could hope to move his fellow-men in that day. We have in his prose plenty of evidence as to his powers of dispassionate and abstract speculation. But this was to be a poem: this was to teach not by argument but by striking home upon the quivering consciences of his hearers. "Whoever has studied medieval art in any of its branches," says Lowell again, "need not be told that Dante's age was one that demanded very palpable and even revolting types. As in the old legend, a drop of scalding sweat from the damned soul must shrivel the very skin of those for whom he wrote, to make them wince if not to turn them away from evil-doing. To consider his hell a place of physical torture is to take Circe's herd for real swine. Its mouth yawns not only under Florence, but before the feet of every man everywhere who goeth about to do evil. His hell is a condition of the soul, and he could not find images loathsome enough to express the moral deformity which is wrought by sin on its victims, or his own abhorrence of it."

It would be difficult to make out an argument of partizanship against Dante on the score of his personal judgments in the *Divine Comedy*. The Guelfs and the Ghibellines as placed in his *Hell* and *Purgatory* are about equal in number. He is often overwhelmed with pitying grief at the spectacle of good and amiable men (as Brunetto Latini) condemned to eternal torture, or long delayed in the enjoyment of heavenly bliss, by reason of one fleshly fault, long repented. If he omits from his category of sinners no name of friend or foe who seems to him justly deserving of inclusion, it is also true that he loses no opportunity to record his gratitude for benefits received, his sense of mitigating virtue among those who had done him personal wrong. Well he might speak, in his sense of the injustice of his fate at the hands of the city which had given him birth, and which had proved so ungrateful a mother, of the salt savor of strangers' bread, and the weary labor of ascending and descending strangers' stairs. But he nevertheless finds place in his masterpiece to express his gratitude to those kind strangers who did what they could for a man in exile.

And through the latter half of the poem shines a serene faith, a benignity, which is hardly connected with the image of Dante in the minds of most of us. From his time to our own too many persons have taken a morbid interest in the horrors of Dante's Hell, in the ghastliness and lifelikeness of his figures of speech, — have been interested perhaps in the Florentine gossip involved,— without in the least caring for the larger meaning of it all. The interest of such a reader naturally wanes as he gets on with the Purgatory, and vanishes utterly in the pure white light of the Heaven of Beatrice. Yet it is here that Dante is to be found at his greatest, here that the deep magnanimity of the man shows forth.

There is, after all, in Carlyle's portrait of him, rather too great insistence upon Dante's tragic aspect. The ending of his poem was, he said, prosperous; and so, no doubt, in all greater senses, he must have regarded the ending of his life. He had passed through the battle, and his wounds continued to trouble him to the end: but it was the end of a victor. He had been for twenty years an exile and a wanderer; but he had come thereby into full possession of himself, and he knew that through his genius he should possess the world. All those later years must have been beatified by the enthusiasm of the great artist who knows that he is doing himself justice. He knew what praise was, and was by no means indifferent to it. In the early years of wandering, he confesses that the fame of his verses was so sweet as to make him almost indifferent to the fact of his exile. Eventually he claimed for himself sixth place among the world's poets. Six centuries later the world awards him second or third place.

Yet there never was a man who, in a superficial sense, wrote more provincially, parochially even. He was intensely occupied with the persons and the events of his day. If it were not for the fact that commentators among his contemporaries sprang up immediately after his death, we should find it hard to follow his meaning half the time. Fortunately they did spring up, and we can follow him fairly well. But even if we knew less than we do about the detail of Dante's *Vision,* the grandeur of its design, the beauty of its style, and the nobility of its tone would still impress it upon us as one of the world's great poems. "Underlying Dante the metaphysician, statesman, and theologian, was always Dante the poet, irradiating and vivifying, gleaming through in a picturesque phrase, or touching things unexpectedly with that ideal light which softens and subdues like distance in the landscape. The stern outline of his system wavers and melts away before the eye of the reader in a mirage of imagination that lifts from beyond the sphere of vision and hangs in serener air images of infinite suggestion projected from worlds not realized, but substantial to faith, hope, and aspiration." Dante drew his inspiration from his time, like all really great poets. Knowing, like Homer, his own heart and the heart of his age, he was able to sing to other ages.

Eight years after Dante's death, a certain Cardinal who had caused the *De Monarchia* to be burnt, proposed that the poet's bones should share the same fate, "to the eternal shame and extinction of his memory." But the Cardinal found himself faced by an opposition which may have surprised him, both from Florence and Ravenna. Dante's fame was not to be extinguished so easily: already it had become powerful throughout Italy. It was not long before Florence was begging for the body she had cast out: as late as within our own memory almost, the plea has been repeated. But little Ravenna has been tenacious of her guest.

Virgil, like Homer, had chosen a man for his theme: Dante's subject was mankind. And quickly mankind gave ear. For never before had that theme been treated with warmer human ardor, with more perfect balance of sympathy and power. "The range of Dante's influence"—to quote from Lowell yet one more passage which needs no re-phrasing—"is not less remarkable than its intensity. Minds, the antipodes of each other in temper and endowment, alike feel the force of his attraction, the pervasive comfort of his light and warmth. Boccaccio and Lamennais are touched with the same reverential enthusiasm. The imaginative Ruskin is rapt by him, as we have seen, perhaps beyond the limit where critical appreciation merges in enthusiasm; and the matter-of-fact Schlosser tells us that 'he, who was wont to contemplate earthly life wholly in an earthly light, has made use of Dante, Landino, and Vellutello in his solitude to bring a heavenly light into his inward life.' Almost all other poets have their seasons, but Dante penetrates to the moral core of those who once come fairly within his sphere, and possesses them wholly. His readers turn students, his students zealots, and what was a taste becomes a religion. The homeless exile finds a home in thousands of grateful hearts. *E venne da esilio in questa pace!*"

SHAKESPEARE

It has always been the amiable habit of English biographers to strain a point a little this way or that in order to connect the object of their enthusiasm with aristocratic or at least gentle birth. So De Quincey and others have done their best to establish a superior ancestry for the great poet of our race. But the simple fact is (and it is not a fact to offend Americans) that Shakespeare came of decent English country stock. We do not know anything of account about his forbears. We do not even know absolutely who his grandfather was. But we are fairly sure that it was a certain Richard Shakespeare, a small farmer who lived in the little Warwickshire village of Snitterfield. He was not a landholder, but seems to have occupied the farm in question as a tenant for many years, and to have been succeeded in the tenancy by one of his sons. His other son, John, left home, probably not long after coming of age, for the neighboring village of Stratford-on-Avon, a small place, but much larger than Snitterfield. Here he entered trade in a small way, and, as it appears, with moderate success from the first.

Our earliest distinct record of him at Stratford gives unsavory evidence as to the physical conditions

WILLIAM SHAKESPEARE

The Jansen portrait

of life in an Elizabethan village. (Sanitary conditions were not so very much better in London, for that matter.) In the year 1552 John Shakespeare was fined twelve-pence for making the public way in front of his house a trifle more filthy than even the Stratford burghers could permit. The streets were not paved; open drains ran through them, and heaps of offal and every kind of household refuse made them a happy hunting-ground for the swine and geese which ran loose in the highways. There were, to be sure, two public places provided by the town for the disposal of offal, and the fining of John Shakespeare is only one of a considerable number of recorded instances going to show that the authorities made intermittent and half-hearted attempts to enforce such a disposal. Stratford seems to have had, under any conditions, more than its share of unhealthfulness. It was a water-logged place, to begin with: drenched with river mist and heavy and sodden of soil. Now and then the town was flooded outright. As the houses had clay floors, at best covered with rushes, the consequences were serious. Shakespeare must have had plenty of experience of those "contagious fogs" about which Titania is so eloquent, with their sequel of flood, rotting corn, distempered cattle, and "rheumatic diseases" among men. Indeed, these conditions persisted for centuries. As late as 1769 Garrick described Stratford as "the most dirty, unseemly, ill-paved, wretched-looking town in all Britain." When we consider what a foul place, from the modern point of view, Garrick's London was, we can imagine what to draw such epithets from him Shakespeare's town must have been. A few months after Shakespeare's birth, the dreaded plague ravaged the town, carrying off something like a seventh of its inhabitants. By chance, or shall we say providentially, the Shakespeares of Henley Street were altogether spared. John Shakespeare, be it noted, is recorded among those who contributed liberally toward the relief of his stricken neighbors.

But the early fine seems to have carried no particular odium with it. By that time he was evidently looked upon as a respectable citizen, and shortly afterward his fortune began to rise in a marked degree. In 1557 he made what was for a small tradesman an exceptionally good match. Mary Arden was the daughter, not indeed of a gentleman, as certain ardent Britons have tried to prove, but of a substantial yeoman-farmer. On his death, but a few months before the marriage, he had left the girl a respectable legacy in money, and the reversion to certain landed estates: one of them, as it chanced, being at Snitterfield, and including the farm rented by Richard Shakespeare. Her social rank was certainly a grade above her husband's, and she would be considered an heiress in any rural community. She brought him both money and prestige. In the following year we find him holding the first of a series of public offices in which he evidently carried himself with credit. He served successively as ale-taster, burgess, constable, chamberlain, and finally, in 1568, as High Bailiff, or Mayor, of Stratford. At this point in this career he is first alluded to in contemporary documents as Mr. Shakespeare, a clear enough sign of his advancement in the world. Mr. Shakespeare, landholder and High Bailiff, was a very different person in the public eye from plain John Shakespeare, butcher, wool-stapler, fellmonger and glover of Stratford. He is credited by fable with all these occupations, and we may as well accept them all, adding those of farmer and sheep-raiser. He probably worked at least part of the land which had come to him with his wife. There is no reason why he may not have grown his own sheep, slaughtered them, sold the carcases and wool, and such of the hides as he did not need in his trade of glover. It is certain that his business throve, so that throughout the great Shakespeare's childhood, his father was a prosperous and honored member of the community. A recently discovered bit of gossip has it that he was "a merry-cheeked man, fond of jesting — valuing his repartee equal to that of his son, whom he called a good, honest fellow." True, he could not read or write, and reckoned his accounts as chamberlain by means of counters; but whatever his method he was evidently looked upon as a skilled accountant, and was certainly not more illiterate than his fellow-chamberlains. His private mark resembled the trademark of

the glovers' guild. When he was constable it was his stated duty to direct the watch, and once a month or oftener from Michaelmas to Candlemas, "as the case requireth, to call to him certain of the council and some other honest men, and keep and have a privy watch for the good of the town." This was some years before Shakespeare's birth, and it was his father's successors in office who must have sat for those richest of all his comic portraits, Dogberry and his underlings.

April 22nd or 23rd, 1564, some seven years after the marriage of John Shakespeare and Mary Arden, the first son, William, was born. Of the boy's early years we have no direct record, but there is little reason to doubt, from what we know of him later and from a hundred allusions in his plays, that he was a healthy and normal child. Who else would have been the prototype of that very robust and natural young person, "with shining morning face, creeping like snail unwillingly to school?" In later life he remembered and made figurative use of such childish games as whipping tops, hide-and-seek, leap-frog, and prisoners' base, not to speak of the older sports of hockey, quoits, ninepins, and football. Nobody can fancy the boy Shakespeare a prig or an idler. Nor can he have had the dreamy childhood of many lesser poets. We may imagine him going actively but without excitement about his work and play, the intensity of his nature not manifesting itself emotionally, but hidden behind his quiet brow and pleasant blue eyes.

A little learning might readily be looked upon as a dangerous thing in those days. A boy must either be content to know nothing of books at all, or run the risk of coming in contact with a good many books of a sort to dash the courage of any incipient tradesman, farmer, or even High Bailiff. If he gave himself to the lesser mysteries of A-B-C, he must find himself exposed to the rigors of Lilly's Grammar, the *Collo-quia* of Erasmus, Cato's *Disticha,* and the like; and these in short order. The elder Shakespeare had not ventured all this upon his own account, or rather it had not been ventured for him; as we have seen, he could not read or write. But it was natural that in his character of leading citizen he should see that his sons had advantage of the very good schooling Stratford afforded.

The most cautious of Shakespeare's biographers admit that he must have gone for some years to the grammar school at Stratford. But attention has been only recently called to the fact that it was an exceptionally good school. It is of course an old and long-honored tradition that Shakespeare's formal education amounted to little, that he picked up what he did know of books in the most careless and casual way, and that the sum of his scholarship was small. The legend dates from the well-known line of Ben Jonson:

> And though thou hadst small Latin and less Greek —

But Jonson was a scholar — one of the giants among classical scholars of his day, when no other sort of scholarship was recognized. It was not to be expected that the university wit and pedant would rate any degree of friendly acquaintance with the literatures of Greece and Rome as comparable with the exact and technical learning upon which he prided himself. Jonson was proud of nothing so much as of his scholarship, and regarded it as a very important ground of superiority over Shakespeare. In writing that famous line he did not consciously try to belittle the man whose eminence as a poet he was whole-heartedly celebrating; he simply stated the plain fact of what he doubtless regarded as Shakespeare's serious limitation. Almost all the other prominent poets and playwrights of the day were university men; Shakespeare's lack of the ordinary training of an educated man would be naturally mentioned by any of them who might be moved to speak of him and his work. But it is worth while to give the line its context:

> And though thou hadst small Latin and less Greek,
> From thence to honor thee I would not seek
> For names; but call forth thundering Æschylus,
> Euripides and Sophocles to us,
> Pacuvius, Accius, him of Cordova dead,
> To life again, to hear thy buskin tread,
> And shake a stage; or when thy socks were on,
> Leave thee alone for the comparison
> Of all that insolent Greece and haughty Rome

> Sent forth, or since did from their ashes come.
> Triumph, my Britain . . .

To minimize this triumphant poet's classical learning is obviously to point the glorifying antithesis.

As a matter of fact, Shakespeare's classical attainments were beyond those of the usual bachelor of arts of to-day, in America at least. The grammar school at Stratford was a very old school when Shakespeare entered it. Richard Fox, who had been its headmaster in 1477, became founder of Corpus College, Oxford. This was the college which chiefly fostered the New Learning; which first introduced the study of Greek at Oxford, and the humane study of the classics as offset against the pedantry, or, as Fox himself called it, the barbarism, of the Middle Ages. Shortly after John Shakespeare came to Stratford, the school was created by royal charter "The King's New School of Stratford-on-Avon." It still exists upon the old spot, and is supported by the ancient endowment of Edward VI. We are not certain of its curriculum in Shakespeare's day, but we may fairly infer the substance of it from what we know of the course in similar schools of the period, and it does not sound like child's play, so far as its attention to the classics is concerned. "The curriculum of Ipswich Grammar School," says Churton Collins, "may fairly be taken as typical of the instruction provided in the best schools of Shakespeare's time. There were to be eight classes in the school. In the first two the pupils were to be thoroughly exercised in the rudiments of Latin, the text-book being Lily's Grammar. In the third form they were to read a Latin version of Æsop, and Terence; in the fourth, Virgil; in the fifth, Cicero's *Select Letters;* in the sixth, Sallust or Cæsar's *Commentaries;* in the seventh, Horace's *Epistles,* and Ovid's *Metamorphoses* and *Fasti;* and they were also required to write Latin verses. In the eighth they were to read the *Commentaries* of Donatus and were to be required to discuss the style and characteristics of Terence. By Shakespeare's time Greek was taught in schools headed by a 'progressive,' as Walter Roche, the Corpus Fellow, undoubtedly was." We may therefore imagine Shakespeare, at the age of seven or eight, entering upon what we should now call a pretty stiff classical course. Whatever we do not know about him, we certainly know that he had powers of acquisition and assimilation for which it is hard to find a parallel. Whatever he found in books or experience he learned, understood, and never forgot. He probably did not love grammar for its own sake; but his poems and plays give evidence that he was familiar with the work of Ovid, Plautus, Seneca, Horace, and Juvenal, at first hand, and, through Latin versions, with Plato, Sophocles, and Euripides, though, curiously enough, he shows no acquaintance with Aristophanes. Shakespeare was in a large sense nature's child, but his "native wood-notes wild" were the reverse of artless.

Everything he did may be referred to precedent, so far as his material is concerned. Nobody was ever so little interested in the process of invention. He took his plots ready-made, he borrowed freely of his contemporaries, and much of his work is in a sense a mosaic of remembered passages from the classics. His indebtedness in a wider way to these sources is incalculable.

The plays give many echoes of his school-boy experience, especially in the portrait of Holofernes (*Love's Labor's Lost*)— such a caricature of the rustic pedagogue as Dogberry is of the village constable. Holofernes and his fellow-pedant, Sir Hugh Evans (*Merry Wives of Windsor*) speak by the card from the *Sententiæ Pueriles,* Lily's Grammar, and Mantuan, the favorite substitute for Virgil in that day. There is no reason to doubt that Shakespeare had the same kind of acquaintance with French and Italian as with Latin and Greek: that is, an easy reading acquaintance. A theory has been not uncommonly held that he knew nothing of these languages, and depended upon translations for his slight acquaintance with a few classical and foreign books. The absurdity of the theory is easily proved by reference to a few dates. A number of the books from which he obtains his plots, Belleforest's *Histoires Tragiques,* Ser Giovanni's *Il Pecorone* and Cinthio's *Hecatommithi,* had not been translated when he used them. The French dialogue in *Henry V.* is as unmistakably Shakespearean as the English dialogue which surrounds it.

John Shakespeare's prosperity hardly outlasted the poet's childhood. We have no way of knowing what caused the lapse in his fortunes: perhaps merely the steady increase in the expenses of a growing family. Two daughters had died in infancy before William was born. Five other children followed, the last born in 1580. Gilbert became a haberdasher in London. Joan, who married William Hart, was the only one of the brothers and sisters to survive the poet, and is named in his will. The house (or houses) now known as the Shakespeare birthplace remained in the Hart family until the nineteenth century. Anne died in childhood, and Richard in middle age, after an unrecorded life at Stratford. Edmund became an actor, and was of sufficient consequence to have the great bell of Southwark rung at his burial. Whatever the cause, the star of the Shakespeares waned more rapidly than it had waxed. Soon after William would have entered the King's School, the turn came. Five or six years later, when the boy was thirteen or so, the serious condition of his father's affairs cut short his schooling. A little later first one and then the other of his mother's estates was mortgaged. By 1586 John Shakespeare had become insolvent, and careless as well of his public duties, for in that year he was deprived of his office of alderman, for repeated absence from the meetings of the council.

Just what the son did " for a living " during the eight or ten years between his leaving school and his setting out for London is matter of surmise, or of vague tradition. One legend has it that he became a butcher's apprentice; another that he taught school; both may be true. The probability is that at first he acted as his father's assistant. John Shakespeare had always killed sheep, and it may be that in his decline he did little else: hence the butcher tradition. From the internal evidence of his poems and plays, it has been argued, and plausibly, that he must have had some sort of legal experience before leaving Stratford, either as apprentice to a lawyer, or in some clerical capacity in connection with the local courts.

Shakespeare's knowledge was encyclopædic: or rather it had an accuracy in many directions which challenges wonder. He had a knack at terminology such as (to compare great things with small), we have recently seen displayed by Kipling: such as, for a fairer analogy, we find in Molière. But we can readily enough trace his information in certain departments to his early experiences in Stratford: for example, his minute learning in the art of venery. He knew all about hunting as it was practised in his day. Every one can quote Theseus's description of the hounds (*Midsummer Night's Dream*) and that of the horse in *Venus and Adonis;* and the plays abound in figures of speech drawn from the technical phraseology of the chase. But the most remarkable and characteristic source of his imagery, a source from which he draws lavishly in the early poems, and which remains inexhaustible to the last, is the phraseology of English law. So in what is probably his earliest known lyric, *A Lover's Complaint:*

> My woeful self, that did in freedom stand,
> And was my own fee-simple.

In *Venus and Adonis:*

> But, when the heart's attorney once is mute,
> The client breaks, as desperate in his suit.

And in *The Rape of Lucrece:*

> The deep vexation in his inward soul
> Hath served a deep arrest upon his tongue.

The sonnets are full of legal terms; four of them (iv., xlvi., lxxvii. and cxxxv.) are nothing if not legal. Here alone is evidence to spare of Shakespeare's intimate knowledge of the technicalities of the English law. Lord Campbell, when Chief Justice of England, was asked for his opinion of Shakespeare's legal acquirement, and had no hesitation in declaring it to be extraordinarily exact and profound. The great jurist's analysis of one of the sonnets is as follows:

Mine eye and heart are at a mortal war
How to divide the conquest of thy sight;
Mine eye my heart thy picture's sight would bar,
My heart doth plead that thou in him dost lie,
(A closet never pierced with crystal eyes,)
But the defendant doth that plea deny,
And says in him thy fair appearance lies.
To 'cide this title is impaneled
A quest of thoughts, all tenants to the heart;
And by their verdict is determined
The clear eye's moiety, and the dear heart's part:
As thus: Mine eye's due is the outward part,
And my heart's right thine inward love of heart.

I need go no further than this sonnet, which is so intensely legal in its language and imagery, that without a considerable knowledge of English forensic procedure it cannot be fully understood. A lover being supposed to have made a *conquest* of (i. e., to have gained by *purchase*) his mistress, his Eye and his Heart holding as joint tenants, have a contest as to how she is to be partitioned between them, each moiety then to be held in severalty. There are regular pleadings in the suit, the Heart being represented as plaintiff, the Eye as defendant.

At last issue is joined on what one affirms and the other denies; and now a jury (in the nature of an inquest) is to be impaneled to 'cide (decide), and by their verdict to apportion between the litigating parties the subject-matter to be divided. The jury fortunately are unanimous, and, after due deliberation, find for the Eye in respect of her outward form, and for the Heart in respect of her inward love.

The legal allusions in the plays are almost innumerable — if, indeed, they should be called allusions. For it is clear that Shakespeare employed this kind of imagery not as a matter of conscious artifice, but because the legal terminology belonged fairly to the texture of his thought. Now Shakespeare left Stratford somewhere about the year 1585, and it is altogether probable that he gained his knowledge of the law during the few years before or after his departure for London.

The first absolutely dated fact we can attach to Shakespeare's name is that of a marriage-bond of November 28, 1582, which is still to be found in the registry at Worcester. Shakespeare was then in his nineteenth year. Anne Hathaway, whose name appears with his on the bond, was in her twenty-sixth. The bond was given to secure a marriage license after once asking of the banns. The names affixed as securities are of friends of the Hathaways, and the seal used is that of the bride's father. No member of Shakespeare's family seems to have been connected with the affair. The natural inference is that the bride's family approved of the marriage, at least as a measure of expediency, while the Shakespeares would have nothing to do with it. This may easily have been so, for the reason that the Shakespeares of Stratford Town, though now no longer at the height of their modest fortunes, may have considered themselves socially superior to the yeoman farmer class from which they had recently sprung. Anne Hathaway's father was merely a poor though thrifty farmer of Shottery, a neighboring hamlet. There would be nothing to attract the elder Shakespeares to the marriage of their eighteen-year-old son to a portionless farm-wench eight years his senior. We have no record of the marriage: six months after the signing of the marriage-bond, a child was born to Anne Shakespeare, which was named Suzanna.

A rather unnecessary amount of emphasis has been put upon this situation. On the one hand we have the general impression that Shakespeare felt himself obliged to marry as a consequence of indiscretion. On the other we have the ingenious explaining away of the difficulty by various learned apologists. "The ceremony of wedlock," says Professor Dowden, "may have been preceded by precontract, which according to the custom of the time and place would have been looked on as having the validity of marriage, though as yet unsanctified by ecclesiastical rites." . . . "The words 'wedded wife' were at this time in no way tautological; a woman duly espoused might be a wife though the priestly benediction of wedlock had not yet been bestowed." In other words the bond which made possible a comparatively hasty religious marriage may have been preceded by a legal civil ceremony. But this is sheer supposition: the fact is that the child was born somewhat sooner after marriage than it should have been. But this was a common occurrence among perfectly respectable people on both sides of the water only a few generations ago. Genealogists know how common it was during our early colonial days. The New England custom of "keeping company" as well as the Dutch custom of "bundling"— both rising from the sense of the sacredness of betrothal — account for this frequency. Whether or not there was any formal "precontract," Shakespeare and Anne Hathaway would be incurring no necessary disgrace in the eyes of their equals by the date of their daughter's birth.

However, it was hardly a marriage that promised brilliantly, and it is impossible not to wonder a little at Shakespeare's choice, if it was a free choice. At eighteen he must have been intellectually a man, he must have had some sort of consciousness of power. Did he deliberately plan to tie himself to a woman who was his social inferior, and who had neither money nor youth to offer him? Or was he haled to this union by force of overwhelming passion? Neither supposition is highly probable. On the other hand, what we know of his later life and work gives us no reason to doubt his affection for his wife.

Why he left Stratford is not positively known. Persistent tradition has it that the reasons were not to his credit. It is impossible to imagine Shakespeare in his twenties as a mere village ne'er-do-well. But it is hardly more possible to fancy him a paragon of staid virtue, rustic or otherwise. The poaching legend recorded by Rowe, Shakespeare's first biographer, has been indignantly denied of late. It cannot be authenticated or disproved, but the chances are there is some truth in it, and there is no real reason why we should shrink from what truth there may be. Poaching was not then regarded with the horror which it inspires in the breast of the modern Englishman. It was looked upon as a peccadillo rather than a serious crime; Halliwell-Phillipps records the fact that "the students of Oxford, the centre of the kingdom's learning and intelligence, had been for many generations the most notorious poachers in all England." The deer-stealing story, as Rowe tells it, runs as follows:

"He had, by a misfortune common enough to young fellows, fallen into ill company, and amongst them some that made a frequent practice of deer-stealing, engaged him more than once in robbing a park that belonged to Sir Thomas Lucy, of Charlcote, near Stratford. For this he was prosecuted by that gentleman, as he thought, somewhat too severely; and in order to revenge that ill usage, made a ballad upon him. And though this, probably the first essay of his poetry, be lost, yet it is said to have been so very bitter, that it redoubled the prosecution against him to that degree, that he was obliged to leave his business and family in Warwickshire, for some time, and shelter himself in London." The chief basis of Rowe's charge seems to lie in the testimony of a country cleric, Archdeacon Davies, who died in 1708, and who declared in his old age that Sir Thomas Lucy had Shakespeare "oft whipped and sometimes imprisoned, and that in revenge of this harsh usage, Shakespeare after held him up to ridicule in his 'Justice Clodpate' and calls him a great man, and that in allusion to his name he bore three louses rampant for his arms." Further may be cited in the matter a certain "very aged gentleman of Stratford" who unfortunately recalled, or fancied he recalled, the beginning of the young Shakespeare's "very bitter" poem. To go by the sample, it was wretched doggerel, owing its mild interest to the "lowsie Lucy" which at least coincides with the testimony of Archdeacon Davies. In disproof of the charge it has been remarked that there was no deer-park at Charlcote, and as for Justice Shallow and the device of the dozen louses "which do well become an old coat," he was created after the death of Sir Thomas Lucy, and one hardly wishes to believe that Shakespeare could have held an old grudge so long, or have taken such petty vengeance. The Lucy family may have judged the cap to fit. A copy of the 1619 *Merry Wives of Windsor* has been found to be the only early Shakespeare edition at Charlcote.

It is barely worth noting that some years after the younger Shakespeare left Stratford, a commission appointed in that neighborhood to inquire concerning Jesuits, priests, and recusants, reported John Shakespeare's name among those of persons who "come not to church for fear of process for debt," and that Sir Thomas Lucy was a member of the commission.

If we are not disposed to discredit altogether the

story that Shakespeare got into some sort of difficulty with the powers at Stratford, we need no such fact to account for his departure. If Shakespeare killed a deer or two within the bounds of Sir Thomas Lucy's park, it was probably done as a boyish prank, in company with other boys of his age. But he must have done with all that long before he went to London. He had then been four or five years married and had three children. His father's affairs were in a hopeless muddle, and he saw no prospect of getting ahead in Stratford. So he went to London, as thousands of other poor fellows have done before and since.

Shakespeare's acquaintance with the stage may have begun very early. It was during the year when the elder Shakespeare was Bailiff that the first licensed play, so far as we know, was heard in Stratford-on-Avon. It could not have been produced without his official sanction, and it is hardly extravagant to suppose that he may have had something personally to do with the innovation. This was in 1568 or 1569. Shakespeare was five or six years old, and as contemporary record shows, may easily have been taken to the play by his father. Witness the record of one Willis, exactly Shakespeare's age, of a play seen by him under similar circumstances in childhood:

"In the city of Gloucester the manner is as I think it is in other corporations, that, when players of interludes come to town, they first attend the Mayor to inform him what nobleman's servants they are, and so to get a license for their public playing; and if the Mayor like the actors, or would show respect to their lord and master, he appoints them to play their first play before himself and the Aldermen and Common Council of the city; and that is called the Mayor's play, where everyone that will comes in without money, the Mayor giving the players a reward as he thinks fit to shew respect unto them. At such a play my father took me with him, and made me stand between his legs as he sate upon one of the benches, where we saw and heard very well."

The two companies which the boy Shakespeare may have heard during that year of his father's bailiffship were under the patronage respectively of the Queen and the Earl of Worcester. For the trial performance to which the public was treated by the town authorities, the Queen's company got a tip from Bailiff Shakespeare of nine shillings, while the Earl's had but twelve pence — a fair indication of the respect held due either to the Queen's players or — their mistress. The play recalled by old Willis was a Morality called "The Cradle of Security," such as Shakespeare may easily have seen in childhood. Rude allegorical arrangements that these were, they more nearly approached true drama than the medieval mysteries the last days of which the boy Shakespeare may also have seen.

In 1587 William Shakespeare's name appears upon the Stratford records as consenting to a new adjustment of the old Asbies mortgage. It was certainly at some time during this period of greatest domestic stress that Shakespeare set out for London. His father was ruined, his wife had brought him no property, and his own apprenticeship in business or the law had led to nothing stable in the way of employment. It was time for him to seek fortune elsewhere. Dr. Johnson seems to be simply reporting a common tradition when he says that Shakespeare "came to London a needy adventurer, and lived for a time by very mean employments"; and that his first connection with the theater consisted simply in holding the horses of gentlemen who were attending the play. This latter legend is traceable (through Pope, Rowe, and Betterton) to Sir William Davenant; that is, to the middle of the seventeenth century. Johnson puts the story in its classic form:

"In the time of Elizabeth, coaches being yet uncommon and hired coaches not at all in use, those who were too proud, too tender, or too idle to walk, went on horseback to any distant business or diversion. Many came on horseback to the play, and when Shakespeare fled to London from a criminal prosecution, his first expedient was to wait at the door of the play-house, and hold the horses of those that had no servants that they might be ready again after the performance; — in this office he became so conspicuous for his care and readiness, that in a short time every man as he alighted called for Will Shakespeare, and scarcely any other waiter was trusted with a horse while Will Shakespeare could be had; — this was the first dawn of better fortune; — Shakespeare, finding more horses put into his hand than he could hold, hired boys to wait under his inspection, who, when Will Shakespeare was summoned, were immediately to present themselves, 'I am Shakespeare's boy, sir'; — in time Shakespeare found higher employment, but as long as the practice of riding to the play-house continued, the waiters that held the horses retained the appellation of Shakespeare's Boys."

This legend has been commonly discredited, but Halliwell-Phillipps, after going into the matter with his accustomed thoroughness, has come to a decision in which we may as well follow him, that there is probably some truth in the tradition that Shakespeare, as he quaintly puts it, did "act in some equine capacity" in the neighborhood of Burbage's theater.

It is hardly probable that Shakespeare went to London with any distinct notion of an employment, or that if he did he succeeded at once in finding it. Halliwell-Phillipps ingeniously demonstrates how naturally this business of horse-boy might have presented itself to the newcomer from Stratford as the first available job. He rode to London on his own horse, and went to Smithfield to sell it, as he would have no means of keeping it. Hardby Smithfield, James Burbage, owner of the Theater (as it was called), "Kept horses at livery for sundry persons."

Shakespeare meets Burbage; Burbage puts him in charge of the horses of his own customers,— and the " equine capacity " is discovered, for the benefit of all concerned. Other traditions dealing with his dramatic progress are to the effect that he was graduated from the post of horse-boy to that of " servitor " or dresser, and thereafter to that of " prompter's attendant," " whose duty," says Malone, " was to give performers notice to be ready to enter as often as the business of the play requires their appearance on the stage." Mr. Halliwell-Phillipps quotes the testimony of one Downes (writing in 1710): " I have known men within my remembrance, arrive to the highest dignities of the theatre, who made their entrance in the quality of mutes, joint-stools, flower-pots, and tapestry-hangings." In some such humble and incidental capacity it is pretty clear that Shakespeare made his first connection with the stage.

English drama at the moment was approaching its highest form. Its development had been so rapid that it had not yet sloughed off its primitive members. Both the Morality plays, with their farces and interludes, and the yet older Mysteries, were produced at Stratford during Shakespeare's boyhood. Shakespeare makes numerous allusions to these primitive but still popular forms,— to the " Vice " of the Morality, and the " black souls " of the Coventry Mysteries. From the Morality, or parallel with it, had developed the Chronicle Play. A year or two before Shakespeare's birth the first English blank verse tragedy appeared in *Gorboduc,* or *Ferrex and Porrex* as it was called in the authorized edition published a decade later. *Ralph Roister Doister* and *Gammer Gurton's Needle* were a few years older — the earliest "legitimate" comedies in English. *Gammer Gurton's Needle* is a development of the farcical interludes whose coarse realism had tempted English audiences to sit through the graver instructions of the Morality plays. To the modern reader it is hardly less dull than coarse, though here and there a spark of true humor is to be discerned shining like a will-o'-wisp in its miry context. *Roister Doister,* on the other hand, is an English adaptation of Plautus's *Miles Gloriosus,* and though written in the same doggerel measure as *Gammer Gurton,* shows traces of its breeding. *Gorboduc* is a Senecan tragedy whose structure as well as its respectable blank verse distinguish it from the inchoate experiments which had preceded it.

It was not by an accident that Seneca became the godfather of English tragedy. He was the model of the Italians to whom English literature then looked for instruction. Seneca's combination of sententiousness and sensationalism was sure to catch a people bred to moral spectacles. Blood and lust are the springs of the Senecan action, as an oracular impressiveness is the chief characteristic of his style. Shakespeare's first tragedy, *Titus Andronicus,* is as Senecan as *Gorboduc.*

But by the time Shakespeare began to write, Seneca no longer remained unchallenged. From the beginning of her reign Elizabeth had encouraged the production of court masques and pageants, and in the hands of Lyly and others a distinctive court drama was developed. John Lyly's allegorical plays had dramatic as well as satirical power. It is to be noted as a sign of the religious origin of the English drama, that up to the very hour of Shakespeare, choir-masters continued to be the most successful managers, and choir-boys the best-trained actors in England. From 1580 to 1591 Lyly's plays were acted by the Children of St. Paul's or those of the Chapel at court: one or other "aery of little eyases" such as Hamlet satirizes. In 1591 the Children of St. Paul's were forbidden to act, and during the eight or nine years of their inhibition Lyly stopped writing. When in 1599 or 1600 he took up his play-writing again, the drama had made such strides that he found himself out of date. The popular play performed by strolling professional players, in town halls and inn-yards, had developed into a drama vastly more powerful and original than the courtly inventions of Lyly and Peele. Under such surroundings rather than at court developed not only the comedy of English manners, and the chronicle play, but the romantic drama which is, after all, the supreme product of the Elizabethan age.

Kyd had summed up whatever of excellence might be in Senecan tragedy in English in *The Spanish*

Tragedy, and there is a vigor and flexibility in him not at all Senecan. At about the time of Shakespeare's arrival in London a *Hamlet* of Kyd's, now lost, had been produced. Marlowe was then at the height of his powers: between 1587 and 1593, indeed, lay his whole brief dramatic career. And in his work the shadow of Seneca began to pass from the English stage of the people. In *Tamburlaine* and its successors, Marlowe displays a passionate energy of conception and of execution which is the quality we peculiarly associate with Elizabethan drama. And in Marlowe's use, English blank verse first assumes that sonority and something of that flexibility and delicacy which were to be perfectly developed during the next two decades by Shakespeare.

Idolaters of Shakespeare have indignantly denied that he could have been in any way responsible for so brutal a play as *Titus Andronicus,* but it is now generally recognized that he must at least have had a hand in it. A tradition recorded in 1678 asserts that the play was not Shakespeare's own, but "brought by a private author to be acted, and he only gave some master-touches to one or two of the principal parts." There seems to be no reason why this should not be accepted as substantially true. There is evidence that *Titus Andronicus* was produced in London at some time between 1588 and 1590: probably toward the latter date if Shakespeare had a hand in it, for he would then have been well on in his dramatic apprenticeship.

And indeed, with all its bombast, its horrors upon horrors, there are passages in it which have very clearly the ring of one who was to become, though he was not then, a master.

In the year 1587 a number of theatrical companies are known to have visited Stratford. Rowe says that Shakespeare returned to Stratford after the Lucy affair blew over. It is not probable that, if he did, he stayed there for any considerable length of time. There is a theory that Shakespeare was among the "Queen's Players" when they went to Stratford in 1587. His name is not upon the list of members of the company for that year; but he may have been with them in the capacity of prompter or what-not. There is little doubt that he was in Stratford at some time that year, for his signature is recorded, giving his sanction to a proposed adjustment of the Asbies estate. In 1578, John Shakespeare had borrowed £40 from a connection named Lambert, the Asbies property being named as security. In 1587 Lambert died, and his son wanted the matter settled. John Shakespeare was then in prison for debt. It was proposed that the mortgage be canceled, and twenty pounds to boot be paid for absolute title to the estate. For some reason this arrangement was not actually made, but Shakespeare's consent to it (he seems to have had a contingent interest which made his signature necessary) shows that neither his marriage nor his departure from Stratford had alienated him from his family. During the years which followed he was active in securing a reinstatement of his father. In 1596 and again in 1599 he applied for the grant of a coat of arms for his father. The heralds seem to have favored the grant, in the second case claiming gentle blood for both the Shakespeares and the Ardens, and proposing to impale the arms of the two families. The device was actually granted in 1599, by which date the younger Shakespeare was already known as a man of substance. The application is only one of many testimonies to Shakespeare's ambition to become a person of consideration in his native town.

September 3rd, 1592, died Robert Greene. In a sort of rambling confession left by him, we have the first distinct record of Shakespeare in London. Greene had been as luckless as most of his fellow-dramatists, and it was almost upon his deathbed that he wrote his now famous *Groat's worth of Wit Bought with a Million of Repentance.* He speaks sadly of his misspent life, and bitterly of the theatrical career. He then warns his colleagues and friends, Peele, Marlowe, and "young Juvenal" (supposed to be Lodge), against the players at whose mercy they were.

"Base minded all three of you, if by my misery ye be not warned: for unto none of you (like me) sought those burrs to cleave: those Puppets (I mean) that speak from their mouths, those Antics garnished in our colors. Is it not strange that I, to whom they all have been beholding; is it not like that you, to whom they all have been beholding, shall (were ye in that case that I am now) be both at once of them forsaken? Yes, trust them not: for there is an upstart crow, beautified with our feathers, that with his *Tiger's heart wrapt in his Player's hide,* supposes he is as well able to bombast out a blank verse as the best of you: and being an absolute *Johannes factotum,* is in his own conceit the onely shake-scene in a country. O that I might entreat you rare wits to be employed in more profitable courses: and let these Apes imitate your past excellence, and never more acquaint them with your admired inventions. . . . It is pity men of such rare wits should be subject to the pleasures of such rude grooms."

Poor Greene! There seems to have been more bile than repentance in him to the last. We can have no doubt as to the identity of the "upstart crow." The specific cause of Greene's rancor is not far to seek. The authorship of the three *Henry VI.* plays has been much discussed by Shakespeare scholars, and it cannot be said that they have come to agreement. However, we have better evidence than in the case of *Titus Andronicus* that Shakespeare's part in them was that of the editor and reviser, and we are pretty sure that Greene was the original author, or one of the original authors. The line:

O tiger's heart wrapt in a woman's hide!

is to be found both in *Henry VI.*, part third, and in the early and crude source of it, the *True Tragedy of Richard Duke of York,* in which Greene has at least part authorship. The Mirst Part of *Henry VI.* was produced certainly as early as March, 1592, by Lord Strange's Company,— the company in which (it was later known as the Lord Chamberlain's Company and yet later as the King's) Shakespeare remained during his whole career as actor.

Greene's attack is particularly interesting for the light it throws on Shakespeare's varied activities as a theatrical man. He has been through all the stages of a dramatic apprenticeship, and now, in 1592, after perhaps five years of experience, has become a *Johannes factotum,* a Jack-of-all-trades in connection with the stage. He acted, adapted, staged plays, and his additions to old plays, and emendations of them, quickly drew attention to his superior ability. He had written three successful comedies: *Love's Labor's Lost, The Comedy of Errors* and *The Two Gentlemen of Verona.* Finally, he had proved himself a capable actor. He never ranked as a great actor: Richard Burbage was the "Shakespearean star" of Shakespeare's day. The few parts legend assigns to the poet are of the minor sort likely to be undertaken by a stage-manager, whose energies are due to the whole play rather than to a single part. The Ghost in *Hamlet,* Adam in *As You Like It,* Old Knowell in Jonson's *Every Man in his Humour,* and in general the stately and quiet parts,— these are the rôles in which tradition places him. Yet he continued to act occasionally even after his work as a playwright was done. There is no more interesting biographical suggestion in the plays than the famous advice to the players in *Hamlet*. It is the advice of a theatrical expert, a manager who has staged many plays, in lifelong combat with the dullness, the conceit, the bombast of the ordinary actor.

That a young and little-educated player should himself attempt to write plays no doubt seemed to Greene a disconcerting fact. Greene, like all Shakespeare's greater contemporary dramatists, was a university man. One Henry Chettle, probably out of pity for Greene, published the *Groat's worth of Wit*. A few months later he printed a pamphlet of his own, *Kind-Heart's Dream,* in the preface to which he took occasion to apologize for the former attack upon Shakespeare. "At that time," he says, "I did not so much spare as since I wish I had, for that, as I have moderated the heat of living writers, and might have used my own discretion, especially in such a case, the author being dead, that I did not, I am as sorry as if the original fault had been my fault; because myself have seen his (Shakespeare's) demeanor no less civil than he excellent in the quality he professes: Besides, divers of worship have reported his uprightness of dealing, which argues his honesty, and his facetious grace in writing, that approves his art."

"With neither of them that did take offense was I acquainted, and with one of them I care not if I never be. . . ."

The two who had taken offense are understood to have been Marlowe and Shakespeare, and the distinction made between them is worth noting. If Shakespeare lacked the learning of his contemporary dramatists, he had evidently more self-control. Most of them were dissolute as well as penniless. There is plenty of evidence that Shakespeare was capable of being a boon-companion, but there is none that he was ever regarded as a disreputable person. For one thing, he had a head for business, and an eye to the main chance if ever author had. His thrift was amazing, his wish for social position a safeguard against the wild living of his rivals. It is not at all unlikely that he caused pressure to be brought to bear upon Chettle in the direction of a public apology for the attack he had made public.

It is to be noted that the publisher knows of Shakespeare's "facetious" (felicitous) grace in writing only through the report of others. Several plays had been given as his, but nothing had been published under his name. The following spring, however, (April 18, 1593) *Venus and Adonis* was entered upon the Stationers' Register, and later in the year it was printed by one Richard Field. Field was the son of a Stratford tanner, whose property the elder Shakespeare, though not yet restored by the industry of his son to solvency and office, is recorded to have appraised in August, 1593 — perhaps at the moment when *Venus and Adonis* was going through the press. The poem had a great success, and many editions were published during the poet's lifetime and thereafter. Its popularity, be it said at once, was no more due to its novelty than that subsequent popularity of the plays. It has been commonly said that Marlowe was Shakespeare's immediate model, whether in lyric or dramatic work; that without Marlowe's *Hero and Leander, Venus and Adonis* would hardly have come into being. But while it is evident that they belong to the same period, it is really impossible to determine which was written first. *Hero and Leander* was published five years after *Venus and Adonis.* Marlowe, dying suddenly in June, 1593, left his poem incomplete; he may easily have seen Shakespeare's, which was finished and probably in the hands of the printer. So that the likenesses which have been noted between the two poems may be due to imitativeness on the part of Marlowe rather than Shakespeare. Lodge's *Glaucus and Scylla,* on the other hand, published in 1589, is Shakespeare's obvious model in versification and even in diction.

An interesting fact in connection with these lyrical experiments of two busy young playwrights is that 1593 was a plague year in London. For some time the theaters were closed by the authorities, and though several companies, undoubtedly Shakespeare's among them, went "on the road," it is probable that he had somewhat more leisure than in other years.

Venus and Adonis was dedicated to the young Earl of Southampton, then only in his twentieth year, but already showing signs of that mingling of taste and generosity which made him the ideal patron. The tone of the dedication is obsequious and formal, but as one of the few bits of prose written in Shakespeare's own person which remain to us, it is worth quoting:

To the Right Honourable Henry Wriothesley, Earl of Southampton and Baron of Titchfield.

RIGHT HONOURABLE: I know not how I shall offend in dedicating my unpolished lines to your Lordship, nor how the world will censure me for choosing so strong a prop to support so weak a burthen, only, if your Honour seem but pleased, I account myself highly praised, and vow to take advantage of all idle hours, till I have honoured you with some graver labour. But if the first heir of my invention prove deformed, I shall be sorry it had so noble a godfather: and never after eare so barren a land, for fear it yield me still so bad a harvest. I leave it to your honourable survey, and your honour to your heart's content which I wish may always answer your own wish, and the world's hopeful expectation.

Your Honour's in all duty,
WILLIAM SHAKESPEARE.

There is a tentative air about this which contrasts sharply with the later dedication to *The Rape of Lucrece,* written a year later: "The love I dedicate to your lordship (it reads) is without end: whereof this Pamphlet without beginning is but a superfluous moiety. The warrant I have of your honorable disposition, not the worth of my untutored lines, makes it assured of acceptance. What I have done is yours, what I have to do is yours, being part in all I have, devoted yours. Were my worth greater, my duty would show greater, meantime, as it is, it is bound to your Lordship; to whom I wish long life still lengthened with all happiness."

Clearly the first appeal had not been without effect. The noble patron must have accepted the dedication with more than ordinary readiness, and we have a tradition that he responded in the way expected of noble patrons. It is indeed a Stratford legend that the Earl of Southampton's bounty enabled Shakespeare to buy property in his native town. Davenant told Rowe that " My Lord Southampton at one time gave him a thousand pounds to go through with a purchase he had a mind to." Probably the amount of this is exaggerated; it is unlikely, as we shall see, that Southampton's generosity would have been necessary to the purchase of New Place (1597).

The Rape of Lucrece was printed by Richard Field in 1594. This is no doubt to be taken as the " graver labor " which the author of *Venus and Adonis* had promised his patron. It is in a sense the obverse of the earlier poem, and was somewhat less popular for too evident reasons. This " graver labor " which the poet has set himself is a companion piece to the *Venus and Adonis,* whose voluptuousness is subdued to a sombre if rather conventional moral.

The phrase "first heir of my invention" has been a good deal discussed. It has been said that though he had done some play-writing, he shared the opinion of his time as to the insignificance of that sort of work from a literary point of view. It has been claimed in other quarters that the words indicate a very early origin of the poem — perhaps even the years before Shakespeare left Stratford. These surmises, as is often true in matters of Shakespearean scholarship, are unnecessarily ingenious. He may very likely have meant nothing more than that it was his first published work. In February of the same year *Titus Andronicus* was entered on the Stationer's Register, and published anonymously.

Attention has been recently called to the fact that Shakespeare's early success had in part a negative explanation. In 1593 Greene and Marlowe were dead; and Lyly had been silenced by the inhibition of the "little eyases" of St. Paul's. Some years were to pass before, with Dekker, Heywood, Middleton, and Jonson, a fresh rivalry began for the public favor. Meanwhile Shakespeare had the field much to himself. There is evidence that during this interval he achieved not only an enormous hit with the common audiences in London and the provinces, but that he was in high favor with the Court. The Queen herself encouraged him: he rode upon the top of the wave. By the close of the year 1593 his apprenticeship had fairly come to an end. *Titus Andronicus* is probably the earliest play with which we can associate his name; it seems to have been retouched by him as early as 1589. His similar connection with the three parts of *Henry VI.* is to be referred to 1590–1592: work of an equally imitative and subordinate sort. The three comedies, *Love's Labor's Lost, The Comedy of Errors,* and *The Two Gentlemen of Verona,* were written at some time between 1589 and 1593. And here also are shown imitativeness and adaptability, the faculty of seizing upon the fashionable thing and improving it. We cannot do better than quote a passage from one of the latest and best of critics of Shakespeare's period, since nothing can better illustrate the relation of Shakespeare to his forerunners and contemporaries, during the first years of his dramatic activity:

"It is common knowledge that in *Love's Labor's Lost,* Shakespeare's first comedy, Holofernes, the pedant, and Don Armado, the vain and boastful captain, are stock figures of the contemporary Italian stage. It is equally well known that his fantastical Spaniard finds his prototype in Sir Thopas of Lyly's *Endimion,* as witty Moth, his page, is paralleled by the all too witty pages of the same and of others of Lyly's comedies. None the less both Shakespearean figures have been said likewise to caricature well-known persons: Don Armado figuring an unhappy Spaniard who haunted the court, and, laboring under the delusion that he owned all the ships that came to London, was known as 'fantastical Monarcho,' while LaMothe was the name of a popular French ambassador to Elizabeth's court. *Love's Labor's Lost,* like nearly all Lyly's plays, is full of word-fence, antithetical conceit, repartee, and quibble. But more important than these particulars, is the circumstance that in this play Shakespeare followed Lyly's ideal of comedy, an ideal which seldom rose to the conception of a drama superior to momentary and local applications. *Love's Labor's Lost* has been well described as a species of 'historical extravaganza . . . travestying known traits and incidents of current social and political life.' In short, in this sprightly and immature effort, the indifferent fabric of which is apparently the only plot of his plays wholly invented by Shakespeare, the young dramatist was hazarding a transfer to the popular stage of Lyly's *drame de circonstance,* already so successful at court. Shakespeare was far from alone at this time in the satirical use of the stage which had rung for years with popular echoes of the pamphlet war known as the Martin Marprelate controversy."

In *The Comedy of Errors* again, the experimenter produced a farce adapted from the *Menaechmi* of Plautus, and it is in the *Two Gentlemen of Verona* alone that we find an approach toward that pure romantic comedy which was Shakespeare's peculiar contribution to the English drama. In *A Midsummer Night's Dream* (1594 or 1595), he once again, and, we suppose, for the last time, endangered his art by direct topical allusion, after the fashion set by Lyly. Leicester's unsuccessful courtship of Elizabeth is prefigured in this play, and the royal fair flattered after the mode of the time. For the rest, the work seems to belong naturally to that excursion into the realm of pure poetry which produced *Venus and Adonis* and *The Rape of Lucrece*. *A Midsummer Night's Dream* is far more poem than play; and its poetry is far more delicate and original than that of the heirs of the poet's invention which had been dedicated to Southampton. It is as if, taking up again his calling of playwright, Shakespeare found himself still carried along by the poetic impulse which he had allowed himself to indulge — and carried much farther than he had traveled hitherto. The *Venus* and the *Lucrece* are the lyrics of a playwright; the *Midsummer Night's Dream* is the play of a lyric poet. And the impulse carried him beyond the achievement of this graceful fantasy. *Romeo and Juliet,* which was given its final form not much later, is likewise so full of poetry that its dramatic action is at times greatly hampered by its lyrical episodes.

In December, 1594, Shakespeare had a part in two performances given before the Queen at Greenwich Palace. Among the other "Lord Chamberlain's Servants" who acted with him, were Richard Burbage, the greatest tragedian of his time, and Kemp, almost as distinguished as a comedian. After this date we know that the company acted often before the Queen. During the Christmas holidays in the year 1597 they played *Love's Labor's Lost* at Whitehall in revised and augmented form. In the spring the First Part of *Henry IV.* had appeared, and the Second Part must have been written within a few months. In this great play Shakespeare came into his own as a historical dramatist. The earlier historical plays showed more or less clear signs of his predecessors. In *King John* (about 1594), he had made use of two old plays, cleverly adapted and welded the material, and infused the whole with life by giving to the *personae* a real discrimination of character. *Richard III.* seems to have been written in 1593 or 1594. Here he shows more strongly than in any other play the influence of a master; and that master is Marlowe. " Not to mention the all but total absence of a gleam of comedy, the likeness extends to a certain fixity of character, a coarseness of stroke, a violence of speech and deed, and to a lyricism which converts whole scenes into the expression of a single emotion." In short, *Richard III.* shows the influence of Marlowe to a greater extent than any play of Shakespeare shows any single influence, and displays to us the young dramatist advanced a further step and seeking to rival his most successful competitor with his own weapons in his own field.

Marlowe's tragic death in June, 1593, put an end to his living sovereignty of the English stage; and the *Hero and Leander* which he left unfinished may have been a tribute in kind to the powers of his younger rivals. In *Richard II.,* which was probably not long in following *Richard III.,* we find Shakespeare using similar material in his own way: not with the finished skill of his later tragedies, but with far more flexibility and pure dramatic power than could have ever been shown by Marlowe, if we are to judge at all from the intimations of the work which his brief career permitted him. In *Henry IV.* these faculties display themselves in full exercise and under full control. In the earlier historical pieces, following Marlowe, there was almost no prose. In the First Part of *Henry IV.* something under one-half, and in the Second Part something over one-half, is in prose. Rhyme, moreover, is for the first time avoided, showing, as Gollancz says, "that he has learned to differentiate between his lyrical and dramatic gifts." Other important signs of advance in this play are the employment of dramatic contrast, the balancing of characters, and the giving to staid political events a flashing background of humor. No wonder good Queen Bess fell in love with Falstaff and commanded his reincarnation in the rôle of lover. It is a tradition that *The Merry Wives of Windsor* was written in a fortnight.

In 1595 or a little later Shakespeare was a property-owner in the Parish of St. Helen's, Bishopsgate, and lived there. He was an important member and part-proprietor of the best theatrical company of the time. He had already set about restoring the family fortunes. A Stratford document of 1596 described John Shakespeare as Yeoman. The authorities of the Heralds' College later in the year entitle him Gentleman.

The history of the granting of arms to the Shakespeares is not without interest. In 1568, John Shakespeare, while in office as Bailiff and justice of the peace, had obtained from the Heralds' College a pattern or sketch of a coat of arms; but had apparently failed to secure the right to bear it. Over thirty years later, in 1599, the right was granted by the Garter King-of-Arms. A draft of the grant is still preserved in the College of Arms. The document amiably asserts that the candidate's "parents and late antecessors were for their valiant and faithful service advanced and rewarded by the most prudent prince King Henry the Seventh of famous memory, sithence which time they have continued at those parts in good reputation and credit." It further states that "the said John married Mary, daughter and heiress of Robert Arden, of Wilmcote, gent." In a later draft, "esquire" is substituted for "gent." as Robert Arden's title; and the heralds plainly withdraw from their original intention to grant the right to impale the arms of Arden (invented for the purpose) with those of Shakespeare. The Shakespeare arms alone appear above the grave in Stratford.

These reasonably successful negotiations were undoubtedly conducted by the dramatist. Whatever hope he may have had of founding a county family was in vain: his only son Hamnet died that same year, and by a series of chances such as seem so frequently to pursue the children of great men, in a few generations no drop of his blood remained flowing in human veins. However, his ambition to establish himself respectably at Stratford was not destroyed by this loss. In 1597 he bought New Place, the largest house in Stratford, with substantial grounds. Tradition has it that his patron, Southampton, made the purchase possible. There is no reason to suppose that this was necessary. Shakespeare's prosperity was by this time assured; and it was by no means without parallel among his fellow-players. The Elizabethan dramatist might starve, but the actor was well-rewarded. During the last decade of the sixteenth century a play brought its author from two hundred and fifty to four hundred and fifty dollars — £6 to £11 in the currency of that day. Sidney Lee estimates that between the years 1591 and 1599, Shakespeare may have made some £20 ($800) a year as an author. He probably made five times that sum as an actor. New Place cost £60 ($2400) which he may easily have had by him after almost ten years' connection with the stage. By this time he was evidently known in Stratford as a man of resources. Later in the same year John Shakespeare filed a bill in Chancery to recover the

Asbies estate, which had been under a mortgage for nearly twenty years. Shakespeare of London was now looked to by his fellow-townsmen as a capable man of business. In January, 1598, Abraham Sturley of Stratford wrote to Richard Quiney, then in London:

"Our countryman, Mr. Shakespeare, is willing to disburse some money upon some odd yard land or other at Shottery. . . . Our father thinketh it a very fit pattern to move him to deal in the matter of our tithes. By the instruction you can give him thereof, and by the friends he can make therefore, we think it a fair mark for him to shoot at, and not unpossible to hit."

Some months later we have on record a letter from Quiney to Shakespeare asking him for a loan of £30. "You shall friend me much in helping me out of all the debts I owe in London, I thank God, and much quiet my mind, which would not be indebted." This was apparently a double request — for a private loan to pay the debts he had incurred upon his mission, and for a public loan, probably to the Stratford Corporation, which was the object of his mission. A little later comes a letter in reply: "Your letter of the 25th October . . . which imported that our countryman William Shake. would procure us money, which I will like of as I shall hear when and where and how; and I pray let not go that occasion if it may sort to our indifferent conditions."

Finally there comes from Quiney *père:*

"If you bargain with Wm. Sha . . . or receive money therefor, bring your money home that you may."

We do not know how the matter came out, but it is evident that Shakespeare already figured in the eyes of his former fellow-townsmen as a man of substance. In this year (1598) Ben Jonson's *Every Man in his Humour* was first produced by the Lord Chamberlain's Company; and tradition has it that Shakespeare was personally responsible for its acceptance. "His acquaintance with Ben Jonson," says Rowe, "began with a remarkable piece of humanity and good-nature; Mr. Jonson, who was at that time altogether unknown to the world, had offered one of his plays to the players in order to have it acted, and the persons into whose hands it had been put, after having turned it carelessly and superciliously over, were just on the point of returning it to him, when Shakespeare luckily cast his eye upon it, and found something so well in it as to engage him first to read it through, and afterwards to recommend Mr. Jonson and his writings to the public." Whatever may be the truth of this anecdote, we know that for many years Jonson and Shakespeare were upon intimate terms. They two were long prominent among the wits of the Mermaid Tavern (the club of the day). What they may have been when pitted against each other, Fuller graphically suggests in his *Worthies:*

"Which two I beheld like a Spanish great galleon

and an English man-of-war. Master Jonson, like the former, was built far higher in learning, solid, but slow in his performances. Shakespeare, with the English man-of-war, lesser in bulk, but lighter in sailing, could turn with all tides, tack about, and take advantage of all winds with the quickness of his wit and invention."

There is a pleasant anecdote relating to Jonson and Shakespeare, the friends, which dates back almost to Shakespeare's lifetime: "Shakespeare was godfather to one of Ben Jonson's children, and after the christening, being in a deep study, Jonson came to cheer him up and asked him why he was so melancholy. 'No, faith, Ben,' says he, 'not I, but I have been considering a great while what should be the fittest gift for me to bestow upon my godchild, and I have resolved at last.' 'I prythee what?' says he. 'I' faith, Ben, I'll e'en give him a dozen good latten spoons, and thou shalt translate them.'" (Latten was an alloyed metal something like brass.)

In 1598 was published a miscellany called *Palladis Tamia,* by one Francis Meres, a Master of Arts at both Oxford and Cambridge. One of the later chapters seems to have been written in the summer of 1598: a "Comparative Discourse of our English Poets with the Greek, Latin, and Italian Poets." Dividing literature into the usual categories, the author names the writers, ancient and contemporary, whom he considers preeminent in each field. Shakespeare is mentioned in every possible instance — nine times in all. One passage has been often quoted for the light it throws upon several moot questions of Shakespearean scholarship:

"As the soul of Euphorbus was thought to live in Pythagoras, the sweet witty soul of Ovid lives in mellifluous and honey-tongued Shakespeare; witness his *Venus and Adonis,* his *Lucrece,* his surged sonnets among his private friends, etc.

"As Plautus and Seneca are accounted the best for comedy and tragedy among the Latins, so Shakespeare in English is the most excellent in both kinds for the stage; for comedy, witness his *Gentlemen of Verona,* his *Errors,* his *Love's Labor's Lost,* his *Love's Labor's Won,* his *Midsummer Night's Dream,* and his *Merchant of Venice;* for tragedy, his *Richard the 2, Richard the 3, Henry the 4, King John, Titus Andronicus* and his *Romeo and Juliet.*

"As Epius Stolo said that the Muses would speak with Plautus' tongue if they would speak Latin, so I say that the Muses would speak with Shakespeare's fine filed phrase, if they would speak English."

The decade from 1588 to 1598, we must remember, was a time of unparalleled activity. If Shakespeare had romantic comedy to himself for a time, there was no other of his chosen fields in which he lacked important rivals. That he should have been named by any one person as eminent in so many ways is an extraordinary tribute to this unlearned provincial from

Stratford town. He now ranked there as a responsible member of the community, a householder and a gentleman. He is recorded on the Stratford books as owner of ten quarters of corn in a famine year (1598). He laid out a fruit-orchard on a part of his grounds, and according to tradition introduced the mulberry-tree in Stratford. Many mulberry-trees were planted in England at about that time, with an eye to the culture of silk-worms. The industry did not develop, but for many years an immense mulberry stood in Shakespeare's garden which loyal tradition asserted had been planted by the poet's own hands. In due time it was murdered, to be cut up into Shakespeare knick-knacks at an enormous profit to the assassin.

But the dramatist can have spent very little time at Stratford until the closing years of his life. No theatrical man can have a permanent country residence, or for that matter a permanent residence anywhere. We know that at about the close of 1598 Shakespeare removed from his lodgings at Bishopsgate to the Bankside, where he lived for some time near the old Bear Garden. It was at this time that Burbage's Theater at Shoreditch was torn down, and its timbers carried to Southwark, where they were used in the building of a larger theater, to be known as the Globe. Here the Lord Chamberlain's Company were to do their city work thereafter; Shakespeare became part proprietor of it, sharing in the profits of the business. And from this time on his income must have greatly increased.

His shares in the proceeds of the Globe probably brought him in some £500 ($20,000) a year for many years, and the market price of plays gradually rose. The Globe was so-called from its sign of Atlas supporting his sphere. It stood a little to westward of London bridge on the Southwark side. Not far away on the Bankside were two rival theaters, the Rose and the Swan. The Globe was burnt in 1613, but was quickly rebuilt; and the incident did little to delay the submergence of the Rose and the Swan under the tide of success which the Globe must have owed mainly to Shakespeare's connection with it in his *factotum* capacity of actor, manager, playwright and proprietor.

The Elizabethan popular theater was a development of the Elizabethan inn-yard, in which the popular drama had its first setting: the courtyard with its single entrance, flanked on the level by offices which served as dressing-rooms, and surrounded by upper balconies in which the spectators — the paying spectators at least — would sit. Says Professor Schelling: "When a structure primarily intended for theatrical performances was planned, the corners and irregularities of the yard were done away with, and an octagonal form in consequence assumed, thus bringing the spectators that crowded in the corners nearer the stage. The rooms were retained, though contracted in size, as they have been retained to the present day, in what are known as the stalls. The stage was made stationary and brought out into the yard, and a pent roof, as it was called, was built over at least a part of it. The stable, too, was enlarged into a tiring-room and given two, sometimes three, entrances to the stage, an advantage at once apparent. Another change consisted in raising the structure above the stage either by the addition of a story above the 'scene' proper or by elevating the entire building a story, making the whole circumference of the same height. The further addition of a cupola, from which a flag was raised when a play was performing on the stage, with a station for a trumpeter to announce the entrance of the prologue, were both obvious devices."

The Fortune, built by the rival manager Henslowe a few years later than the Globe, cost what would now amount to about $30,000. The inside measurement was fifty-five feet square. There were the galleries, extending around three sides of the building. The stage was forty feet wide, and extended twenty-seven feet into the yard or pit.

The galleries and part of the stage were covered with thatch. The building was some forty feet high, and, with standing-room, can hardly have held more than a thousand persons. Shakespeare's Globe must have been considerably smaller. Another theater with which Shakespeare was connected, certainly not much later, was Blackfriars. James Burbage had bought a large house in Blackfriars in 1596, and in spite of the efforts of neighboring dwellers, had converted it into a theater. It was at first leased by Burbage to the

Children of the Chapel, but later it was apparently used by Shakespeare's company, and probably Shakespeare himself acted there. According to Dryden, it was at the Blackfriars that *The Tempest* was successfully produced.

A curious document has come down to us, Henslowe's Diary, as it has come to be called. It is really a book of personal accounts and memoranda extending from 1591 to 1609: thus covering substantially the most prolific period of the Elizabethan drama. Among private matters it details also Henslowe's transactions as a theatrical broker and manager. The manuscript is illiterate in the extreme, but it records the dealings of a man not only of keen business instinct, but of some degree of humanity. He knew when and where to build theaters, and how to attach to himself capable actors and playwrights. He married his stepdaughter to Edward Alleyn, next to Richard Burbage the best actor of the age. And his book contains the names of all the principal dramatists of the period except Shakespeare, Beaumont, and Fletcher. Jonson, Drayton, Dekker, Marston, Heywood, and various others were sooner or later in Henslowe's pay. The work of these men, as it was done for Henslowe, had the same marks of sedulous attention to the supposed wishes of the vulgar as characterize the mass of plays now written for our more powerful metropolitan managers. The well-nigh marvelous fact is that Shakespeare should have outwritten them in their own chosen fields, making himself more popular than they as it were with his left hand, while with his right he gave a richness and power to his work which placed it among the classics of all time. It has been noted as a sufficient indication of the recognized superiority of Shakespeare's company, that between 1594 and 1603 it played twice as many times at Court as all its competitors. Besides the engagements at the Globe and Blackfriars, there was much traveling, so that Shakespeare must have been seen upon the boards in all of the principal towns of England at fairly regular intervals during the period of his active connection with the stage. Sidney Lee has traced the journeyings of the company with which he was identified, during fourteen tours made between 1593 and 1614.

The company played at court during the Christmas seasons of 1599, 1600, and 1602. There is little doubt that the hiatus of a season was due to a real or fancied connection between Shakespeare's *Richard II.* and Essex's rebellion, in which Southampton, Shakespeare's early patron, was implicated. The apparent facts are put as compactly and clearly as possible by Mr. Gollancz:

"The subject of the deposition of Richard II. was regarded with considerable suspicion toward the end of Queen Elizabeth's reign, and the suppression of lines 154–318 in the first scene of the fourth act in the two editions of the play published during the Queen's lifetime must be taken in connection with certain well-known incidents: (1) in 1599 Sir John Hayward was imprisoned for publishing his *History of the Life and Reign of Henry the Fourth, i.e.*, the story of the deposition of Richard II.; (2) in 1601, on the afternoon of the day before the rebellion of Essex, Merrick, one of his adherents, with a great company of others that afterwards were all in the action, had procured to be played before them *the play of deposing of King Richard the Second.* Neither was it casual, but a play bespoken by Merrick; (3) it is recorded how the Queen on one occasion, probably soon after the revolt of Essex, when Lambarde, the Keeper of the Records in the Tower, was showing her his rolls, suddenly exclaimed, on coming to the reign of Richard II.: 'I am Richard II.; know ye not that?' and she told Lambarde how 'this tragedy was played forty times in open streets and houses.'"

It may be that Shakespeare, though he had enjoyed in some measure her favor, had had such experience of the crafty Queen as to look forward with more than equanimity to her abscession. One hesitates to accept the judgment of Professor Schelling that "nothing could have been more natural or more consonant with the worldly thrift that we know to have been Shakespeare's than for him to have arranged thus cleverly to anticipate the patronage of his sovereign to come." But it is impossible to ignore the fact that Shakespeare's voice was almost alone in its silence on the death of the Queen.

Chettle, the publisher of Greene's attack on Shakespeare who had later made so handsome an apology, now called to him vainly to

> Drop from his honeyed muse one sable tear,
> To mourn her death that graced his desert,
> And to his lays opened her royal ear.

At the earliest possible moment after her death the Lord Chamberlain's Company became the King's Company, by royal grant. Elizabeth died March 24th, 1603. Less than two months later (May 19), and less than a fortnight after James's unofficial arrival in London, Shakespeare and his fellow-players received the royal license to play in London and the provinces under the King's name. The following year, when James made his state entry into the City, Shakespeare and eight of his fellow-actors were members of the royal train. Each of them had been presented with four yards and a half of scarlet cloth, "the usual dress allowance to players belonging to the household." Their title was "The King's Servants," and they ranked with the Grooms of the Chamber. Humble rank, surely, for one of the greatest of poets, who was also the greatest of dramatists. But we cannot doubt that Shakespeare took solid satisfaction in the office. Whatever he may have been as an artist, he had the ambition of the yeoman class, to advance himself in the world.

And yet, indeed, there seems to be something little

short of uncanny in this sublime poet's steady march toward a material bourgeois prosperity. Professor Dowden is a little ludicrously complacent over the facts: "It is not always the case," he says beamingly, "that a master in the world of ideas and imagination is a master of prudent husbandry in the material world." It is unfortunate for the impression the diligent grubber among data must get of his later years that so many of the facts at hand have to do with this almost uncanny canniness of the bard. Our knowledge of them, to be sure, is derived from the Stratford records, which naturally chronicle only business matters. In 1602 he bought one hundred and seven acres near Stratford for a price which in present terms would be something under four thousand dollars. In 1605 he bought "the unexpired term of a moiety of a lease of the tithes of Stratford, Old Stratford, Bishopton, and Welcombe," for the equivalent of something over five thousand dollars. In 1610 he bought twenty acres of pasture land. In 1604 he sued one Philip Rogers to recover a debt of something like forty-five dollars. "Again in 1608–9 the author of the ardent idealizing sonnets, published in the latter year, was prosecuting a suit for the recovery of a debt of £6 (about $360) owed by John Addenbroke, and when a verdict was given for the debt and for costs, Addenbroke not being found within the liberty of the borough, Shakespeare pursued his cause against the debtor's bail, a person named Horneby." Other transactions of the sort are recorded, all going to show the poet as a man of affairs, a thrifty householder, and a somewhat exacting creditor.

In 1601 John Shakespeare died, having lived to see his fortunes rehabilitated by the exertions of his thrifty and loyal son. In connection with the land purchase of the following year, the buyer is described as "Wm. Shakespeare of Stratford-upon-Avon, gentleman." It is not to be supposed that Shakespeare as yet found leisure to enjoy to the full his new dignity as a gentleman of Stratford.

He had now reached middle age, was the most successful dramatist of his age both with the people and at Court, and had attained his ambition in becoming a person of respectability and substance. He had no enemies, and if his friends, apart from Jonson, seem to have been chiefly among his fellow-actors, the experience was merely that of most theatrical men. Because he wished to be a country gentleman, it by no means follows that he wished to be a person of fashion or of the court. All the contemporary testimony we have goes to show that he preferred the companionship of simple people — unless, indeed, it be the disputed testimony of his own sonnets — and that the course of his life ran respectably, and even a little monotonously, along the path he had chosen.

The question of the autobiographical character of the *Sonnets* is a very interesting one. It is a question which will never be answered absolutely. Some critics, it should be said, believe that no personal meaning can be wrested from them: that they were written at random during a long series of years, and are purely dramatic or objective in character. Others believe that they constitute a poetical record of actual experience, and that the problem is simply what that experience was. The first mention of the Sonnets is that of Meres in 1598: "his sugred sonnets among his friends," from which it is clear that they had not been published. In the following year two of them were included in that odd jumble of pirated matter called *The Passionate Pilgrim*. The entire sequence was not printed till 1609; and then again without his permission. In fact, nothing of Shakespeare's but the *Venus* and *Lucrece* was ever published by his authority. In that day all publishers were pirates. They depended for copy not upon work regularly contracted for, but upon the offices of a class of men who made a special trade of procuring poems which were being circulated in manuscript, as was common, or from some faithless or careless person; or acting versions of unpublished plays from unscrupulous managers or actors.

In some such way, we may be sure, Shakespeare's sonnets got into print, a fact which renders somewhat absurd a great part of the discussion which has arisen about them. This discussion has been largely founded upon the question of the identity of the person to whom the dedication was addressed. The common inferences have been that Shakespeare himself was responsible for the dedication, and that the recipient of it was plainly the hero of the *Sonnets*. Here is the dedication:

To the onlie begetter of
These insuing sonnets
Mr. W. H. all happinesse
And that eternitie
Promised
By
Our ever-living poet
Wisheth
The well-wishing
Adventurer in
Setting
Forth
T. T.

Now there is no mystery about the initials "T. T." They belonged to one Thomas Thorpe, to whom, on May 20, 1609, the Stationer's Company granted a license to publish the *Sonnets*. But who was Mr. W. H.? "Begetter" has been commonly interpreted as "inspirer," which would identify Mr. W. H. with the beautiful youth to whom many of the *Sonnets* are addressed. Two principal theories have developed with regard to this person: First, that the initials are simply reversed, W. H. standing for Henry Wriothesley, Earl of Southampton, the patron invoked by Shakespeare in the dedications to *Venus and Adonis* and *Lucrece*. This would tally with Sonnet CII.:

> "Our love was new, and then but in the Spring,
> When I was wont to greet it with my rays;"

and the not infrequent assurances elsewhere in the sonnets that he has had no other source of inspiration. So much seems to be true: there is no evidence that Shakespeare ever had any patron besides Southampton; in fact, the evidence is the other way. On the other hand, it is claimed that W. H. was William Herbert, Earl of Pembroke, and a very complete and ingenious story has been built up about the supposed triangular relation between himself, Shakespeare, and Mistress Mary Fitton, a court lady of gay reputation who is known to have been for a time the mistress of Lord Herbert. She, it is alleged, was the dark lady of the *Sonnets* — a statement not borne out by her portraits, which show her fair and blue-eyed.

I need not go at length into the arguments for and against these partizan claims, for it seems to me that Mr. Sidney Lee has shown conclusively that so far as they connect themselves with the dedication they are simply beside the mark. We have no reason to suppose that Shakespeare knew the *Sonnets* were to get into print. They had been circulating in manuscript for many years, but, except the two included in *The Passionate Pilgrim*, they had remained in manuscript. Thorpe was a publisher of a piratical type against which the author of Elizabethan days had little or no protection. Possession was nine points of the law. The Stationers' Company was not an exclusive body, and any member of it who could get hold of an unprinted bit of literature, was practically free to get it printed where he might and to figure upon its title-page not only as its publisher, but as its proprietor. Not infrequently, in his rôle of proprietor, the publisher would write the dedication. At about the same period as his publication of the *Sonnets,* Thorpe succeeded in associating his name with several other works of importance, notably a number of plays by Chapman and Ben Jonson. But before the instance of the *Sonnets,* there is only one case recorded of his acting as dedicator. This was in connection with his first successful venture: the publication of an unprinted translation by Marlowe of the first book of Lucan. How he got hold of the manuscript we do not know, but it was through the services of a fellow-stationer that he succeeded in getting it printed. To this man, by way of recognizing his good offices, he dedicated the book, with some ironical and rather clever advice to him upon his conduct as a patron, which shows an open disdain of noble patronage.

Says Sidney Lee: "Shakespeare, except in the case of his two narrative poems, showed utter indifference to all questions touching the publication of his works. Of the sixteen plays of his that were published in his lifetime, not one was printed with his sanction. He made no audible protest when seven contemptible dramas in which he had no hand were published with his name or initials upon the title-page while his fame was at its height. With only one publisher of his time, Richard Field, his fellow-townsman, who was responsible for the issue of *Venus* and *Lucrece,* is it likely that he came into personal relations, and there is nothing to show that he maintained relations with Field after the publication of *Lucrece* in 1594."

There is no reason, in short, to suppose that Shakespeare had any foreknowledge that the *Sonnets* were to be printed by Thomas Thorpe, or, consequently, could have had anything to do with its dedication. Who then was Thorpe's W. H.? Sidney Lee's argument, which we shall follow, is to this effect:

1. There is no mystery involved in the use of the initials; it was a common fashion of the day.

2. That Thorpe should have inverted the initials to conceal their reference to Southampton is absurd; and they could not have stood for "William Herbert," because the third Earl of Pembroke was always known as Lord Herbert before his accession to the earldom.

3. "W. H." was probably William Hall, a fellow-stationer and procurer (or begetter) of manuscripts, through whom the *Sonnets* had come into Thorpe's hands.

In short, the dedication throws absolutely no light upon the meaning of the *Sonnets.* And, all things considered, there is little reason for our supposing that they have any consecutive meaning, or that they record any absolute personal experience. During the last decade of the sixteenth century sonneteering became fairly the rage in Elizabeth's England. Sir Philip Sydney's *Astrophel and Stella* sequence was published in 1591, and during the next few years appeared collections of sonnets by Daniel, Constable, Barnes (supposed by Mr. Lee to be the rival poet alluded to in the Shakespeare sonnets), Watson, Fletcher, Lodge, Drayton, Spenser and a host of minor rhymers. In the hands of all these the sonnet was a conventional form, dealing with a few recognized themes, "(1) sonnets of more or less feigned love, addressed to a more or less fictitious mistress; (2) sonnets of adulation, addressed to patrons, and (3) sonnets invoking metaphysical abstractions, or treating impersonally of religion or philosophy."

These are precisely the themes of the Shakespeare sonnets. The extravagant terms in which the beautiful youth is addressed (whom we may reasonably take to be Southampton, as Shakespeare had no other patron), are paralleled in many contemporary sonnets by other hands. The dark lady herself, the ill-featured enchantress, is by no means found for the first time in Shakespeare's *Sonnets.* And many of the conceits and turns of expression are borrowed from the poet's contemporaries. The *Sonnets,* in short, are, like the plays, a mosaic of materials derived from various sources. Shakespeare had very little faculty of mere invention. The beauty of his sonnets as of his plays is due to the superiority of his use of familiar material. To assert that they record his own personal experience is merely — to assert. We cannot even be certain that he took his sonnets seriously. There are numerous contemptuous allusions to sonnets and sonneteers in the plays, and it is quite probable that he came to look upon these early exercises and performances in a fashionable vein with the good-humored disdain of a grown man for the trifling effusions of his youth. So, very likely, he may have come to regard the still more youthful *Venus* and *Lucrece*.

We have seen that in 1599, Shakespeare (with several other members of his company), became a shareholder in the new Globe Theater. With this theater he remained thereafter identified, and here his success was greatest. At first the Globe must have had an extraordinary difficulty to face. For about 1597 the Children of the Chapel, who had formerly, under Lyly's tutelage, been so popular, were restored to public practice and favor. By 1600, their vogue was so great that several companies of adult players were fairly driven out of London, and forced to travel in the provinces. That this may have happened to Shakespeare's company seems not improbable from our evidence. In 1601 the Children of the Chapel were playing at Blackfriars, and during part of the year, at least, the Globe company were on the road. *Hamlet* was probably written during the same year, and contains a very intelligible commentary on the whole dramatic situation of the time. Elsinore, it will be recalled, is visited by a company of traveling actors. Hamlet asks Rosencrantz what players they are, and learns that they are his favorite "tragedians of the city."

Ham. How chances it they travel? their residence, both in reputation and profit, was better both ways.
Ros. I think their inhibition comes by reason of the late innovation.
Ham. Do they hold the same estimation they did when I was in the city? are they so followed?
Ros. No, indeed, they are not.
Ham. How comes it? do they grow rusty?
Ros. Nay, their endeavor keeps in the wonted pace: but there is, sir, an eyrie of children, a company of little eyases, that cry out on the top of question and are most tyrannically clapped for it: these are now the fashion, and so berattle the common stages — so they call them — that many wearing rapiers are afraid of goose-quills, and dare scarce come thither.
Ham. What, are they children? etc.

Ben Jonson had involved himself in a characteristic quarrel with Dekker and Marston, and allied himself with the Children of the Chapel, greatly to their advantage. A war of plays ensued, Jonson's *Cynthia's Revels* and *Poetaster* (played by the Children), mercilessly flaying his enemies, to be retorted upon by Marston and Dekker in *Satiro-Mastix,* produced by the Globe players. It is an interesting fact that Shakespeare does not appear to have been involved personally in the controversy; and there is some probability that he may have acted as peacemaker. But what did more than anything else to settle the rivalry in favor of the adult players was the production of *Julius Cæsar* and *Hamlet*. Jonson could provide his little eyases with nothing to compare with these plays, and their vogue rapidly declined. Neither *Julius Cæsar* nor *Hamlet* was fresh in theme, as a *Hamlet* had been played in 1589, and a *Julius Cæsar* in 1594. Never was a writer more indifferent to that trick of invention which now forms the chief stock in trade of the popular novel. *Hamlet* secured recognition for the dramatist in a quarter which was inclined to be none too hospitable to him. It was the only one of his plays to be presented during his life at Oxford and Cambridge.

It is notable that during the five or six years immediately following the accession of James, Shakespeare produced much of his best. Between 1604 and 1609 were written *Othello, Measure for Measure, Macbeth, Lear, Timon of Athens, Pericles, Antony and Cleopatra,* and *Coriolanus*. Circumstances were more favorable than they had been before. If, as Chettle said, Elizabeth had "graced his desert" and "opened her royal ear" to him, James's encouragement was evidently less dictatorial. It was one thing for Elizabeth to give the playwright and actor her haughty patronage, to command a *Merry Wives of Windsor* and what not. But Shakespeare's patron, Southampton, had been severely punished for his connection with the Essex conspiracy, and it may be that

Shakespeare himself felt the weight of her displeasure. At all events, he enjoyed under the protection of James a freedom which was not for the servants of Elizabeth.

After the great tragedies, came a return to romance, or rather the development of a new romance, in *Cymbeline, The Winter's Tale,* and *The Tempest.* Much has been made by Prof. Dowden, M. Darmesteter, and others, of the connection between the marked periods of Shakespeare's work and his personal experience. Sidney Lee has said with characteristic brevity and common-sense all that need be said of this theory:

"In *Cymbeline, The Winter's Tale,* and *The Tempest,* the three latest plays that came from his unaided pen, Shakespeare dealt with romantic themes which all end happily, but he instilled into them a pathos which sets them in a category of their own apart alike from comedy and tragedy. The placidity of tone conspicuous in these three plays (none of which was published in his lifetime) has often been contrasted with the storm and stress of the great tragedies that preceded them. But the commonly accepted theory that traces in this change of tone a corresponding development in the author's own emotions ignores the objectivity of Shakespeare's dramatic work. All phases of feeling lay within the scope of his intuition, and the successive order in which he approached them bore no explicable relation to substantive incident in his private experience. In middle life, his temperament, like that of other men, acquired a larger measure of gravity and his thought took a profounder cast than characterized it in youth. The highest topics of tragedy were naturally more congenial to him, and were certain of a surer handling when he was nearing his fortieth birthday than at an earlier age. The serenity of meditative romance was more in harmony with the fifth decade of his years than with the second or third. But no more direct or definite connection can be discerned between the progressive stages of his work and the progressive stages of his life. To seek in his biography for a chain of events which should be calculated to stir in his own soul all or any of the tempestuous passions that animate his greatest plays is to underestimate and to misapprehend the resistless might of his creative genius."

The Tempest is the only one of the plays the plot of which has not been traced to its source. The setting and much of the machinery are easily referable to the shipwreck upon the Bermudas, in 1609, of an English vessel. News of the adventure came to London in 1610, and Shakespeare seems at once to have made use of it. It has been fancied that the laying aside of Prospero's wand typified the poet's own abdication. Certain it seems that in 1611 he deliberately ended his work as a playwright. In this year he probably sold his shares in the Globe and Blackfriars Theaters. He certainly ceased to act and to write in connection with the stage. But there is good reason to suppose that he left with the company drafts of several other plays. It would be quite characteristic of him to turn over his tools and plans to others, when he left the workshop, with perfect equanimity. *The Two Noble Kinsmen* and *Henry VIII.* were almost certainly items of his legacy: the plan, as we have them, Shakespeare's, the development, Fletcher's.

It was in 1611, then, that Shakespeare found himself free to retire permanently to the life of a country gentleman at Stratford. We must suppose that this had been his aim from the first. We have every reason to think that his primary ambition in setting out for London was not to make himself a great dramatist or poet who should seize his own day and be remembered through the ages, but to establish himself and his family in an honored position in his native town. He never wished to leave Stratford permanently, to make himself a man of the town or of the Court. His wife and children necessarily stayed behind in Stratford. It would hardly have been more likely to occur to him to take his family to London than it would occur to some modern actor to take his family from some quiet place on the Hudson, their natural home, to the hurry and tinsel of Broadway. He could only look forward to an early retirement as the price of hard work. And this is what he achieved. He restored the family credit at home, bought substantial property there, and, when hardly past middle age, retired as decisively as any merchant might have from his business, to the ease and dignity he had made for himself in the place of his birth and of his choice.

There appears to be no sufficient reason for doubting that his thought of Stratford was in part a thought of his wife. To her he certainly returned, and with her he spent the closing years of his too short life. Anne Shakespeare was, like most women and indeed, most men of her day, an illiterate person. Shakespeare's wife could no more read or write than his parents or his daughters. She probably understood little or nothing of the literary quality of his work, but she must have been proud of his success. No doubt this satisfied him. We may be sure that he was quite without intellectual snobbishness. He seems to have had the political opinions of a middle-class conservative. He reverenced the throne, and had due respect for the aristocracy. Also he despised the common people, the laboring classes, so far as they might be supposed to act together politically. They were the mob, ready to toss their nightcaps and hurrah for the favorite of the moment. But as individuals he had endless patience with them, affection for them. Dullness never bores him, mediocrity never provokes him to sharpness. He can spend pleasant hours and days with the Dogberrys and the Audreys, not as a self-conscious and caustic "student of human nature," nor as a person professionally on the outlook for the foibles and absurdities of his inferiors, but because he likes them and values them as companions. So with regard to his wife; it is not the intellectual woman of whom the sum of his dramatic interpretation suggests a kind of worship, nor is it the "dark lady" of the sonnets, that creature of fire and mystery who is so lauded in modern literature, and who is, after all, so ancient a convention. It is the woman of strong and sweet character, the faithful lover and companion, to whom he bows the knee. A few passages have been unearthed from the plays to prove that he was dissatisfied with his marriage, for instance the lines in *Twelfth Night* in which the lover is bidden choose a younger than himself. But why should we seize upon this allusion to a difference in age which nobody, we suppose, would absolutely prefer, and ignore the thousand passages in which the beauty and sweetness of the marriage relation are dwelt upon?

"At Stratford," says the old biographer Rowe, "the latter part of Shakespeare's life was spent, as all men of good sense will wish theirs may be, in ease, retirement, and the conversation of his friends." Tradition assures us how freely and warmly he enjoyed the society of his neighbors, not only in the town, but throughout the countryside. For several years, moreover, he continued to revisit London at intervals, no doubt for the sake of keeping up with his old friends there, more particularly, Heming, Condell and Richard

Burbage among his fellow-actors, and Jonson and Drayton among his old rivals as playwrights.

He seems to have been especially intimate with Burbage throughout his stage career. Burbage was the Shakespearean star of Shakespeare's day, the "creator" of Hamlet, Othello, Lear, and the other great tragic rôles. It would be hard to say how much we owe him, for no doubt Shakespeare had his powers in mind in writing those heroic parts. At all events, they seem to have been upon the best of terms. The only anecdote about Shakespeare which we absolutely know to have been put on record during his life has to do with a jest that passed between him and Burbage: The story goes that once when Burbage was playing Richard III., a lady in the audience made an appointment with him to visit her after the play and to announce himself as Richard III., that Shakespeare got wind of this, anticipated him, ingratiated himself with the lady, and when Burbage arrived sent him word that William the Conqueror was before Richard III. The pair are reputed to have been companions in other amusing adventures.

We have numerous bits of documentary evidence, most of them rather trifling in themselves, as to the normal part which the retired dramatist played in the life of Stratford. In 1611 his name stands upon a list of donors to a fund raised "towards the charge of prosecuting the bill in Parliament for the better improvement of the highways." In 1614 he entertains a Puritan preacher at New Place. This is a fact which may lead to pleasing surmise. The many flings at Puritanism in the plays, as well as our knowledge of the genial and conservative nature of the poet's character, leave no doubt that the rapid growth of the Puritan influence must have been distasteful to him. If Stratford respected him as a prosperous citizen, it did not honor him as an ex-actor and playwright. Plays had been for some time discountenanced there when, in 1612, the town council passed a resolution to the effect that the production of plays within the town limits was illegal, and "the sufferance of them against the orders heretofore made and against the example of other well-governed cities and boroughs, and that players should be fined ten pounds instead of ten shillings as theretofore." Shakespeare's eldest daughter Susanna had married in 1607 a physician, John Hall, of strong Puritan sympathies. It may have been at his instance that the preacher was entertained at New Place; we may imagine that the poet would have had his share of the entertainment.

For the rest, we have sundry legends as to his convivial exploits, of which rather too much has been made. There is said to have been a certain tree near Stratford long known as Shakespeare's crab-tree, on the ground of his having spent the night under it after a bout at a distant inn. And it has long been repeated on the authority of a book of memoranda written by John Ward, Vicar of Stratford, as late as

1663, that a few days before his death, Shakespeare entertained Drayton and Jonson at New Place, and "it seems drank too hard, for Shakespeare died of a fever there contracted." It was a day of hard drinking, but we have no proof that Shakespeare was particularly indiscreet. That he died of the alleged cause seems very doubtful. Halliwell-Phillipps finds sufficient cause in the abominable sanitary conditions of the neighborhood. It is probable that his health had been failing for some time. He had made his will, a very careful document, in January, 1616. He died on April 23, at exactly the age of fifty-two.

As part-owner of the tithes, and consequently one of the lay-rectors, of Stratford, he had right of burial in Stratford Church. Over his grave were written the lines of undeniable doggerel:

> Good frend, for Jesus' sake forbeare
> To digg the dust encloased heare;
> Bleste be the man that spares thes stones.
> And curst be he that moves my bones.

According to a William Hall, who described a visit to Stratford in 1694, these lines were framed by Shakespeare for "the capacity of clerks and sextons, for the most part a very ignorant set of people"; and if they had not been so written, Shakespeare's bones would in course of time have been removed to the charnel-house hardby, where bones from the over-crowded churchyard were commonly disposed of. It seems quaintly characteristic of the man who had so thriftily conducted his affairs during life, this safeguarding of his rights in that last bit of property awarded by posterity to the thriftiest of human householders. His ban was effective. He was buried seventeen feet deep, and his bones have never been disturbed, though his wife wished to be buried by his side.

Shakespeare's will had been signed in March, after the first original draft had received a good deal of revision in the form of interlineation and erasure. By this will his property was left to his daughters and his sister; and there were various legacies to friends. Capital has been made of the fact that his wife is named only in an interlineation, which makes her legatee of his "second-best bed, with its furnishings." It was a natural memento, as the best bed would have been reserved for guests. For the rest, she had rights of dower, and he may have felt it better, in view of her age, and perhaps of her business incapacity, to dispose himself of the property which would in no long time go to the younger generation.

Pope says of Shakespeare that he

> For gain not glory winged his roving flight,
> And grew immortal in his own despite.

What we know of his life and his reputation among his contemporaries, goes to indicate the truth of the couplet. He had no such sense of unique and lofty calling as belonged, for example, to Dante and Milton. He was a busy and thrifty person, looked upon with affection by his fellows, " sweet," and " friendly," " of civil demeanor," " very good company and of a very pleasant and smooth wit "; so we hear of him in the annals of his time. We have no proof that he was conscious of the marvelousness of his powers. The contempt with which he would have regarded the " closet-drama," may be easily imagined. He was far more indifferent to the fate of his plays than to the fate of his bones. Yet he was the greatest of English poets, and perhaps the greatest poet of all time.

NOTE.— A number of documents have been found recently by Professor C. W. Wallace of the University of Nebraska, containing Shakespeare's name. Three of them have to do with a Chancery suit in which Shakespeare was one of several co-plaintiffs to recover certain deeds of property in the Blackfriars district. These are dated in April and May, 1615, the year before Shakespeare's death, and show that he did not retire altogether from active business in his last years. Another document shows Shakespeare living from 1598 to 1604 in the house of a London wigmaker named Montjoy; and presently acting, at the instance of Dame Montjoy, as matchmaker between an ex-apprentice of Montjoy's and the daughter of the house. The match did not turn out very well, but the incident presents the poet as a friendly fellow in private life, in a friendly and engaging light.

MILTON

MILTON'S life overlapped Shakespeare's, but so great changes were taking place during his early years in the national character that the spirit and the product of his maturity might have been separated from the Elizabethan spirit and product by an age instead of a few years. The Englishman of Shakespeare's day was in some respects more like a modern Frenchman, or even a modern American, than a modern Englishman. He was ardent, tolerant, immensely inquisitive, of extravagant manners, of lively and humorous fancy. All these qualities went by the board during the Cromwellian era; even the youthful ardor for the joy of living changed to a hard flame of zeal in the service of the Lord: which largely meant the service of partizan theology and partly meant a high and true impulse toward the life of the spirit.

Much as we know of Milton's life, we know hardly more of his descent than of Shakespeare's. He seems to have sprung from the same class, that of "yeoman-farmer." He, himself, merely says that he came of respectable ancestry. We can trace it back only a generation or two. His grandfather lived in or near the village of Holton, in Oxfordshire. He is said to have been an under-ranger of the forest of

JOHN MILTON
From the painting by P. Van der Plaas in the National Portrait Gallery

Shotover hard-by. Though a churchwarden, he seems to have clung to the old faith. He was twice fined for "recusancy"; and tradition has it that he cast off his son John, for conformity to the established church. So John Milton, Senior, apparently went to London a decade or so after Shakespeare, and in some way prepared himself for the profession of scrivener. A scrivener was a combination of clerical attorney and law-stationer, his chief business being the preparation of deeds. John Milton prospered, and presently bought a house in Bread Street, Cheapside, where he "lived over the shop" at the sign of the Spread Eagle. It is not certain whether this was chosen as a symbol of his family or his profession; but there is a certain quaint appropriateness to the American mind in the fact that the prophet of English civil and religious liberty was born under the wing of the "bird of Freedom." John Milton was born December 8, 1608, the third of six children, only three of whom lived to grow up.

Milton's parentage was clearly superior to Shakespeare's. The elder Milton was not merely the thrifty scrivener of Bread Street, but a man of liberal and accomplished mind, a skilled musician, and a composer of repute. His sympathies were with the growing Puritan movement within the established Church, and from an early age he destined his eldest son for holy orders. From the outset there was evidently a sympathy and understanding between father and son rare in any conditions, but particularly rare in Puritan households. The boy was born with a sense of personal dignity and responsibility which can have left little or nothing in his conduct for an equally serious and dignified father to worry about. A joyous childhood was not provided for in the Puritan program. Superficially the child Milton must have resembled those youthful prodigies who adorn the moral fiction of the seventeenth and eighteenth centuries. He was not a prig; but he may easily have appeared to be. Certainly he took himself, and life itself, very seriously from the start. There is a familiar portrait of him as a little boy, with hair cropped short and square: it is said to have been done by a nonconformist tutor in whose charge he was placed for a time. If the face is not lively, it is certainly not sanctimonious; and there is a suggestion of power in it which hints of a childhood well lost.

His father gave him his first teaching; then would have come the experience away from home with the nonconformist tutor. At the age of twelve we find him day-scholar at St. Paul's school (which stood hard-by the Spread Eagle), provided also with a private tutor. Both the tutor and the Masters at St. Paul's were men of unusual ability. Thomas Young, the tutor, afterward became master of Jesus College, Cambridge, and Milton paid more than one tribute to the part played by him in his early training. The two Alexander Gills of St. Paul's were among the best classical teachers of the day. Milton seems to have had much training in Latin versification, but it is perhaps as well that his school-exercises have not been unearthed. Two psalm-paraphrases, written at fifteen, remain from this period. Milton thought them good enough to print among his minor poems.

At St. Paul's, Milton made his first and closest friend: perhaps the only friend for whom he ever had a very warm personal affection. This was Charles Diodati, son of an Italian physician who had been exiled as a Protestant. The intimacy very likely gave him his special bent toward Italy and Italian literature; certainly it inspired the *Epitaphium Damonis,* most human and impassioned of his Latin poems. But the ruling passion of the poet's boyhood was study, which he carried to such an extreme as would be promptly checked by any modern father. Only a generation or two ago, it was considered blessed to die young of exhaustion upon the slopes of Helicon. "From the twelfth year of my age," says Milton, "I scarce ever went to bed before midnight." . . . "And his father ordered the maid to sit up for him," adds Aubrey.

At sixteen he was ready to go up to the University. The Gills of St. Paul's were Oxford men, but Milton was sent to Cambridge, probably to avoid conflict with the High Church or Arminian movement, then active at Oxford. In February, 1625, he became a "lesser pensioner" of Christ's College, Cambridge. As it chanced, he was assigned to a tutor of strong High Church principles, one William Chappell, a Fellow of Christ's. This man became an ardent henchman of Archbishop Laud's, and was rewarded in time with the see of Cork. It was out of the question that Milton should get on amicably with such a superior. He interfered with Milton's studies, set him irksome tasks, and in the course of a year or so, as far as we can make out, provoked him to open rebellion. There is a somewhat vague tradition that the pair eventually came to blows, and Dr. Johnson records a legend that Milton was the last man to be flogged at Oxford. This is certainly not true, as there is a case recorded as late as 1667. It is probable that Chappell may have struck him, and that Milton may have shown his resentment in some such way as to make a nominal official discipline necessary. He certainly went through something very nearly approaching a rustication during his second spring at Cambridge. But he did not lose a term of residence as he must have if actually rusticated, and on his return he was assigned to another tutor. There is no doubt that during his first years at the University he was unpopular with both his fellow-students and the authorities. His slender and delicate beauty and his refinement of manner and habit gave him the name of "the Lady of Christ's" among the undergraduates; and his free criticism of university methods could not endear him to the dons. But his blameless conduct apart from the matter of speech, and his remarkable scholarship, finally established him in favor in one quarter, as his accomplishments and sheer force of personality did in another. There never was a less lady-like person. His chief characteristics were the fierce mental preoccupation of the scholar, and the stern moral zeal of the reformer. There was nothing soft or engaging about him. He was bound to win esteem and respect, but there was a something aloof and forbidding in his nature which denied him affection.

After his first two years at Cambridge he seems to have come to a practical understanding with the authorities, perhaps involving some added discretion of speech on his part. From that time his course appears to have been smooth and regular. He took his bachelor's degree in March, 1629, and his Master's in July, 1632, both dates being the earliest possible from the date of his matriculation. In later years he seems to have recalled Cambridge as an institution for whose methods he had no great respect, but as a place in which, on the whole, he had personally received honorable treatment. So in 1642 we find him saying of Cambridge the University: "Which, as in the time of her better health and mine own younger judgment, I never greatly admired, so now much less." And yet in the same year he takes occasion to "acknowledge publicly, with all grateful mind, that more than ordinary respect which I found, above many of my equals, at the hands of those courteous and learned men, the Fellows of the College where I spent some years; who, at my parting, after I had taken two degrees, as the manner is, signified many ways how much better it would content them that I would stay; as by many letters full of kindness and loving respect, both before that time and long after, I was assured of their singular good affection towards me." The passage has been taken to mean that he had refused a fellowship. This he would doubtless have done, if it had been offered him, but there is no reason to suppose the offer was actually made. Two fellowships had been bestowed in Milton's time at Cambridge, both by favor rather than merit, to juniors of his — one of them the Edward King whom he was to celebrate as *Lycidas*. His relations with King seem to have been friendly, but without the warmth of his friendship for Diodati. Consequently, of the two elegies, it is the Latin *Epitaphium Damonis* which expresses active grief, rather than the tribute to "Lycidas." Other fellow-students and contemporaries at Cambridge were George Herbert, who was "public orator" of the University, Thomas Fuller, Edmund Waller and Jeremy Taylor.

One obstacle to his accepting a fellowship would have been the necessity of taking orders. He had gone to Cambridge with the distinct purpose of preparing himself for the church. But during his residence political and religious events had taken such a turn as to unsettle if not altogether destroy this purpose. Charles had obtained despotic control of the government, and Laud, one of his chief advisers, had assumed an equally arbitrary power over the Church. Laud's High Church doctrine and autocratic methods were equally offensive to the churchman of Milton's type. It is not clear that when, after taking the master's degree, Milton left Cambridge, he had finally determined to give up the Church; but he was certainly in no mood at the moment to take orders for the sake of academic preferment.

His father had now retired with a comfortable fortune to a country seat at Horton in Buckinghamshire, and on leaving the University, Milton went to live with him there. It cannot have been altogether a cheerful moment for the elder Milton; but he would be the first to respect the scruples which threatened to wreck the high promise of his brilliant son. He himself had sacrificed much in youth for similar scruples. Moreover, the years at Cambridge had not passed without displaying powers beyond those of brilliant scholarship. The musician and lover of poetry must by this time have been aware of his son's poetic promise, now to be nourished by some five years of study, leisure, and contemplation, at Horton. The mood of indecision which attended his last days at the University is expressed in a letter to a Cambridge friend who appears to have remonstrated with him on his inaction. The friend is "a good watchman to admonish that the hours of the night pass on, for so I call my life, as yet obscure and unserviceable to mankind, and that the day with me is at hand, wherein Christ commands all to labor." And to the same period belongs the famous sonnet *On His Having Arrived at the Age of Twenty-three:*

How soon hath Time, the subtle thief of youth,
  Stolen on his wing my three-and-twentieth year!
  My hasting days fly on with full career,
But my late spring no bud or blossom shew'th.
Perhaps my semblance might deceive the truth
  That I to manhood am arrived so near;
  And inward ripeness doth much less appear,
That some more timely-happy spirits endu'th.
Yet, be it less or more, or soon or slow,
  It shall be still in strictest measure even
  To that same lot, however mean or high,
Toward which Time leads me, and the will of Heaven.
  All is, if I have grace to use it so,
  As ever in my great Task-Master's eye.

"I am," he says again, "something suspicious of myself, and do take notice of a certain belatedness in me." His final decision to give up the Church was perhaps arrived at more slowly than his later account of it would lead us to suppose: "The Church," he says, "to whose service by the intention of my parents and friends I was destined of a child, and in mine own resolutions, till coming to some maturity of years, and perceiving what tyranny had invaded in the Church, that he who would take orders must subscribe slave, and take an oath withal. . . . I thought it better to prefer a blameless silence before the sacred office of speaking, bought and begun with servitude and forswearing."

Professor Masson describes Horton as "a rich, teeming, verdurous flat, charming by its appearance of plenty, and by the goodly show of wood along the fields and pastures, in the nooks where the houses nestle, and everywhere in all directions to the sky-bound verge of the landscape." Here were the "russet lawns and fallows grey" of *L'Allegro,* with Windsor in the distance, "bosomed high in tufted trees," the only striking feature of the scene. In Horton, to be accurate, Milton spent five years and eight months. It was a time of ripening. He had now come to a full realization of his calling as a poet, and deliberately set himself to the necessary preliminary training; for he purposed to be no idle singer. "I was confirmed in this opinion," he tells us, "that he who would not be frustrated of his hope to write well hereafter in laudable things, ought himself to be a true poem . . . not presuming to sing high praises of heroic men or famous cities, unless he have in himself the experience and practice of all that which is praiseworthy." Knowledge, purity, and religious faith, were the three accomplishments for which he consciously strove. During the years at Horton his seriousness steadily deepened. Comparatively early in his stay there *L'Allegro* and *Il Penseroso* were written. They represent, not different persons, but varying harmonious moods of a contemplative nature:

Milton's own nature, in short. There is nothing hilarious about *L'Allegro*. At the same time we find in it, as in the Cambridge verses, not a little of the Elizabethan light-heartedness and delight in beauty for its own sake. The *Song on May Morning* gives no presage of the sacred Muse who inspired Milton's great work: it seems to have been written rather by some fellow of Shakespeare:

> Now the bright morning-star, Day's harbinger,
> Comes dancing from the east, and leads with her
> The flowery May, who from her green lap throws
> The yellow cowslip and the pale primrose.
> Hail, bounteous May, that dost inspire
> Mirth, and youth, and warm desire!

Before the end of the Horton experience he seems to have had something too much of solitude. He had made occasional visits to London for the sake of instruction in mathematics and music; and at the end of five years he talked to Diodati of taking lodgings there. "Where I am now," he complains, "I live obscurely and in a cramped manner." But this was by far the most serene period of his life, and we have no reason to suppose that because he was grave he was uncheerful. He is always a little remote from nature as from his fellow-men. He views the landscape about Horton with the eye of a connoisseur well read in poetical description. Yet there are many touches in *L'Allegro* and its companion-piece which show that his remoteness was not unsympathetic. From his correspondence with Diodati and Cambridge friends we see that his discontent was with himself rather than his surroundings. But he was too busy to be often dull and discouraged. "No delay, no rest, no care or thought almost of anything," he writes, "holds me aside till I reach the end I am making for." And his great end set itself before him more and more clearly as time went on. In 1637 he writes to Diodati: "You make many inquiries as to what I am about; what I am thinking of? Why, with God's help, of immortality! Forgive the word, I only whisper it in your ear! Yes, I am pluming my wings for a flight." He was on the whole content to bide his time. Dr. Garnett has called attention to the contrast in this respect between Milton and other poets who have early become conscious of their powers. "He who, like Milton, lisps in numbers, usually sings freely in adolescence; he who is really visited with a true inspiration generally depends on mood rather than on circumstance. Milton, on the other hand, until fairly embarked on his great epic, was comparatively an unproductive, and literally an occasional poet. Most of his pieces, whether English or Latin, owe their existence to some impulse from without: *Comus* to the solicitation of a patron, *Lycidas* to the death of a friend. The *L'Allegro* and the *Penseroso* seem almost the only two written at the urgency of an internal impulse; and perhaps, if we knew their history, we should discover that they too were prompted by extraneous suggestion or provoked into being by accident." It is evident enough that he himself regarded these early poems as incidental, and hardly to be taken into account for themselves. For in 1641 we find him still speaking wistfully of "an inward prompting which daily grows upon me, that by labor and intent study, which I take to be my portion in this life, joined with the strong propensity of nature, I might perhaps leave something so written to after times, as they should not willingly let it die."

It is to be said that there are several of the Horton poems which, however occasional, the world would hardly have let die if no mighty poem had been written. They contain the finest poetry between *The Tempest* and *Paradise Lost.* *Comus* is a very beautiful and perfect thing of its kind. Its occasion is interesting to the student of Milton's life. It was the second of two courtly masques written by Milton during the Horton period. Doubtless through the elder Milton, the poet had become acquainted with Henry Lawes, one of the most accomplished composers of the day. Not long after Milton left Cambridge, Lawes was commissioned to prepare a masque in honor of an aged noblewoman, the Dowager Countess of Derby. Lawes wrote the music, and engaged Milton to write the words. The entertainment (of which a fragment is preserved to us under the title *Arcades*) was successful; and when in the following year Lawes was applied to on a similar occasion, Milton again contributed the lines. Its theme, the praise of chastity, is characteristically Miltonic; and its blank verse often approaches the vigor and sonorousness of his ripest work. Moreover, there are the lovely Elizabethan lyrics, the Echo song, and the Sabrina song: surely without *Comus* we should not know Milton.

It would be interesting to know whether he was present at the performance at Ludlow Castle. It must have been a stately scene. That was the day when the court masque chiefly flourished in England. Endless pains and enormous sums were spent on these productions. In 1634 the Four Inns of Court had given a masque (the music largely written by Lawes) in honor of the King and Queen, which cost £21,000 — a sum which must of course be multiplied several times to put it in terms of to-day. Shortly afterwards another sumptuous entertainment of this kind was given by royalty itself. Lawes was again the composer; and among the actors were the King and various noblemen and noblemen's sons. Among the latter were the sons of the Earl of Bridgewater, who had already been appointed Lord President of Wales, but had not yet been inducted into that office. The ceremony of inauguration took place in the following autumn, and it was natural that a masque should be provided for among the elaborate means of celebration. Lawes was not only the fashionable composer in this kind, but had a special relation of musical instructor to the Earl's family. And he naturally looked for the "book" to the acceptable author of *Arcades,* which had been given in honor of a relative of the Bridgewater family. The chief parts were to be taken by the young sons and daughter of the family, the pupils of Lawes; and Lawes himself probably took the part of the Attendant Spirit, and managed the whole performance. *Comus* apparently attracted more attention at the time than was usual with that sort of occasional performance. It was printed by Henry Lawes in 1637, by Milton's permission but without his name, and in his preface Lawes complains of it as being "so lovely and so much desired that the often copying of it hath tired my pen, and brought me to a necessity of producing it to the public view." Milton, to judge by the Latin motto on the title-page, felt that the publication was premature.

The feeling that his genius is not yet ripe for expression is again suggested in the opening lines of *Lycidas,* written in the same year (1637). The monody is rather a respectful tribute to a worthy acquaintance than a cry of grief. Milton's art is nowhere more formal than in the passages which have properly to do with the memory of Edward King. It is in that digression in which the "dread voice" of St. Peter is heard, with its solemn warning to the English Church, that we listen to a new Milton, the Milton who was destined for twenty years to give himself to the service of a great public cause. "In his earlier poetry," says Pattison, "Milton's muse has sung in the tones of the age that is passing away; except in his austere chastity, a cavalier. . . . In *Lycidas,* for a moment, the tones of both ages, the past and the coming, are combined, and then Milton leaves behind him forever the golden age, and one-half of his poetic genius."

For the moment, however, he seems to have had no premonition of the active part he was to take in public affairs. His mind was intent upon what he no doubt regarded as another important step in his poetic apprenticeship. He had long been anxious to visit Italy. In 1637 the death of his mother had lessened his ties at Horton, and the advent of his brother Christopher, now married though not yet admitted to the bar, made it possible for him to leave his father without a sense of desertion. In April, 1638, Milton, accompanied by a servant, and abundantly supplied with letters of introduction, set out from England. It was not a moment for departure which would have been chosen by a man with a sense of immediate patriotic responsibility at home. The rule of Charles and Laud had become more and more tyrannical, and a month earlier the great remonstrance of the Scottish Covenant had been made. Milton was in sympathy with the rebels, but he saw no active part for himself in the strife that was sure to follow. To broaden his experience was the chief duty which lay before him. He made a short stay in Paris, where he met the Dutch scholar Grotius. Thence, with several brief stops by the way, he went to Florence, where he stayed two months. Here he was warmly received, and "immediately contracted the acquaintance of many noble and learned." He was made free of the numerous "academies" by means of which the Florentine *literati* then nourished the somewhat faint spark of their inspiration. It was not an heroic hour for Italy, even for Florence. Noble artistic achievement had given place to elegant trifling. But they received Milton nobly, and no doubt pleased him by confessing their own limitations. "I have sate among their learned men," he wrote years later, "and been counted happy to be born in such a place of philosophic freedom as they supposed England was, while themselves did nothing but bemoan the servile condition into which learning among them was brought, that this was it which had damped the glory of Italian wits that nothing had been written there now these many years but flattery and fustian." Numerous literary compliments were exchanged between the foreigner and these kindly gentlemen. On a second visit to Florence he succeeded in getting an interview with Galileo, now blind and feeble, but enjoying a partial liberty.

In Rome he spent altogether some four months. Here he was received less cordially than in Florence, though under the wing of Holstenius, a German who had been at Oxford, and was now secretary to Cardinal Barberini, and one of the librarians of the Vatican.

It was not a propitious hour for a talking Protestant in Rome. The inquisition had overreached itself in its treatment of Galileo, but its fangs were not yet drawn. And Milton was not a politic person. His friend and sponsor Sir Henry Wotton had warned him before he left England to be discreet in his speech: "*pensieri stretti ed viso sciolto*" (close thoughts and an open countenance) will go safely over the whole world. But Milton, if we are to believe himself, rather scorned this advice, and talked frankly in Rome as elsewhere. "I had made this resolution with myself, not of my own accord to introduce conversation about religion; but, if interrogated respecting the faith, whatsoever I should suffer, to dissemble nothing."

Strangely, as it seems at first, the art of Italy failed to absorb his interest. He was detained in Rome, he says, by her antiquities. But the music of Italy did not fail to rouse his enthusiasm: least of all in the beautiful person of Leonora Baroni, the first singer of her time. The three epigrams written in her honor suggest the personal homage of a man still young, and, with all his purity of life, undoubtedly susceptible. Similar mementos of this period are the five poems in Italian to an unknown lady of Bologna, which evidently express a real if temporary ardor.

It had been a part of Milton's original plan to visit Sicily and Greece; but news which reached him at Naples determined him to shorten his stay abroad, "inasmuch as I thought it base to be traveling at my ease for intellectual culture while my fellow-countrymen at home were fighting for liberty." Civil war had not actually begun in England, but the Scots had declared finally against Charles and Laud, announced a return to Presbyterianism, and Charles was collecting an army to use against them. Later news probably convinced Milton that affairs at home were not in so serious a state as he had at first understood, and it was some months before, by way of Geneva and Paris, he actually returned to England.

He brought home with him a collection of books and many pleasant memories, less of the scenes and objects he had visited than of the people he had met. The Italian journey had surprisingly little effect upon his poetry, but it was a valuable experience for the man upon whom serious responsibility was soon to fall. One sad lack he found in his home-coming. At Geneva he had heard of the death of Charles Diodati, and soon after his return he must have written the *Epitaphium Damonis.* Diodati had been, as has been said, his only warm personal friend, and the stately lines of the *Epitaphium* express a keen grief. The pastoral figure is employed in it, as in *Lycidas,* but it is perhaps the most spontaneous of his Latin poems, as it is the last. In the concluding lines the poet utters a farewell to the classic Muse, and expresses a determination to use thereafter the harsh [*stridens*] British tongue.

At about the time of his return his brother Christopher was admitted to the Bar, and not long after went to Reading to live, taking the father with him; so that the Horton residence was at an end. Milton took lodgings in London "in St. Bride's churchyard, Fleet Street, at the house of one Russel, a tailor." Here he purposed to take up his quiet life of study again, "with no small delight, cheerfully leaving the conduct of public affairs first to God and then to those to whom the people had committed that task." But though he did not intend to take up any active profession, he very soon drifted into one. His only sister had married, some fifteen years before this, and in 1631 had been left a widow with two sons. She had remarried; a fact which may have had something to do with her now placing these sons in their uncle's charge. The younger came to live with him at once, while the elder for a time visited him for daily lessons, and later, when Milton had taken a house in Aldersgate Street, also became a member of the household. Some of his biographers have taken it for granted that his duties of a pedagogue must have been irksome to him. On the contrary, we have every reason to believe that he felt keen interest in the game of instruction. He developed a theory of education, which may be found set forth in full in his *Tractate of Education,* to Master Samuel Hartlib. His definition of education is impressive: "I call a complete and generous education that which fits a man to perform justly, skilfully, and magnanimously, all the offices, both public and private, of peace and war." His theory is of less account: we need only say of it here that, like so many of his political theories, it is more admirable in motive than in substance. There is no doubt that he enjoyed teaching. We find him a few years later with several pupils beside his nephews, and finally, after another change of residence, virtually the master of a small academy.

However, we are not to suppose that he forgot his earlier purpose. He did not regard teaching at this time, or politics later, as his true vocation. Through these years his vision of a monumental poem never left him. His mind was full of possible themes, which eventually narrowed to two: the Arthurian story, and the subject of *Paradise Lost*. He was long uncertain whether the epic or the tragic method would best suit his purpose; for some time he was inclined toward a *Paradise Lost* in the form of a tragedy. He was actually writing hardly any verses at all. He produced nothing of real importance during the following decade. He had not been long in London before he was swept into the current of political and religious controversy from which it was then almost impossible for any person of active mind to keep clear. England had reached the parting of the ways: the cause of liberty, political and religious, must now be tried and determined. I cannot do better than quote from Professor Masson's summary of the situation as Milton must have seen it in 1641:

"The Long Parliament had, with singular rapidity, in the first months of its sitting, swept away accumulated abuses in State and Law, brought Strafford to trial and execution, impeached and imprisoned Laud and others of the chief ministers of "Thorough," subjected Charles to constitutional checks, made a satisfactory treaty with the Scots, and sent them home with thanks for their great services to England. They had also taken measures for their own security and the permanence of English Parliamentary government. All this having been done unanimously, or nearly so, the Church question had at length emerged as the most difficult of all, and that on which there was most difference of opinion. That the Laudian Episcopacy must no longer exist in England, all, with hardly an exception, were agreed; but for the rest, people divided themselves into two parties. There were the advocates of a Limited Episcopacy, excluding the Bishops, perhaps, from the House of Lords and from other places of political and judicial power, and also surrounding them even in Church matters with Councils of Presbyters, and there were the Root-and-Branch Reformers, who were for abolishing Episcopacy utterly, and reconstructing the Church of England after some Presbyterian model like that of the Scots."

Later on Milton was to become even more radical, advocating the abolition of all church government, but for the present he was of the Root-and-Branch persuasion: determined against Bishops, but in favor of a Presbytery. He plainly saw in the action of the Long Parliament a signal to action for all men of conscience:

"Perceiving that the true way to liberty followed on from these beginnings, inasmuch also as I had so prepared myself from my youth that, above all things, I could not be ignorant what is of divine and what of human right, I resolved, though I was then meditating certain other matters, to transfer into this struggle all my genius and all the strength of my industry." It cannot be said that Milton's genius consented to the transference, but of his industry there was no doubt. Within ten months he flung off five pamphlets against the Episcopacy. Now it may be, as he tells us, that he dreaded "to leave a calm and pleasing solitariness, fed with cheerful and confident thoughts, to embark in a troubled sea of noises and hoarse disputes." But it is certain that, having once embarked, he enjoyed the exhilaration of the voyage. The truth is, he was naturally pugnacious, and in controversy his dignity often left him as completely as it may leave the stateliest of men who finds himself involved in a street scuffle. Milton often vies in shrillness and coarseness with the least humane of his adversaries. Nor can it be said that his argument differs markedly in quality from that of the ordinary controversialist. There is no doubt about the elevation of his motive, the reality of his liberty-worship. But the theories and remedies he proposes have no special mark of inspiration. On the contrary, they display often a mordant hatred of the enemy in the flesh rather than a longing for spiritual victory. He builds upon no broad foundation of philosophical thought. "His opinions," says Lowell, "were heated to the temper of the times and shaped to the instant exigencies of the forum, sometimes to his own convenience at the moment, instead of being the slow result of a deliberate judgment enlightened by intellectual and above all historical sympathy with his subject. His interest was rather in the occasion than the character of the controversy." Consequently he was a spokesman rather than a leader even in the partizan sense.

However, his controversial writings will always be a mine of interest to persons who are concerned with the man Milton as well as the poet. There is a human ingenuousness in their very fallacies that keeps us from forgetting that the English master of the sublime was also mortal. And the frequent narrowness and acrimony of his tone do not deny those equally frequent bursts of eloquence which have hardly their parallel in English prose. So the imaginary apostrophe to himself as a possible recreant:

"Timorous and ungrateful, the Church of God is now again at the foot of her insulting enemies, and thou bewailest. What matters it for thee or thy bewailing? When time was, thou wouldst not find a syllable of all that thou hast read or studied to utter on her behalf. Yet ease and leisure was given thee for thy retired thoughts, but of the sweat of other men. Thou hast the diligence, the parts, the language of a man, if a vain subject were to be adorned or beautified, but when the cause of God or his Church was to be pleaded, for which purpose that tongue was given thee which thou hast, God listened if he could hear thy voice among his zealous servants, but thou wert dumb as a beast; from henceforward be that which thine own brutish silence hath made thee."

There is no doubting the sincerity of the man who could write like this: fanatical he may have been, but none the less sincere. By his five "Anti-Episcopal" pamphlets Milton established himself as a champion of the "Root-and-Branch" faction. As for the public events which followed, we may quote again from Masson: "In August, 1642, Charles having in the meantime assented to a bill excluding the Bishops from the House of Lords, but having broken decisively with the Parliament on other questions, there began the great Civil War. From that date Englishmen were divided into two opposed masses,— the Parliamentarians, taking the part of that majority of the Commons and a small minority of the Lords, which still sat on as two Houses; and the Royalists, taking the side of the King and of the bulk of the nobility, with the adhering minority of the Commons. Milton, of course, attached himself resolutely to the Parliamentarians." During the first year the conduct of the war hardly amounted to more than a series of skirmishes. Milton did not take arms, or, so far as we know, consider the possibility at this or any other time. It is not hard to understand why this is so. He undoubtedly considered himself as more likely to be of service in the struggle at hand as a voice than as a sword or a pike. He was willing to pay the penalty of his honest utterances, but his sense of personal dignity, of high calling, would prevent his exposing himself to the chance quietus of the common soldier. His sense of personal aloofness and of what was his due as a poet, are both frankly displayed in the sonnet *When the Assault was Intended to the City.* In November, 1642, the King's army had approached very near to London, and it was expected for some days that he would march upon the city. It must have been at this moment that Milton wrote the lines in question. He lived outside the city gates, and it has been surmised that the sonnet may have been actually posted upon his doors:

Captain or Colonel, or Knight in Arms,
  Whose chance on these defenseless doors may seize,
  If deed of honor did thee ever please,
  Guard them, and him within protect from harms.
He can requite thee; for he knows the charms
  That call fame on such gentle acts as these,

> And he can spread thy name o'er lands and seas,
> Whatever clime the sun's bright circle warms.
> Lift not thy spear against the Muses' bower:
> The great Emathian conqueror bid spare
> The house of Pindarus, when temple and tower
> Went to the ground; and the repeated air
> Of sad Electra's poet had the power
> To save the Athenian walls from ruin bare.

The patriotic non-combatant is not really a paradox; even in time of war there may be nobler things in life than the willingness to make oneself a target or a rifleman. But there is something absurdly paradoxical in Milton's exploit of the following year. If his dignity and sense of high destiny prevented his enlistment in the Parliamentary army, they should certainly have prevented him from a hasty and frivolous domestic entanglement at such a time. In the spring of 1643, when the public issue to which he had committed his service if not his sword was still all undecided, he made a certain sudden expedition into the country. "About Whitsuntide it was, or a little after," records one of his nephews, "that he took a journey into the country, nobody about him certainly knowing the reason, or that it was any more than a journey of recreation; but home he returns a married man that went out a bachelor, his wife being Mary, the eldest daughter of Mr. Richard Powell, then a Justice of the Peace, of Forest-hill, near Shotover, in Oxfordshire." How it came about we are still at loss to imagine. It is clear that there was little element of romance in the affair, and there was certainly no element of reason: unless the marriage was to be construed as a crude way of collecting a debt. The Powells were Royalists, and the bride was a silly girl just half Milton's age. Mr. Powell was deep in debt, and had a large family to maintain (six sons and five daughters). In some way he owed Milton £500; it is supposed that the debt had been transferred from the elder Milton to the younger fifteen years earlier. Was it simply an instance of Puritan thrift? — at all events, after a month's absence, Milton brought a wife home with him to his bewildered nephews, and, according to the demure account of the biographer-nephew, "there was feasting held for some days in celebration of the nuptials. . . . At length they [certain of the bride's relatives who had accompanied her for this dubious merrymaking] took their leave, and returning to Forest-hill, left the sister behind, probably not much to her satisfaction, as appeared by the sequel. By that time she had for a month or thereabout led a philosophical life (after having been used to a great house and much company and jollity), her friends, possibly incited by her own desire, made earnest suit by letter to have her company the remaining part of the summer; which was granted, on the condition of her returning at the time appointed, Michaelmas, or thereabout." Poor child: a kitten might as well have married a monolith. When the time arrived, the bride arrived not: "Michaelmas being come," goes on nephew Phillips, "and no news of his wife's return, he sent for her by letter, and, receiving no answer, sent several other letters, which were also unanswered, so that he despatched down a foot-messenger with a letter, desiring her return; but the messenger came back, not only without an answer, at least a satisfactory one, but, to the best of my remembrance, reported that he was dismissed with some sort of contempt. This proceeding, in all probability, was grounded upon no other cause but this: viz., that the family being generally addicted to the Cavalier Party, as they called it, and some of them possibly engaged in the King's service . . . they began to repent them of having matched the eldest daughter of the family to a person so contrary to them in opinion, and thought it would be a blot on their escutcheon whenever the Court should come to flourish again. However, it so incensed our author that he thought it would be dishonourable ever to receive her again after such a repulse; so that he forthwith prepared to fortify himself with arguments for such a resolution." Hence the tracts on divorce which were immediately forthcoming: or so we should understand from nephew Phillips. But it has been discovered that the date of publication of the first tract was August 1, very shortly after Mary Milton's permitted departure. The inference is that Milton must have been writing *The Doctrine and Discipline of Divorce,* if not, as has been alleged, during his honeymoon, at least before his young wife had left him. Evidently there had been no golden honeymoon for this ill-mated pair. Mary Powell had very likely found the idea of him tolerable on account of his personal beauty, but the mingled intensity and austerity of his nature no doubt frightened and revolted her when the test of companionship came. If it was a matter of souls, each had affronted the other in the indecorous haste of a nominal union. There was nothing really tragic in the fact of their separation. The tragedy for Milton lay rather in the disappointment of hopes which, however unreasonable, had been real to him. Milton's attitude toward women was that of his class and sect. The woman-cult belonged to Roman Catholicism. The Cavalier inherited and cherished the idea of chivalry, believed in woman as a higher, finer being, to be ministered to and worshiped according to an accepted ritual. But the Puritan had reverted to the Hebrew or Oriental conception of woman as a weaker and inferior being, naturally subject to man. "He for God only, she for God in him" was his motto. It was not a motto likely to make for the happiness of a girl-wife suddenly wrested from the kindlier soil of a Royalist family life.

It was characteristic of the man and of the times that this intimate trouble should at once bear fruit in the form of pamphlets. There is no direct identification in *The Doctrine and Discipline of Divorce* of the author's private experience and public theory. Yet it is more a cry of wrath and anguish than a statement of principles. It must not be forgotten that however limited Milton's conception of women, he had his own high ideal of marriage. However inadvisedly, he had linked himself to one "with whom he looked to be the co-partner of a sweet and gladsome society." There was doubtless something of personal pique in his disappointment at the actual outcome of his marriage, but there was more of real suffering. His belief in the beauty of true marriage remained. It was the canonical theory that false marriage must be perpetuated which stirred his indignation: a domestic aspect of that servitude which he fought in politics and religion. It must have been this aspect of it which made it possible for him to dedicate the *Doctrine and Discipline* to Parliament, urging immediate divorce legislation.

It was hardly the time for invoking the attention of Parliament to trivial matters. At about the time when Milton's wife went back to her family, the entire abolition of the Episcopacy had been decreed by Parliament. A little later the Solemn League and Covenant, providing for the common adoption in both countries of a Presbyterian form of Church government, was signed by the English Parliamentarians and the Scottish people. Very soon, however, a difference arose among the Parliamentarians. Most of them were for the rule by Presbytery, and compulsory worship. But a growing minority pronounced for a principle of absolute independence: the right of every assembly of worshipers to govern itself,—what eventually became known as Congregationalism. Milton's utterances upon divorce had not endeared him to the Presbyterians: a fact which may have hastened, though it would hardly have determined, his alliance with the Independents. The party of greater freedom could not help being the party of his choice.

The first divorce tract was followed by three others. They brought their author no honor; he lived, he says, in "a world of disesteem." Certain ill-advised persons invoked his authority for abrupt domestic revolution. However, he held to his theories, and even thought of putting them into practice. The last pamphlet in the divorce series, *Tetrachordon,* addressed to Parliament, closes with a significant warning. His pleas for proper legislation had been ignored. "If the law make not timely provision," he thunders, "let the law, as reason is, bear the censure of the consequences." In 1645, according to Phillips, he seriously contemplated taking unto himself "a very handsome and witty gentlewoman" named Davis. The lady was of another mind, or at all events had not brought herself to take the step, when a very natural thing happened which effectually put an end to the negotiations. Mary Milton returned to the husband she had deserted two years earlier. Her motive may not have been altogether magnanimous. With the battle of Naseby, June, 1645, the royal cause had received its death-blow. The Powells, already bankrupt, had been driven from their home by the investment of Oxford. The Independents were in power, and Milton was of them. It was no longer a question of a possible blot on the escutcheon, but of possible salvage from the wreck of the family fortunes. Milton was surprised into an interview, the repentant wife seems to have conducted herself with suitable humility, and Milton consented to take her back. And to remove any suspicion of half-heartedness or perfunctoriness on his part, we may note the fact that, upon the sequestration of the Powell estate a year later, he took into his house the whole family, including the mother whom he no doubt considered largely responsible for the original offense of the daughter. It must have been an uncomfortable household. Milton complains of it freely in one of his letters to his Italian friend Dati: "Those whom the mere necessity of neighborhood, or something else of a useless kind has closely conjoined with me, whether by accident or the tie of law, they are the persons who sit daily in my company, weary me, nay, by Heaven, almost plague me to death whenever they are jointly in the humor for it." Mary Milton bore a daughter in July, 1646. Milton's father and father-in-law both died within a few months thereafter.

A more important event to the world was the publication, at the beginning of 1646, of the *Minor Poems*. Most of them had been written long before, but Milton had made no attempt to print them. Their publication at this time was due to the urgency of the bookseller Moseley, who seems to have had a real appreciation of their value. His motive in printing them, he says, "is not any private respect of gain, for the slightest pamphlet is nowadays more vendible than the works of learnedest men, but it is the love I bear to our own language. . . . Let the event guide itself which way it will, I shall deserve of the age by bringing forth into the light as true a birth as the Muses have brought forth since our famous Spenser wrote." It has been suggested that Milton may have been willing that the world be permitted to recognize him as something more than a pamphleteer. Two mottoes are to be found at the beginning of the volume, both undoubtedly chosen by Milton, and each interesting in its own way. The first is from Virgil, and suggests, like the motto prefixed to *Comus* long before, that the poet's real achievement is to come. The other, a Greek quatrain, stands upon the title-page beneath a wretched print, supposed to be a portrait of the author. It resembles no other portrait of him. The lines, engraved carefully by the artist in ignorance of their meaning, whimsically suggest that he, not the author, is responsible for these ill-favored features. It is an instance of the grim humor which is occasionally to be discovered in ambush behind the austere front of the Puritan poet and prophet.

The death of Milton's father left him in easier circumstances; and this fact may in part account for his shortly after giving up his pupils and retiring to a smaller house and a less laborious life. Mrs. Powell and her children were thereafter under allowance from him, but no longer lived with him.

Presbyterian Church government had been nominally established in England; but the army of Fairfax and Cromwell had refused to disband after the defeat of the Royalists, and waited to strike a blow for the Independent cause. In August, 1647, the Army occupied London, and assumed practical control of public affairs. All this was much to Milton's satisfaction. He believed in the principle for which the army strove; and it is certain that the strong establishment of the Presbyterians would have meant personal danger to himself. He had just given up his teaching and become, in a sense, a free man. However, he showed no disposition at the moment to take an active part in the Independent movement. During the next year and a half he was busy with three ambitious literary projects: a Latin Dictionary, a system of divinity, and a History of Britain. Then (January 30, 1649), came the final overthrow and execution of Charles and the establishment of the Republic. Almost at once appeared Milton's *Tenure of Kings and Magistrates,* proving that "it is lawful and hath been held so through all ages, for any who have the power, to call to account a Tyrant, or Wicked King, and, after due conviction, to depose and put him to death, if the ordinary Magistrate have neglected to do it." According to Professor Masson, "it had been begun and almost finished before the King's death."

The chief power of the new Commonwealth was in the hands of a Council of State. Its Committee of Foreign Affairs needed a "Secretary for Foreign Tongues," and Milton was offered the post, with a salary amounting to £1,000 or so in terms of to-day. The chief duties of the office lay in the translation of despatches. He may well have hesitated to accept it. It meant not only giving up his life of retirement, but hard work for his eyes, which were already giving him trouble. But he did not hesitate: two days after the appointment he presented himself for duty. In three years he was blind; but he held his office eight years longer, up to the very hour of the Restoration, and at no time as a sinecure.

There were of course strong arguments in favor of his undertaking the office. He was now in his fortieth year, and in spite of his interest in certain aspects of public affairs, and his pamphleteering, he had lived a life of seclusion. He had experienced little contact with men of action, and had come to feel the need of

> The world . . . her glory,
> Empires and monarchs and their radiant courts,
> Best school of best experience.

The fruit of all his living was to be embodied in that long-planned-for poem of his maturity; but the fruit was still to ripen. Scholarship and contemplation had done what they could for him: what he now needed was to become a part of events. And this he certainly did: during the following dozen years of tempestuous English history, he was very near the storm-center. It was necessary for him to be physically near from the outset. Soon after his appointment he moved to Charing Cross, thence for a time to chambers in Whitehall, then given up to offices and official suites; and finally to a house in Westminster, where he lived for nine years,— as long, that is, as he continued to hold office.

His duties were understood at first to be chiefly clerical: the translation of despatches to and from the Council of State. The total number of letters from the Council to foreign powers or persons translated into Latin by Milton in the course of ten years was one hundred and thirty-seven, and most of them were brief — not a very heavy clerical task. But he undoubtedly composed rather than translated many of them, and other duties gradually fell to him which made the office of Secretary for Foreign Tongues, or "Latin Secretary" a responsible one. He had to be present at interviews between the government and foreign envoys, and sometimes to interview such dignitaries personally, in the name of the Council. Inappropriately enough for the author of the *Areopagitica,* certain duties of censorship seem to have devolved upon him. It was, to be sure, the licensing of books which he had denounced, while the task laid upon him by the council was their examination for seditious utterances. He could hardly refuse the assignment, but he must have found it ungrateful, and there are indications that he exercised all possible leniency.

But the Council came to expect of him still other and more important work. Nine days after the execution of Charles, four days before the appearance of Milton's *Tenure of Kings and Magistrates,* had been published the immediately famous *Eikon Basiliké* (Royal Image), which purported to be a record of the prayers and meditations of the King's later years, set down by himself. It was later found to be the work of Bishop Gauden (who was rewarded for it on the Restoration); but it was then generally admitted to be authentic. The death of the monarch had been a severe shock to the national sense; and the book came at the right moment to precipitate and fix those emotions of pity and horror which were sure to be aroused by such an act even among those who may have been able to consider its possibility with calmness. The effect did not pass off; the book continued to be widely read and wept over; and the Council determined that something should be done to counteract its influence. Choice fell upon Milton as the most promising champion of the Commonwealth. He accepted the commission with reluctance: "I take it on me as a work assigned, rather than by me chosen or affected." But having once undertaken the task, he carried it through with characteristic thoroughness, and, it must be said, with characteristic bitterness. Article by article he takes up the *Eikon Basiliké,* controverts every opinion expressed, and turns every possible item of evidence against the dead King. It is an ungenerous performance, and it can have had little or no effect upon the fortunes of the "King's Book." Milton's *Eikonoklastes* went through three editions in a year to fifty or so for the *Eikon Basiliké.* "His vigorous blows," says Dr. Garnett, "avail but little against the impalpable ideal with which he is contending; his arguments might frequently convince a court of justice, but could do nothing to dispel the sorcery which enthralled the popular imagination." Indeed, there is little dignity in the book to convince any one of anything: it is often trivial and dull as well as ill-natured. It is not greatly to the credit of his superiors that such a performance should have raised him in their estimation; but it undoubtedly did. Consequently, it was not long before he was again called upon to enter the lists, and this time against a redoubtable champion.

In Leyden dwelt at this time a mighty man of letters, one Claude de Saumaise, known throughout Christendom as Claudius Salmasius, the greatest classical scholar of his day. It is hard for us to realize what that meant in the seventeenth century. What the greatest scientist, what the greatest philosopher, is to us to-day, Salmasius was to his Europe. He had read and could quote from a prodigious number of books: he had edited *Solinus* and what not. Consequently he was looked up to with veneration by all right-minded people. His authority was consulted upon all sorts of topics "from episcopacy to hair-powder." Naturally, if one had a bit of literary hectoring to be done, he would apply to Salmasius, and have it done thoroughly, in Latin, for the edification of polite persons the world over. Charles II. had taken up his residence at The Hague, within the direct effulgence of Salmasius's glory. By him Salmasius was presently "commissioned to prepare a manifesto, which should be at once a vindication of Charles's memory, and an indictment against the regicide government." The scholar knew nothing of politics, to be sure, and probably cared nothing for the cause of Charles; but he had a pen, and was fond of exercising it under sufficiently flattering provocation. His *Defensio Regia* was the result. Shortly after it was received in England, the Council of State prohibited its circulation, and ordered "that Mr. Milton do prepare something in answer to the book of Salmasius."

Two months later (March, 1651), Milton's reply to Salmasius appeared. There were excellent reasons why he might have hesitated to undertake such a task at this time. No doubt his midnight studies from early childhood had put a severe strain upon his eyes. For years now they had been actively troubling him. That they were not merely the mousing eyes of the scholar is shown by the fact that he was a skilled swordsman. In 1650 he had lost the sight of one eye completely; and received warning that if he did not take the utmost care of the other he was sure to be totally blind. He seems to have had a premonition that the study necessary in preparing his counterblast to Salmasius would prove fatal to his vision, and to have deliberately decided that it was his duty. "The choice lay before me," he declares, "between dereliction of a supreme duty and loss of eyesight; in such a case I could not listen to the physician, not if Æsculapius himself had spoken from his sanctuary; I could not but obey that inward monitor, I know not what, that spake to me from Heaven. I considered with myself that many had purchased less good with worse ill, as they who give their lives to reap only glory, and I thereupon concluded to employ the little remaining eyesight I was to enjoy in doing this, the greatest service to the commonwealth it was in my power to render." This leaves no doubt that Milton took his reply very seriously. So did the Council, which after offering him a reward in money, which was refused, passed the following vote of thanks: "The Council, taking notice of the many good services performed by Mr. John Milton, their Secretary for Foreign Tongues, to this State and Commonwealth, particularly of his book in vindication of the Parliament and People of England against the calumnies and invectives of Salmasius, have thought fit to declare their resentment and good acceptance of the same, and that the thanks of the Council be returned to Mr. John Milton, and their sense represented in that behalf."

Yet it is difficult to understand on what reasonable grounds either the attack or the defense could have been taken to determine anything with regard to the subject nominally at issue. Salmasius, as we have said, knew nothing of English affairs, and his arraignment of the regicides and their commonwealth was a purely academic exercise. He does not take up the argument, ready to his hand, that Charles was not a bad man but a mistaken one; nor does he make the most of the legal irregularity of his trial and execution. He is content to give most of his space to the bald proposition that all kings, even wicked kings, should be regarded as inviolable. It was a simple matter for Milton to demolish this structure, even then antiquated. It remained for him to seize his great opportunity of enlightening the world as to the principles upon which the regicides had acted, and upon which the Commonwealth proposed to advance. But he did very little in that direction. The main force of his argument is given to personal attack upon a gladiatorial adversary. It is a spirited attack, if not in accordance with the rules of the modern ring. He not only pummels his antagonist thoroughly, he clinches with him, kicks him under the ropes, and follows to throw mud upon his prostrate foe. This is an inelegant figure, but it expresses the situation. Milton is not only truculent in his treatment of Salmasius, he is scurrilous. By way of defending the English people, he jeers at a Frenchman for being hen-pecked, and accuses him, a singularly incorruptible man, of being a hireling. All this delighted the bystanders,— which is to say Europe. Salmasius had had everything his own way too long: at last he had found his match. Wonder was expressed that such excellent Latin as Milton's had come out of England. The question at issue seems to have been lost sight of: the important thing was that an exciting duel was on between persons who could be counted upon to afford good sport.

It seems rather pitiful now: Milton giving his eyes to make a Roman holiday. But to him his achievement cannot have seemed petty or personal. It must be borne in mind, finally, that the established method of disproving a charge was then to assert that the accuser was an habitual liar, thief, or fool: or all three. Milton believed that in humiliating Salmasius, he had vindicated the truth, literally done "the greatest service to the commonwealth that it was in his power to render." This feeling must have comforted him somewhat in the days that followed. By 1652, at the age of forty-three, he was totally blind. His enemies exulted in what they chose to regard as a visitation upon him for his alliance with the Commonwealth. But that connection was not to end. Whatever its merit, his attack upon Salmasius had made him the most famous Englishman throughout Europe, Cromwell excepted. Moreover, he had rendered himself far too useful in his office to be displaced lightly. Assistants were found for him, and he went on to the end of the Cromwellian chapter.

Keenly as he felt his blindness, there is an unfeigned Christian patience in his acceptance of it. "What should prevent me," — he says, before he has quite given up hope that his sight may be restored — "What should prevent me from resting in the belief that eyesight lies not in eyes alone, but enough for all purposes in God's leading and Providence." The further belief grew in him as the years went on that a deeper inward vision was to be vouchsafed him by way of amends for his loss. His earlier emotion of resigned faith in a destiny which was all obscure is expressed in the famous sonnet:

When I consider how my light is spent
  Ere half my days in this dark world and wide,
  And that one talent which is death to hide
  Lodged with me useless, though my soul more bent
To serve therewith my Maker, and present
  My true account, lest He returning chide:
  "Doth God exact day-labour, light denied?"
  I fondly ask. But Patience, to prevent
That murmur, soon replies, "God doth not need
  Either man's work or his own gifts. Who best
  Bear his mild yoke, they serve him best. His state
Is kingly: thousands at his bidding speed,
  And post o'er land and ocean without rest;
  They also serve who only stand and wait."

In this strain we seem to hear once again, at last, the real Milton, the Milton of *Comus* and *Lycidas;* and it is so of the other great sonnets of this decade. His genius has so long remained dormant, its glory obscured by a talent for business, a talent for invective, that it might well have seemed to have been actually extinguished. There is nothing more familiar to human experience than the budding genius that never blossoms, the boyish impulse toward poetic expression which is quickly and finally supplanted by other and lesser impulses. If Milton had died instead of going blind in the year 1652, we should have said that his career represented a sad anticlimax. It would have seemed that his years as a schoolmaster and political secretary had been merely wasted, if indeed they did not prove that he had exhausted his poetic gift before reaching the age of thirty. Plenty of young men in every generation have been confident that they were going to do great things in poetry some day; but most of them have forgotten all about it in middle life. It is very absorbing to grow up, to be married and have children, to take part in the absorbing business of every-day life. But Milton never forgot. The soil of his nature had produced a beautiful young flowering and fruitage. Then for a long time it lay fallow, so far as poetry is concerned, growing deeper and richer: preparing itself for its great hour. Perhaps the shock of his loss of sight was necessary to cast him back upon his deeper self.

At all events, during the next half-dozen years all his greatest sonnets were composed: they are few indeed, but priceless. And it is remarkable that now for the first time the public events and men into whose contact he is thrown inspire in him a pure poetic impulse as offset against the turbid current of his controversial prose. So we have the noble lines on Cromwell and Vane, and the yet nobler sonnet on the Piedmont massacre. He had himself drafted a letter of remonstrance from the Council to the Duke of Savoy on the occasion of the massacre; but it is in his poem that the pure fire of his indignation has best come down to us. Never before or since has so deep a resonance been given to the sonnet form:

> Avenge, O Lord, thy slaughtered saints, whose bones
> Lie scattered on the Alpine mountains cold;
> Even them who kept Thy truth so pure of old,
> When all our fathers worshiped stocks and stones,
> Forget not: in thy book record their groans
> Who were thy sheep, and in their ancient fold
> Slain by the bloody Piedmontese, that rolled
> Mother with infant down the rocks. Their moans
> The vales redoubled to the hills, and they
> To Heaven. . . . Their martyred blood and ashes sow
> O'er all the Italian fields, where still doth sway
> The triple Tyrant; that from these may grow
> A hundredfold, who, having learned thy way,
> Early may fly the Babylonian woe.

There was to be yet another bitter personal controversy, the outcome of his attack on Salmasius. We need not follow him through the mire of it. No new light would be thrown upon the weaker side of his character, and much remains to be thrown upon the stronger and infinitely more important side.

At about the time when his blindness became complete, a third daughter was born to Milton, and soon after the mother died. A son, born two years earlier, had lived only a short time. Milton's grief for the loss of his wife cannot have been poignant. Their uncongeniality must have had deep roots in differences of age, of training, of temperament. She was a Sabine woman in the hands of the enemy. None of her husband's interests or employments, public or private (unless his music) can have appealed to her. And she probably clung to what she could of her traditions, her Cavalier airs and graces. Her daughters,—the two elder daughters, at least — apparently inherited her temperament, and she may have conveyed to them something of her bewildered contempt for the servant of the Commonwealth. But the biographers go too far in taking for granted that there was no bond between the two. No doubt they bore with each other as they could, and their natural antagonism may have been tempered by a real if limited affection, as it often is among housemates. His mate in some sense she was; and to be left mateless with three girl-children to care for must have been a calamity to the blind father.

His subsequent relation to his daughters was not

what it might have been if they had been the offspring of a happy marriage. It could hardly have been a tender relation under any conditions. Our Puritan ancestors in New England were forbidden to kiss their wives on Sunday. The children of a Puritan household were expected to be seen, not heard. Moreover, Milton sincerely believed in the natural subjection of women. And finally he must have had his full share of that domestic ruthlessness which is likely to attend a sense of high calling: the readiness to sacrifice others as well as oneself to the attainment of the great end. He gave them no education: the eldest, it is said, could not write her name. Yet he did not scruple to make servants of them, training them so that they could read five or six languages to his satisfaction, without in the least understanding what they read. The youngest, Deborah, was more like himself, and it is said that he taught her Latin, and had a regard for her above her sisters. But in his old age he included her in a sweeping condemnation of them. That he was not incapable of warm affection is shown in his attitude toward his second wife, the "late espoused saint" of the famous sonnet. He married Catherine Woodcock in 1656; fifteen months later she died in child-birth, and the child with her. It was she, we may suppose, who sat for the portrait of Milton's Eve: a portrait of noble womanhood which must not be forgotten in considering the poet's attitude toward a "weaker sex."

When I approach
Her loveliness, so absolute she seems,
And in herself complete, so well to know
Her own, that what she wills to do or say
Seems wisest, virtuousest, discreetest, best;
All higher knowledge in her presence falls
Degraded; wisdom in discourse with her
Loses discountenanc'd, and like folly shows;
Authority and reason on her wait,
As one intended first, not after made
Occasionally; and, to consummate all,
Greatness of mind, and nobleness, their seat
Build in her loveliest, and create an awe
About her, as a guard angelic placed.

Milton was in his fiftieth year when Catherine Milton died. The eldest daughter, Anne, was not yet twelve years old. "One can fancy," says Masson, ". . . the blind father, a kind of stern King Lear, mostly by himself, and the three young things pattering about as noiselessly as possible, at their own will or in the charge of some servant." It was to be tragic in the end, for him and for them.

An unhappy story, and it may as well be ended here. The two elder girls presently reached an age when they could safely revolt against the authority of a father who was after all dependent upon them in so many ways. The second, Mary, was much like her mother, and her feeling fairly amounted to hatred. They cheated in the domestic accounts, sold his books, and "made nothing of deserting him," as he complained. After four or five years, in sheer self-defense apparently, he married for a third time. The comment of his daughter Mary is too well-authenticated. "That was no news to hear of his wedding," she said, "but if she could hear of his death, that was something." Yet she and her sisters continued to live with him for five or six years longer. Their step-mother, Elizabeth Minshull, was only twenty-four years old on her marriage. But she was a person of ability and tact. She adored Milton, and got on remarkably well, in the circumstances, with the rebellious and ill-trained daughters. It was apparently by her diplomacy that they eventually left their father's house on peaceable terms.

We need not here go further into the details of Milton's service as Latin Secretary. His political attitude during these years has been admirably summarized by Dr. Garnett:

"Cæsar, says Johnson, had not more elegant flattery than Cromwell received from Milton: nor Augustus, he might have added, encomiums more heartfelt and sincere. Milton was one of the innumerable exemplars that a man may be very much a Republican without being at all a Liberal. He was as firm a believer in the right divine as any Cavalier, save that in his view such right was vested in the worthiest; that is, practically, the strongest [This was, we recall, virtually Carlyle's hero-theory]. An admirable doctrine for 1653,—how unfit for 1660 remained to be discovered by him. Under its influence he had successively swallowed *Pride's Purge,* the execution of Charles I. by a self-constituted tribunal, and Cromwell's expulsion of the scanty remnant of what had once seemed the more than Roman senate of 1641. There is great reason to believe with Professor Masson that a tract vindicating this violence was actually taken down from his lips. It is impossible to say that he was wrong. Cromwell was really standing between England and anarchy. But Milton might have been expected to manifest some compunction at the disappointment of his own brilliant hopes, and some alarm at the condition of the vessel of state reduced to her last plank. Authority had actually come into the hands of the kingliest man in England, valiant and prudent, magnanimous and merciful. But Cromwell's life was precarious, and what after Cromwell?" The one matter upon which he betrayed anxiety was the danger of Cromwell's calling himself King. The title of Protector has, he says humbled him from his "real sublimity, and as it were forced him into rank for the public convenience." But the title of King is, he continues, an impossible choice for a man of Cromwell's higher majesty: "For if you in your present greatness were to be taken with that name which you were able when a private man to reduce and bring to nothing, it would be almost as if, when by the help of the true God you had subdued some idolatrous nation, you were to worship the gods you had yourself overcome."

The adversary who was responsible for the attack which he visited upon the luckless Morus had accused him of a rude and dictatorial manner toward Cromwell. Facts do not seem to bear out the theory that Milton had any sort of vigorous influence upon the conduct of public affairs during his secretaryship. He was rather a polished spokesman than a political thinker. The most important event during the period of Milton's public service was the beginning of *Paradise Lost* in the last year of Oliver's Protectorate. But his loyalty to his master extended to his successor, Richard Cromwell, and it was only a short time before the actual restoration of the Stuart dynasty that he was actually "sequestered" from his office. To the end he fought desperately with his pen against the danger of a new kingship: anything, to his mind, was preferable to that. So we find him valiantly pamphleteering to the last gasp. He condemns the suppression of the Rump Parliament by Lambert. When it is restored he drafts a letter of advice. Before it can be published, Monk has arrived in London, and, perceiving which way the wind blows, takes effectual measures to the end that the Rump shall be no more. There are cries of King Charles in the air. But Milton refuses to believe that all is over, and, after necessary revision, publishes his Rump address (March, 1660) under the sufficiently plain title, "The Ready and Easy Way to establish a Free Commonwealth, and the Excellence thereof compared with the inconveniences and dangers of re-admitting Kingship in this Nation." Of course it was a lost cause, and of course Milton's proposals were fantastic and impracticable: but it was at least one of the most recklessly earnest and brave utterances ever put forth by a human being. Twice again in the following month, as the royalist clamor grew ever louder, he lifted his voice, with increased vehemence begging to be heard, and prophesying woes unspeakable (which he yet tries to speak) as the result of the proposed folly. He was answered with ridicule. In May, King Charles II. entered London in triumph, and Milton, with hundreds of others, went into hiding. "The wonder is," says Masson, "that at the Restoration Milton was not hanged. At a time when they brought to the scaffold all the chief living Regicides and their accomplices that were within reach, including even Hugh Peters, and when they dug up Cromwell's body and hanged it at Tyburn, and tore also from the earth at Westminster the body of Cromwell's mother and the other 'Cromwellian bodies' that had been buried there with honor, the escape of Milton, the supreme defender of the regicide through the press, the man who had attacked the memory of Charles I. with a ferocity which even some of the actual Regicides must have thought unnecessary and outrageous, is all but inexplicable." One explanation naturally did not occur to Professor Masson. Absorbed in his study of Milton the political writer as a lesser aspect of Milton the poet, he inclines to overestimate the effect of the controversial writings. Most of these utterances undoubtedly missed the mark, if the mark was public opinion in any large sense.

He was for a time in actual danger. Between May and August, 1660, he remained in hiding in a friend's house near Smithfield. Charles had, to be sure, asked for clemency in the treatment of the enemies of his house, and a "Bill of General Indemnity and Oblivion" had been presented in Parliament early in May. But discussion at once arose as to what persons must necessarily be excluded from the action of such a bill. Fifty-four of the seventy-seven persons who had been active in the trial and execution of Charles I. were listed, but various other persons (between thirty and forty) were named for secondary offenses; and among them Milton. In June an order for his arrest was issued "on account of his *Eikonoklastes* and *Defensio pro Populo Anglicano contra Salmasium*, with a resolution to petition his Majesty for the calling-in of all copies of those pamphlets, that they might be burnt by the common hangman; and on the 13th of August there came forth a royal proclamation calling in all copies of the books accordingly, and ordering them to be burnt." Yet when the "Bill of Indemnity" was passed a little later in the same month, Milton's name did not stand in the list of the excepted persons. It is certain that he had friends at court, among them probably Andrew Marvell, his old associate. Perhaps they urged his blindness; perhaps they pleaded the burning of his offensive pamphlets as a sufficient punishment. The specification of those particular pamphlets in itself suggests adroit management on somebody's part. If, instead of these two, his first important political pamphlet and his last had been called attention to — the *Tenure of Kings and Magistrates,* and the *Ready and Easy Way,* the case against him must have been made to seem far more serious. At all events, his absence from the official list made him once more a free man. The burning of the two works specified, which continued at intervals for some time, began and concluded his relations with the public hangman. He went about again — or was led about again — freely; but he was arrested on one occasion, and only released on the payment of exorbitant fees, and it may easily be that he long felt himself in peril:

> On evil days now fallen, and evil tongues,
> In darkness, and with dangers compassed round,
> And solitude.

So for a time his life must have passed. Public events were no longer anything but a passing show. He no longer torments himself, and us, with his theories and revilings.

Something more than has been said may be said here of his personal relations to the men and women outside his own family with whom, in one way or another, he came in contact. In general the cordiality of these relations depended upon a sense of unchallenged superiority on his part. He had not the kind of nature which brooks a friendly rivalry, or acknowledges authority without an effort. Milton had great admiration, even reverence, for Cromwell, but there is no evidence of any personal intercourse between the two: a fact which is as likely to be Milton's fault as Cromwell's. Regarding himself as the voice of the Commonwealth, and always conscious of his poetic powers, he was probably proud and cold of manner, unready to accept advances toward intimacy on the part of his associates, if such advances were made. In 1657 he writes to a man who has asked for a recommendation to the English ambassador in Holland: "I am sorry that I am not able to do this; I have very little acquaintance with those in power, inasmuch as I keep very much to my own house, and prefer to do so." He had not always been so much a recluse as this. Phillips tells us that in 1641 he had some agreeable acquaintance with men of his own age, even entertaining socially ("keeping a gaudy day," says Phillips) once every three or four weeks, with "two gentlemen of Gray's Inn." He was himself a University man and a gentleman, with none of that contempt for refined manners which belonged to many of his Puritan associates. In later life he seems to have relaxed chiefly in the company of young and receptive persons, upon whom he might allow himself to shine as the sun shines, with the benignance of unchallenged power. He was, says Aubrey, "most familiar and free in his conversation with those to whom most sour in the way of education." He was "extreme pleasant in his conversation, and at dinner, supper, etc., but satirical." His youngest daughter Deborah recalled many years later that he was "delightful company, the life of a circle, and that he was so through a flow of subjects, and an unaffected cheerfulness and civility." Altogether we get the impression of his social manner as that of a solitary Don, self-exiled from his equals, but capable of geniality in the presence of certain favorite pupils. He had had a group of such young admirers about him during the Commonwealth, notable among them the Cyriack Skinner and "young Lawrence" of the sonnets. These sonnets were written about 1655, after he had become blind, but before the decline of the Commonwealth had begun to distress him. The lines to Lawrence (who was hardly more than a boy), with their pleasant and even light-hearted invitation, give very clear evidence of Milton's sociability under the right conditions:

Lawrence, of virtuous father virtuous son,
  Now that the fields are dank, and ways are mire,
  Where shall we sometimes meet, and by the fire
  Help waste a sullen day, what may be won
From the hard season gaining? Time will run
  On smoother, till Favonius reinspire
  The frozen earth, and clothe in fresh attire
  The lily and rose, that neither sowed nor spun.

What neat repast shall feast us, light and choice,
  Of Attic taste, with wine, whence we may rise
  To hear the lute well-touched, or artful voice
Warble immortal notes and Tuscan air?
  He who of these delights can judge, and spare
  To interpose them oft, is not unwise.

The first sonnet to Skinner is in similar tone: certainly not the voice of an ascetic or misanthropist. Mirth, he says, has her place as well as "deep thoughts" and "solid good":

  For other things mild Heaven a time ordains,
And disapproves that care, though wise in show,
  That with superfluous burden loads the day,
  And, when God sends a cheerful hour, refrains.

As Milton had no near acquaintance with the leading statesmen of the time, even of his own party, so it is equally true that he knew little or nothing personally of the leading scholars, men of letters, or men of religion. If his early intimacy with Charles Diodati had any parallel in later life, it was his friendship with Andrew Marvell. Marvell was, like Milton, a Cambridge man, but twelve years younger. When the Latin Secretary's blindness made an assistant necessary, Milton recommended Marvell for the post; but it was not till five years later, on the removal of Philip Meadows, that it was given him. Marvell's connection with the Cromwellian government was not of a kind to bring him into danger after the restoration. He was a member of the Commons which passed the Bill of Indemnity; and, as we have said, is supposed to have been one of the members who brought about the erasure of Milton's name from the list of those who were excepted from the operation of the bill. His friendship for Milton continued to the end of the poet's life. Unfortunately he has left no record of the intimacy, only some rather poor verses in which he expresses his admiration for the author of *Paradise Lost*.

We know a good deal of Milton's later life from his nephew Edward Phillips. It has been said that the character of his nephews was a plain commentary on Milton's theories of education, which encouraged contact with a great many things rather than thorough mastery of a few. But he was not responsible for their natural endowment; they were both shallow and flighty by nature. Milton must have been pretty thoroughly ashamed of them in later life. No doubt the stern moral atmosphere of his training had its provocative effect upon them. Once released from his control, they drifted with the fashionable current of the times. "The generation of young men," says Pattison, "who grew up under the Commonwealth, were in intellectual revolt against the restraint of Puritanism before they proceeded to political revolution against its authority. Long before the reaction embodied itself in the political fact of the Restoration, it had manifested itself in popular literature. . . . The press began timidly to venture on books of amusement, in a style of humour which seemed ribald and heathenish to the staid and sober covenanter. Something of the jollity and merriment of old Elizabethan days seemed to be in the air. But with a vast difference. Instead of 'dallying with the innocence of love,' as in *England's Helicon,* or *The Passionate Pilgrim,* the sentiment, crushed and maimed by unwise repression, found a less honest and less refined expression." In short, books of studied indecency began to be written. They could not be ignored by the Puritan authorities. And in 1656 we find Cromwell's Council of State censuring a book called *Sportive Wit, or the Muse's Merriment,* as containing "much lascivious and profane matter." This book was by John Phillips, Milton's younger nephew; and the elder brother, Edward, though he was considerably the staider of the two, published a book two years later called *Mysteries of Love and Eloquence* which Godwin declared to be "entitled to no insignificant rank among the multifarious productions issued from the press, to debauch the manners of the nation, and to bring back the King." These must have been grave offenses in Milton's eyes. Strangely enough, there seems to have been no open breach. Edward Phillips, at least, continued to visit his uncle to the last: in part, no doubt from the Boswellizing motive. As a literary hack in search of copy (if in no more generous guise), he already had it in mind to become his uncle's biographer. He can hardly have understood the real elements of Milton's greatness, but he purrs over his memory as that of a man to whom other men looked up. After the Salmasius episode, Milton's reputation was greater on the continent than in England. He became one of the British institutions which foreigners wished to see. "Learned foreigners of note could not part out of this city without giving a visit" to the uncle of Edward Phillips.

During the last fifteen years of his life Milton had to live frugally, though never poorly. First went his salary as secretary, then considerable sums invested in securities which became worthless on the Restoration. However, he had left something like six or seven hundred pounds income, in terms of modern money, which enabled him to support himself and three daughters, to marry again, and to keep two servants. After he became blind, his habits naturally changed. He no longer sat up late, and he rose very early: at four in summer and five in winter. His man read the Bible to him, then he "contemplated" till seven, when his man attended him again, and read to him or wrote for him till dinner. Then he walked in his garden (there was always a garden, wherever he might live), or, if the weather was bad, exercised in a swinging chair. Then came music: he played the bass-viol as well as the organ, but the organ principally. Often some one sang to his accompaniment, perhaps his young wife, who he said had a good voice, but no ear, or Edward Phillips, whom he had taught to sing. Then came more reading. From six to eight he received his friends, and at eight had a light supper. He was already troubled by gout, and had to be careful of his eating and drinking. After supper he smoked a pipe, drank a glass of water, and went to bed. He sometimes composed in bed, sometimes while walking in the garden. Often he could do nothing, occasionally he worked very fast. He was at his best " from the vernal to the autumnal equinox." He would carry his verses in his mind till the chance came to dictate them to one of his daughters, or to some visitor.

I think something too much has been made of Milton's loneliness and distress of spirit during these years. The cause with which he had identified himself for twenty years, was, to be sure, now lost; and the indifferent or hostile presence of his daughters in his household no doubt deepened that sense of helpless discomfort which seems to be recorded in *Samson Agonistes:*

> I dark in light exposed
> To daily fraud, contempt, abuse, and wrong,
> Within doors, or without, still as a fool
> In power of others, never in my own.

But his third marriage paved the way to greater domestic tranquillity, and pleasant human companionships fell to him. Above all, he was at last free, and ready, to undertake the great task which he had proposed to himself early in life, and which he had never ceased to ponder. That satisfaction was of a kind to outweigh a multitude of minor dissatisfactions. Shakespeare probably realized little or not at all the wonder of his achievement; but Milton knew very well what he was about: that he was now actually producing that masterpiece which coming generations would not willingly let die. Those quiet days with their opportunity and their achievement must have been in many ways the happiest of his life. One imagines the calm elation with which he must have composed, pacing his garden on summer afternoons, this matchless passage or that in a vein of sublimity hitherto unapproached by any poet of his race. Let those who may, pity the old blind Milton: to me he seems one of the most enviable of men.

Milton attended no church or congregation in these later years. His age and his blindness have been urged as excuses. But the pretty evident fact is that he outgrew the desire for formal worship. This was a perfectly natural outcome of his religious development. He was first a Church of England man, then a Presbyterian, then an Independent. Finally not even the latitude of Congregationalism was enough for him. Having rid himself first of episcopacy and second of all church government, he still found himself confined to a form of public worship which put him under tutelage. "A profound apprehension of the spiritual world," says Pattison, in this connection, "leads to a disregard of rites. To a mind so disposed, external forms become, first indifferent, then impertinent. Ministration is officious intrusion. I do not find that Milton, though he wrote against paid ministers as hirelings, ever expressly formulated an opinion against ministers as such. But as has already been hinted, there grew up in him, in the last period of his life, a secret sympathy with the mode of thinking which came to characterize the Quaker sect. Not that Milton adopted any of their peculiar fancies. He affirms categorically the permissibility of oaths, of military service, and requires that women should keep silence in the congregation. But in negativing all means of arriving at truth except the letter of Scripture interpreted by the inner light, he stood upon the same platform as the followers of George Fox."

It is significant that among the friends and helpers of his later years was a young Quaker, Thomas Ellwood, between whom and Milton there sprang up a real attachment. For some time Ellwood acted as volunteer reader, visiting Milton regularly. In connection with Milton's attitude toward religious observance may properly be mentioned the last two pieces of work with which he busied himself. The first was a tract, published before his death, dealing with the subject of religious toleration. He names various nonconformist sects as to be tolerated on account of their habit of drawing their faith direct from the Scriptures. For the rest, it is remarkable that the Roman Catholic faith alone is named as not to be tolerated. Against English Episcopacy he has nothing to say. The second was a long-projected *Treatise of Christian Doctrine.* The manuscript, finished in rough draft only, at his death narrowly escaped destruction, was lost sight of, and not printed till a century and a half later. Here he sets forth, mainly in Scriptural language, the body of doctrine which he has evolved at first hand from the study of the Bible. This doctrine, it is enough to say, the reader will find far more nobly expressed in the great poems, *Paradise Lost* and *Paradise Regained.*

Paradise Lost was begun in 1658, the last year of Cromwell's Protectorate. Professor Masson thinks the first two books were written before the Restoration. It was probably finished in rough draft five years later, and finally revised (according to Ellwood) in 1665. The general project of a great poetical work on that theme had been in his mind a quarter of a century before. At thirty he had nearly determined that his subject should be drawn from the Arthurian legends, and was planning for the epic form of treatment. Then he became uncertain as to whether the dramatic form would not be better — by which he meant the Greek, not the Elizabethan form; and later he abandoned the Arthurian theme for that of *Paradise Lost.* He drafted several plans for a heroic drama on this subject. In one of his early tracts, at a time when he felt himself drifting into the current of public controversy, he confides in his readers to this effect:

"Neither do I think it shame to covenant with any knowing reader that for some years yet I may go on trust with him toward the payment of what I am now indebted, as being a work not to be raised from the heat of youth, or the vapours of wine, like that which flows at waste from the pen of some vulgar amorist, or the trencher-fury of a riming parasite, nor to be obtained by the invocation of Dame Memory and her Siren daughters, but by devout prayer to that Eternal Spirit who can enrich with all utterance and knowledge, and sends out his Seraphim with the hallowed fire of his altar to touch and purify the lips of whom he pleases. To this must be added industrious and select reading, steady observation, insight into all seemly arts and affairs,—till which in some measure be compassed, at mine own peril and cost I refuse not to sustain this expectation from as many as are not loth to hazard so much credulity upon the best pledges that I can give them." At about the same time Edward Phillips, then a pupil in his uncle's house, heard read a passage, planned for the proposed tragedy, which was finally incorporated in the fourth Book of the poem. The lines are especially interesting because they show that already Milton had the figure of his chief person, Satan, clearly in mind.

The publication of the poem was probably delayed by the two great calamities which visited London: the Great Plague of 1665, and the Great Fire of the following year. The summer of the plague-year Milton spent in a cottage in the country, which had been found for him by the young Quaker Ellwood, and here Milton submitted the complete poem to Ellwood's judgment. The official licenser of such books was the Archbishop of Canterbury, and to him the author of *Areopagitica* had to submit his poem. But the great prelate could not be expected to attend to such matters in person, and the examination fell to a favorite chaplain of his, the Reverend Thomas Tompkins. He is said to have objected to certain passages, notably to the perilous figure of speech,

> As when the moon
> Looks through the horizontal misty air,
> Shorn of his beams, or, from behind the moon,
> In dim eclipse, disastrous twilight sheds
> On half the nations, and with fear of change
> Perplexes monarchs.

This, coming from the old Commonwealth's man might certainly be taken as seditious. But the Reverend Mr. Tompkins seems to have been (though something of a gladiator with his pen) a good-natured young cleric: at all events, he finally gave the manuscript his imprimatur, and it was presently published by one Samuel Simmons. A business arrangement was made by which Milton received five pounds down for the manuscript, five pounds more on the sale of a first edition of thirteen hundred copies, and five pounds each for two subsequent editions, if they should be called for. This has often been spoken of as a ridiculous bargain, as of course it was if poetry could ever expect to be paid for in accordance with its quality. I doubt if Milton would have made any better terms to-day. Five pounds then was not far short of twenty pounds, or one hundred dollars now. Such a work could not be expected to be popular; no publisher could count upon a large sale. Milton lived to receive the second five pounds, so that he had in all two hundred dollars on a sale of thirteen hundred copies. It would be a good sale for a book of poetry in our day, and an exceptionally good royalty. After the poet's death, his widow received eight of the ten pounds which might possibly, by the terms of the contract, have come to her. The weak side of the arrangement was not the smallness of the payments as far as they went, but the virtual relinquishment of rights by Milton after the three editions should have been published. After making his last payment to the widow, Simmons obtained a release from her, clinching his absolute ownership of the poem. He later sold his rights for twenty-five pounds to another bookseller, Aylmer, who in turn disposed of them at a profit to Tonson, the most enterprising and liberal publisher of the day. Tonson issued three elaborate editions before the close of the century. This publisher and his successors had a strict monopoly till 1750 of all of Milton's work.

But how was it possible for such a work to be listened to with any sort of favor in those cynical and dissolute days of the Restoration? Did it not "fall on evil days and evil tongues"? Would not its pure tones be obscured or submerged utterly in "the barbarous dissonance of Bacchus and his revellers," the laughter and indecent jests of Charles and his crew? It certainly did not "make a sensation." The serious Puritan remnant who recalled Milton as their former champion doubtless bought most of the few hundred copies of the poem which were printed before his death. But here and there in less likely quarters enthusiastic admirers were found: Sir John Denham, Lord Buckhurst,— above all, John Dryden. Dryden was a notable poet and a great critic. In his poetical work he showed himself a time-server, a pandar to the licentious tastes of Charles and his court. He was not without conscience, as his fits of remorse show; but he allowed himself to drift with the stream, and in due time had his reward of the laureateship. But as a critic he was incorruptible, and his wonder at the genius of Milton is tinged with that genuine humility which makes of Dryden so human and appealing a figure. "This man cuts us all out, and the ancients too!" he exclaimed after reading *Paradise Lost*. His opinion of it improved with time. In

1674 he wrote of it with high praise, and in his old age he deplored the fact that when that praise of the poem was written, he "knew not half the extent of its excellence." Worse, he had stooped to parody it in his *State of Innocence;* that must have been a humiliating memory for the ripe and wise old John Dryden whom Addison knew.

It will be recalled that Milton spent part of the plague-year in the country at a house found for him by Ellwood. That young friend was not able to welcome him to it, being just then in jail as a result of a row at a Quaker funeral, of all places! But as soon as he was released, he went to Milton, and had the reading of *Paradise Lost.* After reading it, Ellwood said one day, "Thou hast said much of Paradise Lost, but what hast thou to say of Paradise Found?" . . . "He made no answer," records the questioner, "but sat some time in a muse, then brake off that discourse, and fell on another subject." A year or two later, when Ellwood visited Milton in London, he "showed me his second poem, *Paradise Regained,* and in a pleasant tone said to me, 'This is owing to you; for you put it into my head by the question you put to me at Chalfont; which before I had not thought of.'" Milton himself thought highly of this sequel, and disliked to hear it called inferior to *Paradise Lost.* Wordsworth and Coleridge declared it better in execution. But the truth remains that it is comparatively dull. Satan is present, but no longer as the splendid rebel. The poet Blake said that "the reason why Milton wrote in fetters when he wrote of Angels and God, and at liberty when he wrote of Devils and Hell, is because he was a true poet, and of the Devil's party without knowing it." That is, no tragic or epic fabric can be wrought out of philosophical disquisition or elaborate description. The real theme must be the struggle of the human heart. And to this theme Milton returned, though with a restraint almost amounting to coldness, in *Samson Agonistes,* which shortly followed *Paradise Regained.* Both poems were published in a single volume in 1671. Thereafter Milton wrote no more poetry, contenting himself with the revision of his minor poems. It remained for him to conclude the several prose tasks which he had kept before him as firmly as that of his great poem.

Old age now came rather quickly upon him; there was a steady weakening of his constitution. The daughters had left home "to learn some curious and ingenious sorts of manufacture that are proper for women to learn, particularly embroideries in gold and silver." The poet and his young wife thereafter lived by themselves, with a single maid. Jonathan Richardson, the painter, has left a note upon him as he appeared during these last years:

"I have heard many years since that he used to sit in a coarse gray cloth coat at the door of his house near Bunhill Fields, without Moorgate, in warm sunny weather, to enjoy the fresh air, and so, as well as in his room, received the visits of people of distinguished parts as well as quality: and very lately I had the good fortune to have another picture of him from an aged clergyman of Dorsetshire, Dr. Wright. He found him in a small house, he thinks but one room on a floor. In that, in a room up one pair of stairs, which was hung with a rusty green, he found John Milton sitting in an elbow-chair, black clothes, and neat enough; pale but not cadaverous; his hands and fingers gouty, and with chalk-stones. Among other discourse he expressed himself to this purpose, — that, was he free from the pain this gave him, his blindness would be tolerable." He suffered comparatively little, however, and had still his hours of cheerfulness; so that we find him reported in the summer of 1674 as "very merry and seemed to be in good health of body." But on November 8, of the same year, he died, after a brief relapse, of "gout struck in." He was buried beside his father in the Church of St. Giles, Cripplegate: at his funeral service were "all his learned and great friends of London, not without a friendly concourse of the vulgar."

I have been able here simply to attempt a sketch of the man Milton, as he lived in the body. Such an attempt has special risks in his case: there is so much about his life that appears unamiable, the man was so little ingratiating, and had so little the knack of endearing himself in any intimate way. It is, after all, only through his poetry that we can know the best of such a man. We may best revere the memory of Milton not as the harsh sectary, the zealot and egotist of the divorce pamphlets and the quarrel with Salmasius, but as the most nobly inspired and deepest-toned of English poets.

JOHANN WOLFGANG GOETHE

From the painting by J. K. Stieler, 1828

GOETHE

NOT much more can be said of Goethe's ancestry than of Shakespeare's or Milton's. His great-grandfather was a Thuringian blacksmith. His grandfather was a tailor, who after an apprenticeship and some wandering, made his way to Frankfurt. Here he found work, prospered, became in due time a citizen of Frankfurt and a member of the tailor's guild; and presently married the daughter of the Master-tailor. Several children were born and died, to be followed shortly by the mother. Five years later he married again, this time a hearty widow, owner and hostess of an inn, whereupon he promptly ceased to be a tailor and became mine host. The younger of his two sons by this marriage was the father of the poet, who traces certain of his own characteristics direct to the inn-keeping pair. His grandfather, he says, was a ladies' man, and his grandmother was fond of finery and display. But he makes no direct mention in the autobiography of his horseshoeing or tailoring forbears. This is sufficiently explained by the fact that he had never known his father's father.

The tailor-innkeeper at least gave his son every possible advantage. Johann Caspar Goethe was educated well, allowed to travel, and became an

Imperial Councilor at Frankfurt. This, as we shall see, was unfortunately an honorary position. Henceforth he lived in his mother's house, with no other occupation than the management of his family. In 1748 he married the daughter of the chief magistrate, Johann Wolfgang Textor. It was this grandfather whom Goethe knew, and whose memory he affectionately cherished. For his father he evidently had more respect than affection. He was a stern man, without humor, rigid in his beliefs and his behavior; in short, a good deal the pedant and martinet. To him Goethe attributes his vigorous frame and methodical habit: "from my dear little mother my happy disposition and love of story-telling." The mother indeed had something close to genius — the genius, at least, of cheerful and even buoyant living under conditions which must have dispirited most women. A girl of very romantic nature, she was married by her family at the age of seventeen to the grim and in petty ways tyrannical councilor. She was eighteen at Goethe's birth. Five other children followed, of whom only one girl, Cornelia, lived to grow up. If there is any fact thrust upon the biographer, it is that until almost our own age, to be born into this world, even into a family in comfortable circumstances, meant hardly to be given an even chance of actually experiencing human life. The infant mortality in these families now pointed to by prophets of "race suicide" was shocking. The early loss of four children out of six cannot have seemed an unusual affliction to the mother of Goethe. It must indeed have been an exceptional sorrow which could have cast a permanent gloom over her cheerful nature. The two children who survived her were more than commonly lovable; and she made the most of them.

"On the 28th of August, 1749, at midday, as the clock struck twelve, I came into the world at Frankfurt-on-the-Maine. My horoscope was propitious; the sun stood in the sign of the Virgin, and had culminated for the day: Jupiter and Venus looked on with a friendly eye, and Mercury not adversely; while Saturn and Mars kept themselves indifferent; the Moon alone, just full, exerted her reflex power, all the more as she had then reached her planetary hour. She opposed herself, therefore, to my birth, which could not be accomplished till this hour was past."—With these words, characteristic in their quaintly humorous detail, begins Goethe's autobiography, that invaluable, if not always accurate, commentary on his youth and early manhood. The moon's untoward influence exerted itself beyond the moment of birth: the child showed slight signs of life, and was revived with difficulty. However, the favor of the other planets pulled him through.

His mother has recorded various traits of his childhood; that he was "much more easily moved to anger than to tears"; that he was devotedly fond of his little sister Cornelia, the only one of his brothers and sisters to grow up with him. Perhaps more significant is her account of his precocious love of beauty: how at three he refused to play with ugly children. He himself records his mischievousness, his night fears, his melancholy in the presence of a lovely landscape, or a scene of domestic merrymaking. His mother did what she could to make her children happy, and his father to make them — like himself. The father was, he says, "altogether of a didactic turn." He even played the pedagogue to his young wife during the early years of their marriage; and when the children came, determined to teach them himself. Goethe seems to have been a precocious child; a fact which of course has nothing to do, in one way or another, with his subsequent greatness. Exercises have been preserved which show him at the age of seven composing in German, Italian, French, Latin, and Greek. He could write Latin dialogues of merit, and turn off moral axioms with the ease of a philosopher in his dotage: "Horatius and Cicero were indeed Heathens, yet more sensible than many Christians, for the one says silver is baser than gold, gold than virtue, and the other says nothing is so beautiful as virtue. Who was truer in friendship than Damon? more generous than Alexander? more just than Aristides? more abstinent than Diogenes? more patient than Socrates? more humane than Vespasian? more industrious than Apelles and Demosthenes?"

The father, grim and self-centered as he was, did

not fail to see his son's superior promise. He expected him to become a jurist like himself, but a greater one. "He prized my natural endowments the more, because he had himself been wanting in them; for he had acquired everything only by means of unspeakable diligence, pertinacity, and repetition. He often assured me, early and late, both in jest and earnest, that with my talents he would have become something quite different from what he was, and managed the affairs of life to much better purpose." The father grew increasingly ambitious for the brilliant boy, as his education went on, and would talk to him of his future studies at Leipsic, his own university,— or at any other except Göttingen — for which the listener had a natural preference. Travel was also planned for, with Italy as its goal: "He dwelt upon it emphatically that Paris should first be seen, because after coming out of Italy nothing else could be pleasing." About Italy he would become eloquent: "His at other times serious and dry manner seemed on these occasions to relax and quicken." He had himself seen Italy, and had a deep love for all things Italian. He had some good engravings of Italian buildings and scenes, with some marbles and "natural curiosities" which he would expound. Certainly he inspired his children with "a passionate wish to become a part of the Paradise he described."

Italy came to mean more even to the son than to the father — or rather his enthusiasm meant more to the world. But there was much in the Frankfurt of his childhood to determine the bent of his imagination. It was a city full of the memories of ancient Germany, and yet already touched with the new industrial spirit. Goethe describes it all with lingering affection: the bridge over the Maine, on which he liked to walk as a boy, the Saalhof, standing on the site of Charlemagne's Castle; the old trading quarter with its crowded market-place; the Roman Hill. Above all, "what chiefly drew the observation of us children were the many little towns within towns, the fortresses within fortresses: viz., the walled monastic enclosures, and several other castle-like precincts, remaining from earlier times . . ." A certain liking for the antique thus seized the boy, which was specially nourished and promoted by old chronicles and wood-cuts, like those of Grave relating to the siege of Frankfurt. At the same time a quite different taste was developed in him for observing the actual conditions of mankind, in all their manifold variety and naturalness, without regard to their importance or their beauty. A favorite walk lay along a path that ran on the inner side of the city wall. Here they could see the real life of the city: "many thousand people amid their little domestic and secluded circumstances"; the courtyards, the gardens, the graveyards, the factories. "A many-colored, wonderful, ever-changing spectacle passed before us, with the enjoyment of which our childish curiosity was never satisfied. In fact, the celebrated Devil-upon-two-sticks, when he lifted the roofs of Madrid at night, scarcely did more for his friends than was done for us by the bright sunshine, in broad daylight."

Several incidents of childhood emerge with special distinctness from the level of his reminiscent narrative: most clearly perhaps a Christmas puppet-show at his grandmother's house which made a strong impression upon the fancy of the boy. This is all Goethe says of it in the *Wahrheit und Dichtung* (usually called in English the autobiography); but in *Wilhelm Meister's Apprenticeship,* a book almost equally autobiographical, there is a full description of the occasion and of the effect it had upon his childish imagination. The city fairs too, and various ancient observances in which the grandfather had an official part of some prominence, are among his sharp memories. The Lisbon earthquake brought him, at six, his first great mental shock. He had inherited from his mother a sensibility so tender that he found it necessary to cultivate a repression of feeling which led to the charge of coldness in mature life. Those public and private casualties which seem to act as an agreeable stimulant upon most members of the Teutonic race inspired in him a shuddering horror and pity. He would have found difficulty in reading a modern yellow journal. But we have so supped on horrors that a fresh one is simply a glut: we can barely taste. The Lisbon disaster, bad as it was, was not half so frightful in extent as the recent overwhelming of Sicily. But how many of us, at our safe distance, were profoundly moved by it? The child Goethe was fairly unstrung by the fate of Lisbon, and was moved (at six) to grave doubts of the justice and goodness of God.

The problem of existence was presently brought home to him in other ways: "I neither escaped measles, nor smallpox, nor any other complaint of childhood; and I was assured each time that it was a great piece of good luck that the evil was now past. But alas! still another threatened in the background, and advanced." There was nothing for it but the virtues of the Stoics, which he proceeded to practise.

These virtues were doubly necessary because the methodical father insisted on their making up for lost time in their studies as soon as they were convalescent. As is common in such instances, the mother indulged the children as much as the father domineered over them. She was a woman of remarkable quality, warm-hearted, humorous, a delightful companion and a lively letter-writer: above all determined to be happy and to make others happy. "I am fond of people, and that every one feels directly — young and old. I pass without pretension through the world, and that gratifies men. I never demoralize any one — always seek out the good that is in them, and leave what is bad to him who made mankind, and knows how to round off the angles. In this way I make myself happy and comfortable." This philosophy, as we shall see, the son inherited. The bond between them was very close: "I and my Wolfgang," she declared in later days, "have always held fast to each other, because we were both young together." His character is in an unusual sense traceable to these oddly-matched parents: his intellectual solidity and persistence comes plainly from the one, his high spirit, in many senses of the term, from the other.

During Goethe's seventh year began the Seven Year's War. Here a family difference arose, the grandfather siding with Austria, the father and small son with Frederick. Then came a French occupation of Frankfurt by the French, enemies of Frederick, and the quartering upon the Goethes of an accomplished officer who endeared himself to the children, but failed to ingratiate himself with the father. Altogether it was a lively episode: a French theater was established, and at ten Goethe had the use of a card of free admission, given to his grandfather. Of course the plays were in French, but he went nearly every afternoon, and picked up some acquaintance with the versified comedies which were then in vogue. He presently got to know a boy of the theater, made love to his sister, fought a duel with him, and submitted to him his first play. He had earlier shown instincts for verse-making and story-telling — the latter, as he says, derived directly from his mother. His stories were admitted by his companions to be superior to theirs; but he was astonished and disconcerted to find that they were as confident of the superiority of their verses as he was of his own.

In 1761 the French left Frankfurt, and the father, who had given himself up to gloomy retirement during their stay (which no doubt accounts for the freedom of his son's theatrical experience)—had in fact sulked—again found himself in the mood to look after his children's training. Under his supervision they took up drawing, music, mathematics, and English. Goethe had little interest in mathematics. He learned to play the harpsichord (and later the violoncello) very indifferently. Languages still absorbed him most, and he presently hit upon a plan for practising all his tongues at once, "by contriving a romance concerning several members of a family, who, separated from each other and scattered over the world, should communicate with each other in turn as to their conditions and prospects. The eldest brother writes German. A sister replies to one or the other of the family after the approved fashion of women, in short sentences and nothing but stops, all about domestic affairs, and the love-scandal of the neighborhood. Another brother studies theology, and writes very formal Latin, to which a Greek postscript is often appended. To the next brother, holding the place of clerk at Hamburg, the English correspondence naturally falls, while a still younger one at Marseilles has the French.

The Italian is imposed on a musician, on his first adventure in the world; while the youngest of all, a sort of pert little busybody, applies himself to Jew-German, other languages having been exhausted, and by means of his frightful cyphers brings the rest of them into desperation, and the old folks into a hearty laugh at his conceit." Evidently this was an exercise in dramatic humor as well as linguistics. Most boys of his age would be satisfied with the idea, or at most with an experiment or two toward its execution. But Goethe, as we have said, had his father's steadiness as well as his mother's quick fancy. He went at the thing in a very thorough-going way, studied the "geography of the countries to which my creations referred," invented incidents in character with his imaginary correspondents, and by hook and crook, got together a body of workmanlike notes. But this was not all, for finding himself awkward in handling the "jaw-breaking Jew-German," he made up his mind to study Hebrew by way of foundation, and actually got his father to provide him with a tutor. But Hebrew very soon interested him for its own sake; or rather, for the sake of the new acquaintance it gave him with the Old Testament. He grew absorbed in it as literature, and read deeply in the commentaries which belonged to his tutor: "In the long summer days I sat and read as long as I could, many times alone, until by-and-by he suffered me to take one volume after another home with me." This, it must be remembered, was no prig or mere bookworm, but a lively, normal boy. These scriptural studies were at the moment his favorite sport. One result was a Biblical prose epic on the story of Joseph, which he had copied out fair and bound up with some religious verses which he thought would please his father — as they did.

There were a dozen things he was as much interested in as Hebrew. He was always picking up knowledge in connection with various crafts — making the acquaintance of artisans and watching them at work. And he was by no means content to find companions of his own age only among the members of his own class. At fourteen he had somehow become intimate with a group of young people who lived somewhat precariously as copyists and tutors among the lower class. Through his acquaintance with them he got into his first love-affair and his first serious scrape. Among them was a beautiful girl some two years older than Goethe, a sweet and modest girl with whom he promptly fell in love. He was above her class; his attentions pleased her, and she allowed herself some little familiarities with him which she would not let him return. Suddenly one of these associates was accused of forgery, and the rest were indirectly implicated. Goethe's acquaintance with them was discovered, and he was called upon to give an account of his relations with them. Boylike, he blurted out the whole matter, including his romantic attachment for Gretchen. She was promptly sent away from Frankfurt, and he never saw her again. His grief was softened by the affront to his boyish pride in Gretchen's forthcoming testimony that she had known him, but had done him no harm: "I always treated him as a child, and my affection for him is only that of a sister." Yet his grief was real, and he never forgot her. She is supposed to have been, more than anyone else, the model of the Margarete in *Faust*.

Frankfurt was the most important of the cities which, up to the middle of the nineteenth century, ranked as free or independent cities of the Holy Roman Empire. "The imperial crown could strictly only be received at Rome. But the crown of the subordinate dignity of 'King of the Romans' was conferred at Frankfurt (formerly Aix-la-Chapelle); and the emperors of modern times dispensed with the imperial coronation. Sometimes the emperor caused his successor to be elected and crowned during his own lifetime." At the time of the affair with Gretchen, (1763) such a coronation took place — that of Archduke Joseph as Joseph II., heir to the Empire and King of the Romans. Goethe gives a very full description of the ceremony and attendant festivities in his autobiography.

The Gretchen experience apparently led the Imperial Councilor to feel that stricter oversight of his son was advisable. He was placed under the supervision of a tutor, who tried to interest him in philosophy without great success, but at all events did not seriously antagonize him. Goethe still mourned Gretchen, or rather, perhaps, cherished the luxury of loving her without hope. He walked much, sketched much, and did a little traveling with the tutor. He was really waiting to be old enough to go to the university. He went to Leipsic in October, 1765, destined by his father to study jurisprudence, though he would have preferred the humanities and Göttingen. He carried a letter of introduction to a professor of law; and ingenuously confided to him his preference for literary studies. Naturally he received no encouragement, and he seems for a time to have devoted himself faithfully to the studies in law and logic laid down for him. But his distaste for them soon reasserted itself, and his activity found natural outlet in the amusements of the ordinary undergraduate. His letters of the period show a disposition to affect a wildness and irresponsibility beyond what he really displayed. A Leipsic lady, wife of the law professor, takes him in hand and reforms his provincial dress and manners. He becomes something of a fop, and the "ladies' man" develops in him rapidly. His letters to friends of his own age whom he has left in Frankfurt display, among much that is undeniably clever, a youthful facetiousness and a worldly pose which show how much he has in common with the typical undergraduate. He alludes mysteriously to sentimental attachments, writes long rigmaroles in verse, is melancholy, — is, on the whole a perfectly natural if voluble Freshman. His attendance on one of his courses is interfered with by the discovery that near the Professor's house "the most delicious fritters came hot out of the pan just at the hour of lecture."

Presently he became intimate in the family of a wine-merchant named Schönkopf. His wife was of Frankfurt, treated her young fellow-townsman hospitably, and he was not long in falling in love with the eldest daughter, Anna Katharina, commonly called Käthchen, though in the autobiography Goethe calls her Annete or Annchen. She was a beautiful and lively girl, who seems to have been worthy of him. After some mystification and pretense of being attached to some one else, he confided in his friend, Horn, who describes her enthusiastically in a letter to a third friend. "He loves a young lady beneath him in rank, but a girl whom — I do not think I say too much — you would love yourself if you saw her. I am no lover, so I shall write entirely without passion. Imagine to yourself a woman well-grown, though not very tall; a round, agreeable, though not extraordinarily beautiful face; open, gentle, engaging manners; a very pretty understanding without having had any great education. He loves her very tenderly, with the perfect, honest intentions of a virtuous man, though he knows that she can never be his." It is not clear that he conveyed this latter bit of knowledge to

Käthchen. But very likely she divined it (like Gretchen, she was somewhat his senior) and so protected her heart from his attentions, while, womanlike, making the most of them. After a time he allowed himself to tease her with a jealousy to which he had not acquired the right. Their intimacy, whatever it may have amounted to, became less, and not long after she married a man to whom Goethe had introduced her. It is impossible to suppose that his feeling for her was deep. His letters of the time do not ring true. But there is no doubt of his conviction that his heart was broken. For a time after their first break he took to dissipation (in the form of coffee, beer, and late hours) and at least succeeded in wrecking his digestion, which was no doubt a vast satisfaction to him. The result was a serious hemorrhage, from which, with proper care, he slowly rallied. In the summer of 1768 he returned to Frankfurt.

As the autobiography shows, his years in Leipsic had been devoted only incidentally to the study of jurisprudence. He had won permission to attend the courses of Gellert in literature and morals, and gave much better attention to his lectures than to those on logic and jurisprudence. Gellert was apparently one of the rare teachers who inspire a personal affection and devotion in their pupils. He gave little attention to them individually, and yet they all loved him. Goethe received little encouragement from him or from anybody else in his attempts at poetry while he was in Leipsic. Madame Böhme (wife of the law professor) took charge of his improvement not only in dress and social manners, but in literary taste. Goethe's poetic enthusiasms hitherto had been for a crude German school of which Madame Böhme and others showed him the defects; and they probably did him good service by giving his own attempts very little praise. But it was a serious matter to him at the time. "I found myself in the miserable situation in which a man is placed, when a complete change of mind is required of him, a renouncing of all that he has hitherto loved and found good. After some time, however, and many struggles, I conceived so great a contempt for my labors, begun and ended, that one day I burned up poetry and prose, plans, sketches, and projects all together in the kitchen fireplace, and threw our good old landlady into no small fright and anxiety by the smoke-clouds that filled the whole house." On the whole the Leipsic years seem to have been good for him; it was a refining experience such as he would hardly have got at the universities,— Jena or Halle, for example,— where the unruliness of the student was taken much as a matter of course. Self-assertion, crudeness, extravagance of any sort, were frowned upon in Leipsic, and Goethe returned to Frankfurt a very different person from the callow young provincial who had set out so complacently a few years before to take the world by storm.

He did not find matters running very smoothly at

home. His sister Cornelia had turned bitter and sullen. His father had "concentrated all his fondness for teaching upon her in Goethe's absence. He had pretty much confined her to the house for three years, and forced her to spend all her time in study. He had even virtually dictated her letters to her brother. He was, in short, one of those most miserable of domestic pests, a man of busy instinct with nothing to do (his councilorship being purely honorary) but harass the members of his own household. What a commentary there is in Goethe's remark, after enlarging upon his sister's wretchedness: "My father was personally pretty comfortable. He was in good health, spent a great part of the day in my sister's instruction, wrote at the description of his travels, and was longer in tuning his lute than in playing on it." He was naturally little pleased with the return of the son, from whom he had expected so much, a semi-invalid, by no means ready for his degree, and with "mind still more out of order than his body." But, to do him justice, there seems to have been nothing really harsh in his attitude. Under the devoted care of his sister and mother Goethe gradually improved mentally and physically. His father cannot have regarded his studies in law at Leipsic an absolute failure, for it was finally decided that he should go on toward his degree at Strasburg, with jurisprudence still as his object. Meantime his holiday had not been wasted. He seems to have pondered upon his faults to some purpose, and once more, before leaving for Strasburg, made a general sacrifice of all his verses, and some dramatic fragments.

He kept two plays, the first of them inspired by his treatment of Käthchen Schönkopf, and mercilessly dissecting himself in the character of a jealous lover. He had also done some drawing and etching, and dabbled in alchemy, in which there were still educated believers. Here again we discern a trace of *Faust* in the making.

He had chafed a good deal in the narrow atmosphere of Frankfurt, and a quarrel with his father, over a matter of taste, made him very ready to set out for Strasburg, as he did in the spring of 1770. From Strasburg he writes gloomily at first: "It is indeed all twilight in this world: a trifle more or less; one may console oneself with that. . . . I have now been a fortnight here, and find Strasburg not a hairsbreadth better or worse than all that I am acquainted with upon this earth,— that is to say, very ordinary." After a few months he begins to be more cheerful: he even finds a good word to say for his law studies: "Jurisprudence begins to please me much. Thus it is with everything as with Merseburg beer: one shudders the first time, but if one has drunk it a week, one cannot give it up again. . . . And alchemy is still as ever my secret love. Still as ever the old madcap. . . ."

Other loves he had outside his proposed course of

studies. There were medical students at his table, and with his faculty of interesting himself in what interested his associates, it was not long before he was attending lectures in chemistry and anatomy. And there were loves of a less abstract sort. Goethe was in his twenty-first year, and had reached his physical prime. He was of middle height, but so well-built, deep-chested and erect of carriage as to appear tall. His features were commanding, and his eyes dark and brilliant. He dressed fashionably, talked well, and had his mother's faculty of the sympathetic listener. The effect of all these attractions upon the maiden hearts of Strasburg was what might have been expected. To perfect himself in the character of ladies' man he took dancing lessons of a French master who had two pretty daughters as assistants. Goethe seems to have flirted with one of them, who was barely safe from him on the score of being betrothed. The other fell desperately in love with him, and there was a melodramatic scene which is whimsically described in the ninth book of the autobiography. There are certain love-poems of the period which indicate other experiences of the kind: he was soon to have a much more serious affair.

Strasburg was nominally a French town. It was there, a month after Goethe's arrival, that Marie Antoinette, the bride-elect of the Dauphin, was formally given over to the French ambassador. But the tone of the university and of the town itself was defiantly

German, and it was a German culture that Goethe there received. Goethe had been taught to sneer at Gothic art, and at least permitted to acknowledge the German literary genius as essentially inferior to the French. He now came to love the Strasburg Cathedral and what it stood for — a strong and native German art. And he now found himself in contact with active minds which did not hesitate to exalt German ruggedness over French refinement. Lessing, Klopstock, and Herder were hailed as forerunners of a mighty national movement. Goethe read a life of Götz von Berlichingen, and the idea of turning him to dramatic account was already in his mind. Some vague notion of a Faust drama had also occurred to him.

After a year at Strasburg, Goethe passed his examinations for his degree, remaining to prepare his thesis. It was at this time that he made an acquaintance which meant much to his intellectual life, and indeed did much to mature him in every way. Johann Gottfried Herder was but five years older than he, but had already made a reputation as a critic of the new school. He had come under the influence of Rousseau, had adopted his humanitarian philosophy, and had proceeded to apply it to the criticism of literature as well as of life. Like Rousseau, he had a greater regard for his fellow-man than for his fellow-men. The reverse was true of Goethe. Herder was bitter against actual human beings because they did not come up to his theory of them; Goethe had endless tolerance and affection for the individuals with whom he came in contact,— himself included. Fortunately Herder could not change Goethe's nature in this respect, but was of real service in leading him to feel that great poetry is the product of a national force, and not only of a single talent. He set Goethe studying the Bible, Homer, and Shakespeare from this point of view; and perhaps gave him for the first time a sense of safety in following his natural instinct of self-expression. At this time, too, *Percy's Reliques* came into his hands, and taught him the dignity of folk-literature. He soon began a collection of German popular ballads and songs, which yielded much poetic material as time went on. Herder had an enthusiasm for various English authors, among them Goldsmith. He read the *Vicar of Wakefield* to Goethe and a number of others.

It happened that Goethe had a fellow-boarder named Weyland, a native Alsatian, who knew the country about Strasburg intimately, and often acted as Goethe's guide. On one of these expeditions they visited the family of a country clergyman, who appealed to Goethe as strikingly like the Primroses of Wakefield. The younger daughter, Frederike, was a charming girl, and she and Goethe, aided by some boy-and-girl fooling, not only fell in love at first sight, but came to a sufficiently good understanding at second. There is a delightful description of the whole episode in the autobiography, of which only the description of Frederike may be quoted here: "A short, white, full skirt, with a furbelow, not so long but it left the neatest little foot visible up to the ankle; a tight white bodice and a black taffeta apron,— there she stood, on the boundary between country beauty and city belle. Slender and airy, she tripped along as if she had nothing to carry, and her neck seemed almost too delicate for the luxuriant braids of flaxen hair on her elegant little head. A free, open glance beamed from her calm blue eyes, and her pretty little turned up nose peered inquiringly into the air with as much unconcern as if there could be nothing like care in the world; her straw hat dangled on her arm, and thus, at the first glance, I had the delight of seeing her perfect grace, and acknowledging her perfect loveliness." Goethe made a virtual declaration on his first visit to Sesenheim, wrote an undeniable love letter on his return to Strasburg, and lost no time in paying other visits, undisguisedly on Frederike's account. Her parents seem to have regarded them as virtually betrothed. It must be said that Goethe's conduct in this affair was not upon a plane to give him satisfaction as he recalled it in later life. Between his first sight of Frederike and his first letter (the briefest possible intervals) we find him writing to another and unknown lady in a vein of gallantry. "And you, my dear friend," the letter closes, " whom, amongst many, I can so name especially, accept this letter as a new pledge that I shall never forget you." Clearly he is not to be off with the old because on with the new. Next day he composes his letter to Frederike, calls her his dear new friend. If she is not his friend "there is no truth in glances." "My eye found in yours the hope of this friendship, and for our hearts I could swear." As usual, it has not been hard for him to conquer or to be conquered.

But presently, as he says, his love was put to "a severe test." During the winter he was kept in Strasburg by the necessity of working hard upon his dissertation. It was probably by arrangement between the lovers that the mother brought her two daughters for an extended visit at the house of a rich relative. Here Goethe saw his beloved in a different setting. She was too proud or too simple to abandon her country dress or manners, and Goethe, with the snobbishness of his age, found both unbecoming in the city. It may be that Frederike's innocent air of proprietorship put him out. At all events, he seems to have thought better of the whole bargain. It was a relief to him when she went back to Sesenheim, and he seems never to have followed her there. According to the code of the time, a match between the son of the Imperial Councilor of Frankfurt, a man of substance (thanks to his inn-keeping mother), and the country parson's daughter, would no doubt have been regarded as unequal. No better excuse can be urged in Goethe's favor than this sufficiently paltry one. His desertion of the loving girl, whose devotion to him there is no cause to doubt, evidently caused him much mental suffering; but it was not the less a desertion. Even his suffering (as in the instance of Käthchen) may have been chiefly due to his sense of having lost the delicious experience called love. A letter written to another fair unknown in the spring of this year is to the point: "When I talk of love, I mean that agitation of feeling in which our heart floats ever hovering to and fro around one spot, whenever any attraction has shifted it out of the ordinary path of indifference. We are like children on their rocking-horses, always in motion, always at work, yet never leaving the spot. That is the truest picture of a lover." In this same epistle he laments the lack of "a light, free heart," makes a sentimental allusion to Käthchen, and sends the following uncompromising message to a further charmer of whom we know nothing else: "Tell my Franzchen that I am still ever hers. I am very fond of her, and am often angry with myself because she tortures me so little. When one is in love, one wishes to be in fetters."

There is no mistaking in all this the note of the professional eighteenth century philanderer: the complacent male who, with the most extravagant adoration and reverence for the sex, found no woman worth being faithful to. Up to this point, certainly, and including the Frederike episode, Goethe's affairs had been affairs of self-love in a guise which he did not himself recognize. He had yet to become a man in his relations to woman. There are, at least, a few fine lyrics which the world owes to Frederike. Something less than a year after their first meeting, shortly after taking his degree, he parted with her, leaving her, as he has recorded with scrupulous accuracy, in tears. Nothing seems to have been said at the moment to suggest that it was a final parting, but Goethe doubtless meant it to be so. The real fact is probably that he had allowed himself to drift into a romantic relation, without any serious thought of marriage. They met once again, eight years later. Frederike seems to have come to feel that the separation had been necessary for him. She lived in the memory of their relation, and there is a tradition that she turned away all suitors with the words: "The heart that Goethe has loved cannot belong to another."

In Strasburg he had come for the first time strongly under the spell of Shakespeare, not only by Herder's influence, but through association with a group of young Shakespeare enthusiasts, who had met often in the name of the great English master.

The influence of the new Shakespeare-cult upon the younger German minds at this time was prodigious. His name afforded them a mighty battle cry in their war against the classical French drama. The force and exuberance which were an offense to French taste were precisely what recommended him to these young rebels. An oration by Goethe delivered before the Shakespeare circle has been preserved. It is interesting not only as a personal manifesto, but as a sign of the times: "The first page of his that I read made me his for life; and when I had finished a single play, I stood like one born blind, on whom a miraculous hand bestows sight in a moment. I saw, I felt, in the most vivid manner, that my existence was infinitely expanded, everything was now unknown to me, and the unwonted light pained my eyes. By little and little I learned to see, and, thanks to my receptive genius, I continue vividly to feel what I have won. I did not hesitate a moment about renouncing the classical drama. The unity of place seemed to me irksome as a prison, the unities of action and of time burthensome fetters to our imagination; I sprang into the open air, and felt for the first time that I had hands and feet."

In August, 1771, he returned to Strasburg, and at once applied for a license to practise as advocate. He had now satisfied his father, and at once turned his energies toward something very different from the practice of the law. This was a drama upon the subject of the German sixteenth century hero whose autobiography he had read at Strasburg, and who no doubt seemed to him fit to represent the revolt against accepted authority of which he and his associates regarded themselves as champions. The first version of the play, *The History of Gottfried of Berlichingen with the Iron Hand, Dramatised,* was written during the following winter. It is a work of irregular power, and simply what it claims to be — a dramatized chronicle. The second version, called *Götz von Berlichingen,* was published two years later, and made a great impression as one of the first forcible utterances of the Sturm und Drang (Storm and Stress) movement in German literature. It was, as we have seen, a movement of conscious revolt; in 1772 the *Frankfurter Gelehrter Anzeigen* was founded as its declared organ. Goethe joined its staff of reviewers, and many of his contributions are to be found in his collected works. His father had been inclined to take pride in his literary ability as well as in his legal acquirements, but he must have found little satisfaction in his son's connection with what he would have looked upon as a foolish demonstration.

Father Goethe was nothing if not persistent, and true to his determination to make a great advocate of his son, he presently despatched him to Wetzlar, so that he might observe the majesty of the law in its actual workings. As a matter of fact, it was the last place to impress a mind like Goethe's. The Imperial Court of Justice at Wetzlar was, says Lewes, "a Court of Appeal for the whole empire, a sort of German Chancery. Such a chaotic accumulation of business as this Wetzlar Kammer-Gericht presented was perhaps never seen before. Twenty thousand cases lay undecided on Goethe's arrival, and there were but seventeen lawyers to dispose of them. About sixty was the utmost they could get through in a year, and every year brought more than double that number to swell the heap. Some cases had lingered through a century and a half, and still remained far from a decision." It is not to be imagined that Goethe spent many hours attending these unconscionable sessions. Fortunately a commission had been appointed by the different states of the Empire to inquire into the affairs of the court, and Goethe found himself thrown with a lively group of secretaries and attachés belonging to this commission. They had got up a burlesque Order of Knighthood, of which the members were called by such fanciful names as St. Amand the Opinionative, Eustace the Prude, and so on. Goethe evidently talked of his hobby of the moment, and was dubbed Götz von Berlichingen the Trusty. He entered into this nonsense with gusto for a time, but his melancholy moods returned. He spent many days rambling alone about the country with his sketch-book. It was the "Ewigweiblichheit"— the ever-womanly — for which he unconsciously searched, and which he presently found in a new guise.

All that he needed to free him from the memory of Frederike was a fresh enchantment; and he found it in the person of a certain Charlotte Buff, the original of the Charlotte in *Werther*. She was of the same general type as Käthchen and Frederike,— a sweet and merry and feminine type,— but with greater dignity and self-command. Moreover, she was already betrothed, though informally, to a Dr. Kestner, Secretary of the Hanoverian legation. Certain letters of his, published long after by his son, show how extraordinary the relation of these three became.

"It happened that Goethe was at a ball in the country where my maiden and I also were. I could only come late, and was forced to ride after them. My maiden, therefore, drove thither in other society. In the carriage was Dr. Goethe, who in the carriage here first saw Lottchen. . . . No woman here had pleased him. Lottchen at once fixed his attention. . . . He did not know she was betrothed. I came a few hours later; and it is not our custom in public to testify anything beyond friendship for each other. . . ."

The next day Goethe called on her, and found her the center of a charming group. She was the oldest of a large family of orphans, and took the best of care of them. Charlotte, to be sure, seems to have had really nothing to recommend her that Frederike lacked. If she had not been protected by her attachment for Kestner, another episode of the familiar kind might easily have followed. Probably Goethe would not have married anybody at all. The fact of her engagement gave him a sense of safety. But indeed, the conduct of all three was romantically generous, if not wise. Kestner accepted Goethe's feeling for Lottchen as a tribute rather than an affront to his beloved.

The two men became really intimate friends. Goethe was constantly at Charlotte's house, and undoubtedly made such love to her as he could without actual treachery to his friend: and a good deal of leeway was permitted in that sentimental day. She grew fond of him. "But," says Kestner, "Lottchen knew how to treat him so that no hope could germinate within him. His peace of mind suffered much in consequence"— apparently nothing could disturb Kestner's —"there were remarkable scenes, in which Lottchen gained in my opinion; and he must needs become dearer to me as a friend, though I was often forced to wonder what strange creatures love can make of even the strongest and otherwise most self-contained people."

It was just as well that the situation was not too greatly prolonged. Goethe put an end to it by making off without taking leave. Both Charlotte and Kestner regretted him sincerely; and the whole affair terminated with honor to all parties. "I leave you happy," reads his parting note to Charlotte, "and shall remain in your heart. And shall see you again; but *not to-morrow is never!*" There is no doubting the sincerity of his emotion; yet he had not even now experienced the passion of love. He missed Charlotte Buff, as he had missed Käthchen and Frederike,— less for what she was than for what she stood for in his poetic fancy. In a month or two he is consoling himself with the dark eyes of the pretty Maximiliane

Laroche. The von Laroches were a family with whom he stayed in Coblentz, on his way back to Frankfurt. The mother was something of a blue-stocking, and Goethe corresponded with her for a long time.

He now pleased his father and surprised his friends by actually practising as advocate, and that with a good deal of energy. However, he kept up his writing for the *Gelehrter Anzeigen,* and began to revise the *History of Gottfried von Berlichingen.* The second version was much more compact and dramatic than the first, but Goethe regarded it also as a preliminary study, and published it only by the urgent advice and with the financial help of his friend Merck. In spite of Herder's lukewarm and really ungenerous judgment of it, its projectors were confident of the book's success, and arranged to share the profits. They were right as to its success, which was immediate and astonishing. "Its bold expression of the spirit of freedom," says Lewes, "its defiance of French criticism, and the originality no less than the power of the writing, carried it triumphant over Germany. It was pronounced a masterpiece in all the salons and all the beer-houses of that uneasy time. Imitations followed with amazing rapidity; and the stage was noisy with the clang of chivalry, the bookshelves creaked beneath the weight of resuscitated Middle Ages." In short, it was the "Storm and Stress" masterpiece. Profits there were none for the author and his sponsor, on account of the numerous pirated editions which at once appeared, and against which there was then no protection. Nevertheless, a bookseller offered him a handsome sum for a round dozen of plays in the same style: the mere prestige of the poet's name was now a marketable commodity. *Götz von Berlichingen* expresses whatever was noblest in the Storm and Stress movement, as well as much of its sound and fury. So the *Sorrows of Werther,* which was shortly to follow, expresses (in far less offensive form than it is to be found in many other works of the time) that strain of mawkish sentimentalism which marked this same movement.

The success of *Götz* undoubtedly did much to establish Goethe's faith in his future. The qualities of daring or of revolt against outworn conventions, with which he had invested his hero, were also his own. But he was soon to express, in Werther, another side of his nature, another and more characteristic aspect of his time. For the unrest reflected by the Storm and Stress movement, the unrest which permeated the life of Europe in that day, more often took the form of despairing vacillation than of strong and decided revolt. The evolution of Werther is not hard to follow. The affair of Charlotte and Kestner had not ended abruptly like those of Käthchen and Frederike. There was a permanent charm in her inaccessibility. He could safely indulge in a vague romantic feeling for the promised bride of his friend. The long series of letters from Goethe to Kestner, after Goethe's retreat from Wetzlar, could hardly have been so written and so received in any other age. They embody, in fact, a sort of prolonged and air-drawn flirtation with the girl by way of her lover. He has her silhouette on his wall and kisses it before he goes to bed; he asks for some little memento, something she has worn. He takes it amiss that she has not dreamt of him: "Have I not been with her body and soul, and dreamt of her day and night?" Gradually he becomes calmer, admits that he is happy, admits even that he is pleased with this maiden and that. The approach of Charlotte's marriage in the following spring brings about something of a relapse. He demands mournfully that he be allowed to choose the wedding rings. The news of the marriage comes a little sooner than he has expected, and he writes: "God bless you, for you have surprised me. Good Friday I was going to make a holy sepulchre, and bury Lotte's silhouette. So she hangs there still, and shall hang there, too, until I die. Farewell. . . . I wander in deserts where no water is, my hair is my shade, and my blood my well. And yet your ship, just in port, with gay flags and shouts, makes me glad." We have no cause to doubt the generous reality of his gladness; and his woe is no doubt real to his poetic fancy. But three days later, on the Good Friday which was to have been a day of sacrifice, "as I sprang to my window, and heard the little birds, and saw the budding almond-trees, and the hedges all green under the glorious sky, I could no longer withhold the good spring feelings of warm youth." The world was not over for him yet. But it was a lonely summer in many ways. His sister Cornelia was married and went away. His best friend, Merck, left Frankfurt.

He had at this time a plan for a drama on Mahomet, of which he wrote only a few fragments. From what he tells us of its scheme, it might have proved an imposing poem, and his mind was full of other schemes. It may be that an experience of the following year hastened the writing of *Werther,* which had for some time been taking shape in his mind. Maximiliane Laroche, whose society had helped him to bear the first pang of his parting with Lotte, married a middle-aged widower of Frankfurt. Goethe's relation to the Laroches seems to have been founded upon a real affection. He corresponded regularly with the mother, addressing her as "Mama," and he alludes to "dear Max" in precisely the same tone before and after her marriage. His natural attentions to the daughter after her marriage seem to have been misinterpreted by her husband, greatly to Goethe's rage and distress. *Werther* was written, by his own account, in four weeks. He shut himself up during this time, and would see no one, so that Merck thought the success of *Götz* had turned his head.

In the following September *Werther* had been printed but not published. And now Goethe does an amazing thing. He has outlived whatever was painful in his feeling for Charlotte, has made shameless copy of it, and now sends his effusion first of all to her and Kestner, apparently confident that they will be pleased with the performance. "Lotte," he writes, "how dear this little book is to me thou wilt feel in reading it, and this copy is as dear to me as if it were the only one in the world. Thou must have it, Lotte; I have kissed it a hundred times; have kept it locked up that no one might touch it. O Lotte! And I beg thee let no one except Meyers see it yet; it will be published at the Leipsic fair. I wish each to read it alone, thou alone, Kestner alone,— and each to write me a little word about it. Lotte, adieu, Lotte."

But *The Sorrows of Young Werther* (as its full title ran) was too much even for the long-suffering Kestner: he and his Lotte were unfeignedly angry at the public exhibition, in highly embellished form, of an episode which had been sufficiently trying. For the story of Werther is, up to a certain point, the story of Goethe and Charlotte and Kestner: Lotte is there to the life, to the very name. Albert, the inconvenient betrothed, is, by all accounts, a feeble travesty of Kestner, who was by no means a weakling. Lotte is represented as in the end struggling almost hopelessly against a growing passion for Werther; and Werther shoots himself as the only way out for all concerned. Yet the Kestners did not enjoy it! There has seldom been such an illustration of the pitiless egotism of genius. The fact probably is that Goethe felt the importance of the story as a work of art, and took it for granted his friends would take pride in their share in it.

The effect of *Werther* was immense; but not wonderful. It took all Europe by storm because it gave Europe a voice. "And here," says Carlyle, "lies the secret of Goethe's popularity. In his deep, susceptive heart he felt a thousand times more keenly what every one was feeling; with the creative gift which belonged to him as a poet, he bodied it forth into visible shape, gave it a local habitation and a name; and so made himself the spokesman of his generation. *Werther* is but the cry of that dim, rooted pain under which all men of a certain age were languishing: it paints the misery, it passionately utters the complaint; and heart and voice all over Europe loudly and at once respond to it. True, it prescribes no remedy; for that was a far different, far harder enterprise, to which other years and a far higher culture were required; but even this utterance of pain for the present is grasped at, and with eager sympathy appropriated in every bosom . . . the first thrilling peal of that impassioned dirge which, in country after country, men's ears have listened to till they were deaf to all else."

So *Werther* "became a people's book, hawked about the streets, printed on miserable paper, like an ancient ballad; and in the Chinese empire, Charlotte and Werther were modelled in porcelain." Some voices,

Lessing's and a few others', deprecated the extravagance of the book and its effect. It represented the mingling of insatiable desire and feeble will which marked the intellectual life of the Europe of that day. It was a diseased condition, mentally and physically, which the study of *Werther* revealed to the life. Goethe understood it, shared it up to a certain point: went to bed on one occasion with a dagger by his side, and tried its point upon his breast, and so on. But his will never actually failed him; when *Werther* was written he had outlived the Werther phase of his own experience. But his nature was still in turmoil; or rather his mind was seething with different and often conflicting projects. And his heart, or his romantic fancy, was by no means at rest. It is not long before we hear of his falling in love anew with some unnamed maiden of Frankfurt, and barely escaping betrothal. There is a literary relic of this intimacy also in *Clavigo,* a prose drama written at the maiden's suggestion. This play and its successor, *Stella,* are written in prose and carefully observe the unities for which Goethe had expressed total contempt a few years earlier, in his first enthusiasm over Shakespeare. *Clavigo* was mediocre literature, but good drama; it is said to hold its place still on the German stage. Of *Stella* and other minor works of the time we need say nothing. The important fact is that by this time *Faust* had so far shaped itself in his mind that he had actually begun its composition, though we hear little of it till some time later.

Whatever he wrote, he was living all the time, eagerly and actively. He rode, fenced, skated, with inexhaustible energy. He was to be seen in all circles, — at dances and all kinds of public functions. He makes friends everywhere. Of the poet Klopstock, of the philosopher Lavater, of the dirty and inspiring disciple of Rousseau, Basedow, we hear much. And he is still responsive to the charm of the maiden — the very young maiden, as always. In 1775 he was somehow introduced into a circle at Frankfurt above that in which his family moved, and met there a Lili (Anna Elizabeth) Schönemann, who was evidently a young person of his favorite age and favorite type,— pretty, sixteen, and innocently coquettish. He at once laid siege, had as usual no difficulty in making himself beloved, and actually became engaged. It may be that his social inferiority and the moderate opposition of the girl's parents to the match were what unconsciously led him to desire the engagement. At all events, the matter was no sooner settled than he found his mind all unsettled. There were, in fact plenty of sensible objections to his marriage such as had not existed in the case, for example, of Frederike Brion. Lili could hardly have been happy in the Goethe household: "How would they welcome a fine lady, inured to luxury, elegance, and gay society; and how would she reconcile herself to the homely ways of their old-fashioned and unpretentious household?" However, for a time Goethe tried to make the best of his happiness, and settled down to his profession with the determination of one who proposes to work in domestic harness for the rest of his days. Lili seems to have made matters a little hard for him by enjoying the attentions of other young men in a manner not uncommon in good society, but hardly pleasant to a lover of Goethe's jealous temper. And the exuberant young poet must have found it hard enough to keep within bounds in the calmly correct atmosphere of the aristocratic circle in which his betrothed had been born. In a letter (to a lady) he describes the two Goethes of this period, the bound and the free: "If you can imagine a Goethe in braided coat, from head to foot in the gallantest costume, amid the glare of chandeliers, fastened to a card table by a pair of bright eyes, surrounded by all sorts of people, driven in endless dissipation from concert to ball, and with frivolous interest making love to a pretty blonde, then will you have a picture of the present Carnival-Goethe. But there is another, in gray beaver coat, with boots, and a brown silk neckerchief, who, ever living in himself, working and striving, now throwing the innocent feelings of youth into little poems, now the strong spices of life into dramas, sketching his friends in chalk, asking neither right nor left what will be thought of his doings, because he always rises through work a step higher, because he springs at no ideal, but lets his nature develop itself fighting and playing." He is still very young: as conscious of one costume as of the other. The real Goethe is as independent of the brown silk neckerchief as of the braided coat. But the young man of twenty-six in whom the real Goethe dwells has the innocent pleasure in make-up of his type and of his time.

So we find him presently setting off with two young Counts of Stolberg, all three in Werther costume — green cloth coat with brass buttons, leather breeches, and top-boots — which, "originally adapted from the English country gentleman's dress of the period, was then considered to express in its wearer all that was romantic and sentimental." He was already corresponding with the sister of these two young men, on romantic terms apparently proposed by her: one of the fruits of *Werther*. They were on their way toward Switzerland, and he determined to go with them, without saying good-by to Lili, "as an experiment to see whether he could renounce her." The three seem to have had a harum-scarum journey. The Stolbergs were a wild pair, intent upon proving their enlightenment by shocking respectability in every possible way. In the course of the expedition Goethe visited his sister, who did all she could to dissuade him from marriage with Lili. And he was presented by the Stolbergs to the Prince of Weimar, soon to be Duke, and was urgently invited to visit Weimar. His father, who was also against the marriage, now urged him to go on, and make his long-talked-of visit to Italy. He arrived at the St. Gotthard pass on Lili's seventeenth birthday. "Lombardy and Italy lay before me as a strange land; while the dear home of Germany lay behind, full of sweet domesticities, and where — let me confess it — she lived who so long had enchained me, in whom my existence was centered. A little golden heart, which in my happiest hours I had received from her, still hung about my neck. I drew it forth and covered it with kisses"— and so turned toward Frankfurt. But his return was more futile than his departure; for he had no real and active desire to marry Lili or anybody else. The "sweet domesticities" which he loved in fancy would have bored him in fact. Enough opposition had arisen in her family and his to make it possible for him to retire with dignity, as he presently did. It must be recognized that good sense characterized these withdrawals of Goethe's. It is far worse to marry foolishly than to think foolishly of marriage. Only in the case of Frederike, apparently, was real suffering the result of his philandering.

He was working upon the tragedy of *Egmont,* (which was not to be finished till years later) when the Duke of Weimar passed through Frankfurt and again urged Goethe to come to Weimar. It was an invitation sure to tempt him at the moment. He was still uneasy over the break with Lili, and anxious to leave Frankfurt; and a real liking had sprung up btween him and the Duke. His father did not wish him to go. The recent love-affair had not increased his willingness to have his son mix with social superiors; and he prophesied that the Duke's favor would not last long, and that Goethe would be sorry to have submitted himself to humiliation. But Goethe decided to go. It was arranged that an official of the court should convey him to Weimar. He did not come at the time appointed, or for some days after; and Goethe, with characteristic impatience, determined that he would neither go to Weimar nor stay in Frankfurt. Once more he turned his face toward Italy. But he was routed out in the middle of the night at Heidelberg by a message that the escort was awaiting him at Frankfurt. He hastened back, and in due time (November, 1775), was ushered into the court at Weimar. Weimar was to be practically his home for the rest of his long life, and to this fact it chiefly owes its fame. It was one of the smaller German principalities. The ducal family was poor, and the court conducted upon a modest scale. The place itself was a small walled town, of six or seven hundred houses. Nobody could go in or out of the gates without registering. The streets were ill-paved and unlighted.

At Weimar, in short, Goethe found himself in friendly and sympathetic rather than magnificent surroundings. The Dowager Duchess Amalia was only ten years older than he, and a woman of unusual qualities,— of keen mind, wide cultivation, high spirits, and warm heart. She and Goethe became good friends from the outset. She came to have a great affection and regard for Goethe's mother, called her by her family name, and sent her little gifts not as from a superior, but as from an intimate friend. She had a faculty of gathering superior minds about her. Goethe found Wieland at the court in the capacity of tutor. Goethe had ridiculed Wieland rather unfairly in print, and Wieland had humiliated him by taking his attack in excellent part. But they no sooner saw each other than they became excellent friends. The young Duchess at first hardly shared the Dowager's liking for Goethe. Indeed, it seems probable that the Duke was first attracted to the poet as a boon-companion; they had been introduced by those scamps, the von Stolbergs. The Duke was only nineteen, a lad of good mind and strong character in many ways; but just then "feeling his oats" as his own master, and ripe for all sorts of mischief. The first weeks of Goethe's stay at Weimar seem to have been given to carousal and tomfoolery of one kind or other, in which the guest took his full part. They played practical jokes on members of the court. "They spent days and nights together in each other's society; they hunted, drank, and gambled together. On one occasion they were seen cracking sledge-whips in the market-place of Jena, for a wager. "At night they finished up with carousals, in which wine was drunk from skulls." No wonder the young wife looked askance at this honeymoon companion, no wonder the report went abroad that Goethe was corrupting the young Duke. Goethe, who had entered into it all in a spirit of pure boyish thoughtlessness, of which he was quite capable on occasion much later in life, had enough of it in a few weeks, and went off by himself, much to the Duke's discomfiture. In one way or other he had made himself indispensable to Weimar, and must be brought back at all costs. So the Duke offers him the post of Privy-Councilor, with a salary amounting perhaps to two thousand dollars, modern money. And Goethe, after no long hesitation, accepts and returns to Weimar, for good — in all senses.

Goethe had made himself very popular during his visit at the court; but his appointment necessarily met with some protest. Neither his birth nor his training qualified him, in the minds of the Duke's advisers, for the office in question. A formal protest was sent to the Duke, but he was firm, and the event justified his choice. Formal decorum was never observed between the Duke and his Privy-Councilor, and they were still to have some escapades in common. But in the long run Goethe proved to be a restraining influence. The judgment of the Dowager was vindicated, and that of the young Duchess in part at least revoked. And it was not hard for Goethe to overcome the opposition among the courtiers, for he soon proved that he was not a mere irresponsible favorite.

Nevertheless, there is no doubt that the Duke at first wanted him at the court as a friend rather than an adviser. In writing to the senior Goethe, he made it clear that the office might be resigned at any time: "Goethe can have only one position — that of my friend. All others are beneath him." This friendship had its moments of strain during the years to come; both were impetuous and opinionated men. But it survived for half a century,— to the death of the Duke.

Goethe did not adopt the grave manner, to be sure. What he was at this time, in the flesh, may be best suggested by an anecdote told by one Gleim: "Soon after Goethe had written *Werther* I came to Weimar, and wished to know him. I had brought with me the last *Musen Almanach,* a literary novelty, and read here and there an article to the company in which I passed the evening. While I was reading, a young man, booted and spurred, in a short green shooting-jacket thrown open, came in and mingled with the audience. I had scarcely remarked his entrance. He sat down opposite to me and listened attentively. I scarcely knew what there was about him that particularly struck me, except a pair of brilliant black Italian eyes. But it was decreed that I should know more of him. . . . During a short pause, during which some gentlemen and ladies were discussing the merits of the pieces I had read, lauding some and censuring others, the gallant young sportsman (for such I took him to be) arose from his chair, and bowing with a most courteous and ingratiating air to me, offered to relieve me from time to time in reading, lest I should be tired. I could do no less than accept so polite an offer, and immediately handed him the book. But oh, Apollo and all ye Muses — not forgetting the Graces — what was I then to hear? At first, indeed, things went on smoothly enough . . . the somewhat more solid, substantial fare of Voss, Stolberg, and Burger was delivered in such a manner that no one had any reason to complain. . . . All at once, however, it was as if some wild and wanton devil took possession of the young reader. . . . He read poems that had no existence in the *Almanach;* broke out into all possible modes and dialects. Hexameters, iambics, doggerel verses one after another, or blended in strange confusion, came tumbling out in torrents. What wild and humorous fancies did he not combine that evening! Amidst them came out such noble, magnificent thoughts, thrown in detached and flitting, that the authors to whom he ascribed them must have thanked God on their knees if they had fallen on their desks. . . . 'That is Goethe or the Devil,' cried I to Wieland, who sat opposite me. 'Both,' he replied."

But if Goethe kept his faculty of startling people by his unconventionality, he at once showed his sense of responsibility in important matters. The magnanimous Wieland (between whom and Goethe there was never a suspicion of jealousy) testified very soon after the appointment of the Privy-Councilor as to the change in his behavior. "From the moment that he decided on becoming a man of business," he says, "he has conducted himself with blameless σωφροσύνη and all worldly prudence." And: "Goethe, with all his real and apparent *sauvagerie,* has in his little finger more *conduite* and *savoir faire* than all the court parasites, Boniface sneaks, and political cobweb-spinners have in their whole bodies and souls. So long as Karl August lives, no power can remove him." This prophecy was verified.

An instance of Goethe's magnanimity is his treatment of Herder, who had dismissed *Götz von Berlichingen* with something like contempt, and had since shown himself the reverse of friendly. By Goethe's influence, against strong opposition, Herder was given the post of court preacher at Weimar, and thereafter he and his sponsor were excellent friends. The Duke had given his friend a house with a garden outside the city gates, and pleasantly situated. Here Goethe lived for several years with his servants. Later he lived in the town during the winter. He had not been long in Weimar before a new attachment sprang up; this time one which had, on the whole, a beneficent influence in his life. The lady was a Charlotte von Stein, who had been married eleven years and had seven children. She knew and admired his work. He had seen her silhouette in Frankfurt, and had written under it, "It would be splendid to see how the world reflects itself in this soul. She sees the world as it is, yet through the medium of love." She was six years older than he, and not especially brilliant; but she was beautiful, discreet, and sympathetic. The morals of the court of Weimar were not above the morals of the day. The intimacy between Goethe and Frau von Stein caused comment but no censure, though it was probably suspected of amounting to more than it actually did. The lady was a finished woman of the world, and apparently knew very well how to manage Goethe. They met continually. Hundreds of letters and notes passed between them. It is a sign of the lady's canniness that she got all her own back and burned them, but kept Goethe's with the greatest care. On the whole, regulated as it was by her, the relation seems to have been a good thing for the poet. It prevented the danger of more serious intrigues, for which the court life gave plenty of opportunity, and it brought him valuable discipline. Self-discipline became a passion with him during these years. On the 7th of August, 1779, his diary contains this entry:

"A calm glance back on my past life, on the confusion, restlessness, lust after knowledge, of youth, — how it roams about everywhere to find something satisfying. How, especially, I found delight in mysteries, in dark, imaginary relations. How, when occupied with anything scientific, I only half attacked it, and soon let it pass; how a sort of humble self-complacency goes through all I then wrote. With how little insight I moved round and round in human and divine things. How there was as little of action as of thought and poetry directed to an aim; how many days were wasted in time-destroying sentiment and shadow-passions; how little good came to me therefrom; and how, now that the half of life is past, there is no way back, but I simply stand here as one who has saved himself from the water, and whom the sun begins beneficently to dry. The time I have spent in the rush of the world, since October, '75, I do not yet trust myself to review. God help further and give light, so that we may not stand so much in our own way; cause us to do from morning to night what is fitting; and give us clear ideas of the consequences of things, so that we may not be like men who complain all day of headache and dose themselves for headache, and every evening take too much wine."

Goethe was not quite thirty when these words were written, but how far behind he has left his Wertherism, how true ring these manly utterances! From this time he grew steadily in self-command and firmness of aim. His self-discipline included discipline of the body, he avoided all excesses, and in a country where windows were always closed and water used as little as possible, he took daily baths in the Ilm, even in winter, and often slept out-of-doors. And he made no sinecure of his office. It is recorded that he was scrupulous in attending all meetings of the Privy Council, and that he not only gave careful attention to all business brought up, but showed unusual ability, especially in matters of finance. Moreover, he was detailed by the Duke for certain important diplomatic duties, which he performed with skill. When the question came up of reopening certain disused mines, it was Goethe who brought it about, " studying the principles of mining, consulting with men who had a right to an opinion on the subject, and finally seeing that the undertaking was organized in accordance with the most advanced methods. Public works, education, the army, all benefited by his zeal and thoroughness. He became the mainspring of the administration." " Goethe," wrote Merck, during a visit at Weimar, " directs everything, and everyone is pleased with him, for he serves many and hurts none. Who can resist the unselfishness of the man? " All this activity was very good for him, it had a calming and steadying effect upon his eager nature. " The pressure of affairs is very good for the mind," he said. " When it has disburdened itself, it plays more freely and enjoys life. There is nothing more miserable than a comfortable man without work." He had seen what this meant, in the case of his own father.

It may have been the study of the mining problem set before him that directly quickened his interest in science. Both at Leipsic and at Strasburg he had varied his law studies by attendance on sundry scientific lectures. He now took up science as eagerly as he had been wont to pursue literature. Mineralogy led to geology; but his chief interest came to lie in osteology and botany. His garden and the forests near Weimar were his botanical laboratory; and the neighborhood of the University of Jena, with its men of science and its collections, gave him facilities for his anatomical studies. He was not a mere dabbler. He was to make several scientific discoveries of importance, the first of which was perhaps the most striking. This was the discovery of the intermaxillary bone in the human jaw, the lack of which had been hitherto supposed to prove a fundamental difference in structure between man and the other vertebrates. The discovery was essential to the later discovery of the law of evolution.

The literary product of the ten years passed at Weimar before the Italian journey was not as large as it might have been under other conditions, but it was not inconsiderable. Some striking poems and much of *Wilhelm Meister* were written during this period. Of more direct local origin were the prose dramas written to be presented by the company which was composed chiefly of members of the court, including the Duke, the Dowager Duchess, and Goethe himself. Private theatricals were then very much in vogue throughout Germany. There were many regular companies which not only performed at home, but now and then went "on the road," visiting the other private theatres (which were many of them out-of-doors). The Weimar theater was one of the best. For this theater and the company of which he was a leading actor he wrote not only various prose trifles, but *Iphegenie* (in prose), a drama of dignity and restraint. The extravagance of his early manner is gone. The changes which have been taking place in his habits are reflected in his style. The difference between the freedom of his early manner and the measured conduct of his later style was not primarily the result, as has been held, of his journey to Italy. The prose *Iphegenie* shows that the change belongs to the early years at Weimar. *Werther,* and the mood for which it stood, had now long been distasteful to him. He had grown away from all that, and it troubled him that everybody else had not. As a fact, Wertherism was strong as ever; mawkish sentimentalism characterized the popular literatures of the day; and Goethe could not help being conscious that he was himself in part responsible for the situation. He continued to receive letters from professed disciples of *Werther.* A girl who had been disappointed in love drowned herself in the Ilm near Goethe's house, and a copy of *Werther* was found in her pocket. It is a pity that Goethe, in his new mood, should not have published a counterblast for all Europe to hear. Perhaps it seemed hopeless to him. In *Werther* he had expressed a general mood. An anti-*Werther* at this time would merely have expressed his own. Besides, he no longer wrote for a public and with the idea of gain (an idea which had been proved vain by his experience with *Götz* and *Werther*), but for a circle of intimates. At all events, he contented himself with writing a burlesque for the Weimar theater, the hero of which is a caricature of Werther, and in which that manual of mistaken sensibility is itself held up to ridicule. Goethe was then studying Aristophanes, and the manner of this skit plainly shows his influence.

With the early sentimentalism, the early self-absorption slipped away from him. There are many anecdotes of his warm-heartedness and his benefactions. We may cite one. In 1778 "an unknown correspondent wrote to him, under the assumed name of Kraft, for assistance. From the history of his circumstances it appeared that he had fallen from a respectable position to complete destitution. Goethe in reply sent him money and clothing. In the correspondence which ensued it became evident that the man was one of those morbid and suspicious natures whose misfortunes are usually of their own making, and who attribute to the world the fault that is in themselves. Goethe saw this, but did not therefore give him up. Regarding him as more to be pitied than blamed, he made provision for his living economically, and endeavored to provide him with some occupation. He ultimately made him an allowance of two hundred thalers a year, one-sixth of his official income, and continued it until the death of the man in 1785. It should be added this was done without the knowledge of any of his friends, and was only brought to light with the correspondence after Goethe's death." From this time he was frequently charged with coldness and haughtiness of manner. But however true this may have been of his manner toward silly or presumptuous persons of the ruling class, he had a warm affection for goodness and sincerity wherever they might be found. From his mines he writes, "How strong my love has returned upon me for these lower classes which one calls the lower, but which in God's eyes are assuredly the highest!" Later, he finds it impossible to go on with *Iphegenie* because news has come of a famine in a certain district: "The drama will not advance a step: it is under a curse; the King of Tauris must speak as if no stocking-weaver in Apolda felt the pangs of hunger!" He had little regard for "high society" as such. In 1778 he went to Berlin with the Duke, and, having little respect for the literary parasites of the Great Frederick, would have nothing to say to them, greatly to their offense. When the visit was over (it lasted only a few days), he said, "I have got quite close to old Fritz, having seen his way of life, his gold, his silver, his statues, his apes, his parrots, and heard his own curs twaddle about the great man." There may have been a touch of pique in this on account of the fact that Frederick paid no attention to his presence in Berlin. They were the two greatest men of the day, but they had no literary ground in common. There was no German literature for Frederick. His ambition to distinguish himself as a writer in French and his subjection to Voltaire must have disgusted Goethe. And in the year of the Berlin visit, Frederick had made it quite clear what he thought of Goethe. After sneering in good Voltairean French at the "abominable pieces" and "ridiculous farces" of Shakespeare, he intimates that that unfortunate writer had an excuse, "for the birth-time of the arts is never the point of their maturity. But pray consider a *Götz von Berlichingen* appearing on the scene, a detestable imitation of these wretched English pieces, and the audience applauding and calling enthusiastically for a repetition of these disgusting platitudes."

After ten years of the busy life at Weimar Goethe grew restive. He felt the need of rest and change, the half-conscious desire to give himself up once more to creative work. He determined to make the journey to Italy which had been so many times postponed. He seems to have had a superstitious fear that if his plans became known they might be again blocked in some way; and when he applied for leave of absence to the Duke, he said nothing about what he was going to do with his time. His impulse toward a new relation to the world extended itself to a renewed desire for a larger audience than Weimar afforded. Before he left Germany, he had arranged with a

Leipsic bookseller to publish a collected edition of his works in eight volumes; and had actually got four volumes ready for the press.

Goethe set out for Italy in September, 1778, intending to make a comparatively short journey of it. But his enthusiasm for what life in Italy meant to him increased, his leave of absence was indefinitely extended, and it was over a year and a half before he returned to Weimar. His activities during this period were as varied as ever. Most of his time was spent in Rome, and his interest in Roman antiquities and art steadily deepened. He lived for some time in the house of a German painter, and under instruction took drawing and painting in earnest, becoming so absorbed in the work that he seems to have had serious thoughts of turning painter. He wrote his poetical version of *Iphigenie,* and much of the first part of *Faust.* His studies in anatomy and botany were kept up to such effect that he discovered the "metamorphosis of plants," and the relation between the bones of the skull and the vertebræ: two more important steps toward the development of the theory of evolution.

Throughout his absence he was writing voluminously to Frau von Stein, who fortunately kept this series of letters. Many years after, he edited and published many of them under the title *Italian Journey.* "I count as a second birthday, the day of a real new birth, that on which I entered Rome," he says. He returned to Weimar with a mind greatly broadened and a spirit greatly calmed. He was not disposed to take up the full burden of his old duties, and the Duke readily lightened them. From this time on he was comparatively free to do his own work in his own way. His intimacy with Frau von Stein could not be wholly resumed; he had in a sense outgrown her during his absence. She resented the change in him, and their relation became strained. He felt himself once more free, and it was at this moment that the abiding love of his life began.

Shortly after his return a girl came to him with a letter from her brother, who had studied at Jena, had literary ambition, and wanted Goethe's advice and help. Christiane Vulpius was young, pretty, and frank: she had the charm which had belonged to most of the women who had touched Goethe's heart. But this girl he not only loved at first sight, but continued to love. It was not long before they entered into a relation which he undoubtedly considered a marriage, though eighteen years passed before it was given religious sanction. He was a high court official, he had been ennobled, and was entitled to write himself von Goethe; he could not give this girl of low rank the name of his wife. Weimar was scandalized as it was, not at the irregularity of the relation, but at the impropriety of his choice. Frau von Stein was very angry, and wrote to him in so outrageous a tone that he made no reply. They afterwards became friendly in an ordinary way. Christiane's attitude toward Goethe seems to have been altogether wifely. She was not only a good housewife and mother, but an intelligent and sympathetic companion. After the birth of their son, Goethe took Christiane's mother and sister into his household. His own mother called Christiane her "dear daughter"; however their relation during the first eighteen years of their public life together may be judged on grounds of public morality, there was no element of vulgar intrigue connected with it from first to last. For her his *Roman Elegies* were written, and to her he dedicated his *Metamorphosis of Plants.*

His theory in this connection that "the foliar organs of flowering plants are all to be regarded as various forms of the leaf," has been accepted by botanists. The speculations in which, at about this time, he became interested as to a theory of colors had little practical result. He believed that Newton's theory was wrong, and that he was on the track of the true one. He reverted to the subject from time to time to the end of his life, and it is one of the ironies of genius that in the end he came to pride himself especially upon his work in this field. In old age he once declared that "he did not at all pride himself on his poetry, but that his theory of colors did seem to him something to be proud of."

The hour of the French Revolution was now at hand, and there is evidence in Goethe's literary work of the period that he watched with concern the outcome of the democratic theories to which, under the tutelage of Rousseau, he had once been so ready to subscribe. He believed that the recourse to violence would prove futile in the long run, but he held that revolutions were the fruit of oppression, and not of depravity in the individuals who revolted. Certain dramatic sketches of the period make clear his conviction that the French nobility needed only to be generous, in the large sense, to be safe. But the hour struck: French monarchy was challenged at the cannon's mouth, and for the divine right of kings the armies of Prussia and Brunswick took the field. The Duke of Weimar was made a Prussian general, and Goethe accompanied the army of invasion (August, 1792). There were minor successes, then the major reverse at Valmy. Here they discovered the strength of the revolutionary movement, and, as they had set out on the adventure without proper military precautions, as against a band of desperadoes, they were forced to retreat. It is characteristic of him that, anxious to learn what "cannon-fever" meant, Goethe deliberately exposed himself to fire during this engagement. On the evening of that day, which marked the first distinguished success of the French forces, he wrote, "From this place, and to-day, begins a new epoch in the history of the world, and you may say that you were there." Several German cities were captured thereafter by the revolutionaries, and Goethe was with the Duke when, in the following year, Mainz was retaken. This experience of actual warfare interested him greatly; but he was glad to return to Weimar, to his family and his natural employments.

In 1794 began the remarkable intimacy between Goethe and Schiller. There had seemed to be little promise of it. Schiller was ten years younger than Goethe. When he had published *The Robbers* (1781) Goethe had been disgusted with its extravagance — all the more so because it recalled too clearly the exuberance of his own early work. If *Götz* and *The Robbers* had been written at the same time, the two authors would no doubt have admired each other mutually. But Goethe had left the Storm and Stress movement far behind, and it distressed him that it should still persist. When in 1788 Schiller came to the neighborhood of Weimar, Goethe paid him a visit, but they parted without having made any approach toward a friendship. Schiller was exuberant, Goethe dogmatic. "I doubt," wrote Schiller, "whether we shall ever come into any close communication with each other. Much that still interests me has already had its epoch with him. His whole nature is, from its very origin, otherwise constructed from mine; his world is not my world; our modes of conceiving things appear to be essentially different. From such a combination no substantial intimacy can result." This was a great disappointment to Schiller, who looked upon Goethe as his superior in many ways. Schiller was in the midst of a hard struggle to live; his plays had brought him fame, but little money. So he set himself to write *The Revolt of the Netherlands,* chiefly as a pot-boiler. But the first volume attracted attention, and made it possible for Goethe to procure him the chair of History at Jena. Goethe, however, was still lukewarm toward him personally, and it was several years before they actually became friends, in spite of the fact that Schiller presently married the daughter of a family with which Goethe had long been intimate. Schiller was always delicate, and in 1793 he had to leave Jena. During his absence he arranged for the publication of a periodical to be called *The Hours.* He wrote to Goethe about the project, and asked him to become a contributor. Goethe responded cordially, and the next time the two poets met there seems to have been more sympathy between them. Shortly after, Schiller was Goethe's guest for a fortnight. From that time on they were devoted friends and allies. There was no more danger of their imitating each other than in the instance of Virgil and Horace, but each of them greatly influenced the work of the other, Goethe supplying Schiller with a needed curb, and himself receiving an equally needed spur.

Goethe's poetic powers had seemed for some years to be in abeyance. He had been occupied with affairs and scientific work. Schiller's poetic fire and enthusiasm roused him — brought to him, as he said, "a second youth," "a new Spring." *The Hours* was not favorably received, much to Schiller's vexation, and more, it seems, to Goethe's amusement. Together they got up a series of epigrams upon their critics and other writers of the day who needed to be put in their places. These epigrams were printed in Schiller's annual, the *Musen Almanach,* of which we have heard, and made exactly the sensation they were intended to make. This was by-play of a not altogether dignified sort. The first work of importance to be done under Schiller's inspiration was the completion of *Wilhelm Meister's Apprenticeship.* This, it will be recalled, had been begun during the reign of Frau von Stein, and worked upon at intervals thereafter, but now laid aside for some time. Schiller showed great interest in it, and the fact that it was carried to any sort of conclusion is probably due to him. It is easy to understand how Goethe might have given it up, since the conception of it belonged to his own youth. Meister is one of his emotional, irresolute heroes: a Storm and Stress figure of Goethe's early imagination — and experience. Schiller's suggestions of detail were not all of them happy; and towards the last Goethe's fancy flags. But if *Meister* is antiquated long since as fiction, it is still alive, if only for the sake of Mignon, elf among heroines. Next came *Hermann and Dorothea,* many of his best lyrics, and a series of ballads written in friendly rivalry with Schiller. He admitted Schiller's superiority as a ballad-writer, but now and then, as in the *Erl-könig,* he strikes a note beyond Schiller. A letter of Schiller's written at the time of *Meister's* publication shows his fine feeling toward Goethe and his work: "It is one of the greatest blessings of my life that I have lived to see this work of yours completed — that it has been written while my faculties are still in a state of growth, and that I may draw inspiration from this pure source. Further, the beautiful relation that exists between us makes it seem to me a kind of religious duty to make your cause my own, and so to develop all that is real in my nature, that my mind may become the clearest mirror of that which exists beneath this covering, and that I may deserve the name of being your friend in the higher sense of the word. . . . Calm and deep, clear and yet incomprehensible, like nature, your work makes its influence felt. It stands there, and even the smallest secondary incident shows the beautiful equanimity from which it has all emanated." Schiller's contact with this beautiful equanimity was the best possible thing for his art, especially as it was a warm and nourishing equanimity. Goethe encouraged Schiller in turn in the writing of *Wallenstein* and *Wilhelm Tell.* Goethe was director of the Court Theater, and in the last year of the century produced the great trilogy of *Wallenstein* with such care and enthusiasm that a remarkable success was scored for the author. Soon after, Schiller left Jena for Weimar, and from that moment till Schiller's death the friends were hardly separated. Under these favorable conditions, Schiller produced during these six years *Maria Stuart, The Maid of Orleans, The Bride of Messina,* and *Wilhelm Tell.*

In April, 1806, Schiller, who was consumptive, caught cold at the Theater, and died a few days later. Goethe was himself sick, and could not see Schiller during these last days. When the news of Schiller's death was brought to the house, nobody could muster up courage to tell Goethe. He seems to have read the truth in the manner of his family, but he asked no direct question, merely saying to Christiane, "I see Schiller must be very ill." In the night he, the most self-contained of men, was heard sobbing. The next morning he asked Christiane, "It is true, is it not, that Schiller was very ill yesterday?" Christiane broke down. "He is dead!" said Goethe, and covered his eyes with his hand.

Goethe had been at first less interested in the philosophical movement which stirred Germany toward the close of the eighteenth century. One of his first points of difference with Schiller had been the latter's preoccupation with Kant. Kant's successors, Fichte and Schelling, appealed to Goethe more than Kant. By his influence they became professors at Jena, and so members of the remarkable group of men who lived in the neighborhood of Weimar. The leaders of the new romantic school, August and Frederick

Schlegel, also became lecturers at Jena, and were encouraged by Goethe, who went to the length of producing two rather mediocre plays of theirs at the Weimar theater. Whatever was best in this romantic impulse might not unfairly be traced to Goethe; but he was not responsible for its later extravagances.

While Schiller was producing the brilliant series of plays which brought his career to a close, Goethe was comparatively unproductive. He had in mind a trilogy of plays "dealing with the ideas on which the French Revolution had been compelling all the world to reflect." He wrote only the first part, *The Natural Daughter,* which may have dissatisfied him as less a drama of human character than of circumstance and fate. Through all these years the idea, and to some extent the form, of *Faust* was slowly maturing. He had first worked upon it in the Frankfurt days before he set out for Weimar; he had taken it up again in Italy, and in 1790 *Faust: a Fragment,* was printed in one of the later volumes of his collected works. Schiller had been greatly impressed with this fragment, and never during his life stopped urging Goethe to go on with it. Goethe himself felt that this was to be his great work; but it was not a work to be hurried; and it was not completed till twenty years after Schiller's death. The First Part was at this time finished; and the manuscript may have narrowly escaped destruction in the course of certain days of terror which visited quiet Weimar.

The summer of 1806 brought the Confederation of the Rhine, the downfall of the Holy Roman Empire, and — Napoleon. Prussia was doomed as an independent kingdom. The decisive engagement was fought near Jena, October 14, 1806; and Goethe and his family could hear the boom of the cannon. Later in the day of the battle a skirmish took place very near the garden by the Ilm. The Prussians were routed, and Weimar was broken into by the French soldiery. Goethe's house was entered, and it seems to have been through some adroitness of Christiane that no actual damage was done. The next day Napoleon himself entered Weimar, and soon afterward the looting was stopped. The Duke's territories were saved to him by the Duchess much as Goethe's property had been saved by Christiane; but he had to leave the Prussian army, to join the Confederation of the Rhine, and to pay a large indemnity. The French left Weimar in sad havoc, and Goethe, roused by the emergency, resumed his old activity in the management of the restoration of the town to order. It was not the only way in which he at this time asserted himself. Five days after the entry of Weimar by the French troops, Christiane became legally his wife, the only persons present at the ceremony being their son and Goethe's secretary. By the German law the son became legitimate. He was a handsome boy of seventeen, and Goethe was both fond and proud of him. Two years later he went to study at Jena.

This formal marriage no doubt made Goethe much happier during the years that followed. He had come to see the value of the convention of marriage as he had not in earlier years. The unfortunate social position of Christiane must have been a continual rebuke to him. He was always most sensitive to any slight put upon her or his son, and this sensitiveness was in the nature of the situation kept perpetually raw. In the end it seemed to him better to brave the displeasure of the court rather than remain uneasy in his own conscience. A good deal has to be said, in telling the story of his life, about his susceptibility to youthful charm. This he never outgrew. But it is to be recorded that his real love was for Christiane. They had their differences, but he remained faithful to her in spite of the fact that his world would have countenanced him in casting her off at any time. And it was after she had lost her youthful charm and acquired an unfortunate habit that he chose to make their relation permanent.

Among the many visitors who came to Weimar and sought Goethe's acquaintance was the mother of Schopenhauer, herself a novelist and a brilliant woman. "He is the most perfect human being I know," she wrote of Goethe, "even in appearance. A tall, fine figure, which holds itself erect, very carefully clad, always in black or quite dark blue, the hair tastefully dressed and powdered, as becomes his age, and a splendid face with two lustrous brown eyes, which are at once mild and penetrating." Another was Madame de Staël, who very quickly gave up her attempts to patronize him; he seems to have found her rather a bore. A third was Bettine Brentano, daughter of Goethe's old friend Maximiliane. This girl imagined a resemblance between herself and the Mignon of *Wilhelm Meister;* and romantically set herself to love Goethe as Mignon had loved Meister. At twenty-two she came to Weimar, and displayed her devotion rather openly. No doubt Goethe was touched in a way, as what man would not be? — he would treat her kindly for the sake of her mother, if for no other reason. There is no reason to suppose that he encouraged her, however. Later she married a lesser poet, von Arnim, and as a young matron insulted Madame Goethe. Christiane, now Goethe's wife, promptly banished her from Goethe's house, with his full approval. After his death Bettine published a book called *Goethe's Correspondence with a Child,* purporting to be a series of letters of a sentimental cast from him to herself. They were proved to be chiefly fictitious.

Yet another visitor was Napoleon. In 1808 the Congress of Erfurt was held, and Goethe was present at the attendant festivities. Napoleon had read a French version of *Werther,*— seven times, he said; and wanted to see its author. So Goethe was summoned to the conqueror's breakfast-table. The quaintness of the situation does not seem to have struck any of the chroniclers of this incident: Goethe presents himself: the Emperor stares him in the face for some seconds, and stops munching long enough to remark approvingly, "Vous êtes un homme." He then talks about *Werther,* that youthful ebullition which Goethe recalls with contempt, and for which Napoleon, ignorant of his mature work, insists upon admiring him. It must have been an irritating interview. It ended by Napoleon's asking him to come to Paris, promising him a welcome; and remarking again, as he went out, "Voilà un homme!" A few days later Napoleon was present at a performance of Voltaire's *Mort de César,* a strange choice for the occasion. At a ball after the play Napoleon talked much to Goethe. "He condemned Voltaire's drama, and suggested that Goethe should write a better one on the subject, showing how Cæsar, if he had been allowed to live, would have done great things for Rome."

In 1805 a new collection of Goethe's works had been arranged for. A volume published in 1808 contains the First Part of *Faust,* in its completed form. It will be remembered that a "Fragment" had appeared in 1790 which had made a great impression on Schiller and a few others, but had attracted little general attention. But the First Part made a veritable sensation. Goethe had come to be regarded as beyond his prime; but *Faust* could not but be looked upon as his masterpiece. His acknowledged rank in German letters, already very high, now became supreme.

There is little doubt that *Faust* had originally presented itself as a tragedy, to be normally completed in a single drama. As the First Part stands it is a drama complete in itself. But before it was finished Goethe had evidently conceived the idea of a further development: a Second Part which should interpret and conclude the action upon a plane broader than that of merely human experience.

Not long after, he began to write his autobiography, the proper title of which is *Aus Meinem Leben; Dichtung und Wahrheit* (From my Life; Poetry and Truth). The first three parts had appeared by 1810; the fourth was not published till seventeen years later. The whole narrative only brings him to the age of twenty-six, Goethe's theory being that the formative period of a man's life is the period of real interest. It is not one of the great autobiographies: its tone is too reticent and impersonal. It is rather a delightful commentary on the Germany of Goethe's youth, illustrated by many detached incidents of his own life.

The year 1815 was marked by two events of importance in Goethe's life. Goethe had not sympathized with the movement which resulted in the War of Liberation. It seemed to him too early to strike a decisive blow for German independence. Napoleon, though crippled by the Russian campaign, was still very powerful; and the German powers had not as yet shown great ability or great disinterestedness. But the war was fought, and fought successfully, for Germany. And Goethe was of course the first to rejoice that his predictions had been proved wrong. The Duke of Weimar now became a Grand Duke, and his territories were extended. A constitutional government was established, and Goethe, somewhat to his surprise, was made First Minister of State. He had not been consulted about the formation of the new government, and it would seem that at this time his relations with the Duke had become less intimate. An actress, Fräulein Jagemann, made some trouble between them by persuading the Duke to produce several plays at the Court Theater of which Goethe disapproved. In consequence Goethe resigned his directorship. But the old friendship was never really broken. When, in 1825, the fiftieth anniversary of the Duke's accession was celebrated, Goethe was the first to offer his congratulations, and the Duke, grasping both of his hands, cried, "To the last breath together!" A little later the fiftieth anniversary of Goethe's coming to Weimar was also celebrated. The Duke had a gold medal struck as a memento of the occasion, and published a letter expressing his own and his people's gratitude for Goethe's long and devoted service to the Duchy.

In 1816 Christiane Goethe died, to Goethe's deep and sincere grief. Yet he had not outgrown his susceptibility to feminine influence, and there were several intimate friendships with other women during his wife's last years. Seven years after Christiane's death, at the age of seventy-two, he fell romantically in love with yet another maiden, a mere girl, the daughter of an old friend. In feeling he was as young as ever, and it meant a bitter fight with him to overcome his infatuation, as it must after all be called.

Goethe's son August had married in 1817 a bride of the father's choice, and had taken up a minor official position at Weimar. He was a man of ability, but moody and excitable, and in the course of a dozen years he had become a drunkard. After his death, in 1830, his brain was found to be malformed. Of four other children of Goethe and Christiane, three were born dead, and the fourth lived but a short time. His two grandchildren, however, remained to comfort him. During his last years he had as secretary that Eckermann who published after his death the *Conversations with Goethe*. These conversations cover an astonishingly wide range of theme, and the tone of his speech is always serene and humane. Heine, at twenty-five, visited the man whom even he was ready to call master. He said that while he talked with Goethe he was always expecting to see the eagle of Zeus at his side; that it would have seemed natural to address him in Greek; but that though he had prepared a number of wise things to say, all he could think of was that "the plums by the wayside between Jena and Weimar were uncommonly good." Apparently this is not the whole truth, for

Goethe discerned Heine's promise, and told Eckermann that with all his brilliancy he lacked but one thing for the highest success,— love. As it was he would be greatly feared.

The Grand Duke died in 1828, and the Grand Duchess in 1830. Goethe was now pretty much alone in the world, so far as his own contemporaries were concerned, but his doors were besieged by members of the younger generation, or rather generations, which had sprung up since the beginning of his fame. His greatness was now beginning to be recognized in England. On his last birthday a group of Englishmen including Scott, Wordsworth, Southey, and Carlyle, sent him a seal inscribed with a motto of his own, "Ohne Hast, aber Ohne Rast" (without haste, but without rest). Carlyle had translated *Meister,* and a good deal of friendly correspondence followed. About 1830, according to Thackeray, "at least a score of English lads used to live at Weimar for study, or sport, or society: all of which were to be had in the friendly little Saxon capital." Thackeray was among these lads, and he has left a vivid sketch of the aged Goethe of his remembrance.

"In 1831, though he had retired from the world, Goethe would nevertheless very kindly receive strangers. His daughter-in-law's tea-table was always spread for us. We passed hours after hours there, and night after night, with the pleasantest talk and music. We read over endless novels and poems in

French, English, and German. . . . He remained in his private apartments, where only a very few privileged persons were admitted. . . . Of course I remember very well the perturbation of spirit with which, as a lad of nineteen, I received the long-expected intimation that the Herr Geheimrath would see me on such a morning. This notable audience took place in a little antechamber of his private apartments, covered all around with antique casts and bas-reliefs. He was habited in a long gray or drab redingote, with a white neckcloth, and a red ribbon in his buttonhole. He kept his hands behind his back, just as in Rauck's statuette. His complexion was very bright, clear, and rosy. His eyes extraordinarily dark, piercing, and brilliant. I felt quite afraid before them. . . . His voice was very rich and sweet. He asked me questions about myself, which I answered as well as I could. I recollect I was at first astonished, and then relieved, when I found he spoke French with not a good accent." Thackeray's impression of the court is also worth quoting: "Though his sun was setting, the sky round about was calm and bright, and that little Weimar illumined by it. In every one of those kind salons the talk was still of Art and Letters. The theatre, though possessing no very extraordinary actors, was still conducted with a noble intelligence and order. The actors read books, and were men of letters and gentlemen, holding a not unkindly relationship to the

Adel. At court the conversation was exceedingly friendly, simple, and polished. The Grand Duchess, a lady of very remarkable endowments, would kindly borrow our books from us, lend us her own, and graciously talk to us young men about our literary tastes and pursuits. In the respect paid by the court to this Patriarch of letters, there was something ennobling, I think, alike to subject and Sovereign."

Toward the last, Goethe's interest in contemporary events, especially political events, became less, and there is a quaint anecdote illustrating his indifference, and his preoccupation with his own intellectual affairs: "On the day when the tidings of the French Revolution of 1830 reached Weimar, his friend Soret went to see him. When Soret entered his room, Goethe began to talk of the mighty volcanic eruption at Paris. Soret replied that nothing was to be expected from such a ministry. Goethe looked at him in astonishment. What had the ministry to do with the matter? He had not been speaking of 'those people,' but of the contest in the French Academy between Cuvier and Geoffroy St. Hilaire — a contest in which St. Hilaire had supported Goethe's ideas as to the true way of conceiving organic Nature."

But, far from being in its dotage, his genius had never been more active. It was shortly before his last birthday that he finished the Second Part of *Faust,* after which he told his secretary Eckermann that he should look upon whatever life might remain to him as a pure gift. With this great poem, which is also a great confession of faith — faith in the power of unselfish service to transform the world of the human spirit — the man's life really closes. He died after a brief illness on March 22, 1832.

THE END

INDEX

I

J

N

O

T

U